The Superfluous Men

Conservative Critics of American

Culture, 1900–1945

Robert M. Crunden is professor of history
and American civilization at the University of
Texas at Austin.

CHOICE JULY/AUG.'77

General

THE SUPERFLUOUS MEN: conservative critics of American culture, 1900–1945, ed. by Robert M. Crunden. Texas, 1977. 289p bibl 76-18060. 14.95 ISBN 0-292-77527-X. C.I.P.
A collection of writings selected as representative of conservative think-ing in the United States from 1900 to 1945. The defining characteristic of conservatism for editor Crunden is the view "that the best things in life are not political and cannot be obtained by political means" (p. xv). The scope of that definition is narrowed considerably, however, by not-ing the centrality of the additional conservative positions of opposing government activity in general, escaping the unpleasant present by turn-ing to the past for values, and advocating that an intellectual elite run our institutions and teach people what they should know and want and how to behave politically. Five of the twenty-eight selections are by Santayana and four by Mencken, with the others by Nock, Davidson, Cram, Owsley, Babbitt, Ransom, More, Tate, and Lippmann. The current revival of conservatism noted by the editor is neither clarified nor forwarded by this volume, but undergraduates might profit from exposure to this grouping of articulate, though frequently dis-gruntled, intellectuals. A short bibliographic essay.

The Superfluous Men

Conservative Critics of American

Culture, 1900–1945

Edited by Robert M. Crunden

University of Texas Press, Austin & London

Library of Congress Cataloging in Publication Data

Main entry under title:

The superfluous men.

   1. United States—Intellectual life—Addresses, essays,
lectures. 2. Conservatism—United States—Addresses, essays,
lectures. I. Crunden, Robert Morse.
E169.1.S964   973   76-18060
ISBN 0-292-77527-X

Printed in the United States of America

Set in Primer by G&S Typesetters, Inc.

For Marjorie Morse Crunden,
who has long had her doubts about the modern world

Contents

Introduction

To the surprise of many observers, conservative thought has revived
in the 1970s. Men and women who once regarded themselves as liberals, radicals, Marxists, Trotskyists, or some other variety of critic
from the left have reversed themselves in the public media and come
out for ideas and policies that would scarcely have seemed conceivable during the 1940s and 1950s. Conservative ideas that once influ-
enced only religious and literary figures have spread into the social
sciences and into practical politics and seem likely to be a force in
American life for the next generation, something which has not really
been the case within the memory of most Americans. Names like
Daniel Boorstin, Edward Banfield, Irving Kristol, Nathan Glazer, Sey-
mour M. Lipset, and Daniel P. Moynihan are simply too prominent in
the 1970s to be ignored, and their works and the works of like-minded
critics have already had an impact on the presidency, the Supreme
Court, the FBI, the CIA, and the implementation of social policy from
the busing of young school students to the distribution of poverty
funds.

The failure of the liberal war to extend the benefits of American
democracy and President Johnson's Great Society to Asia has provided
Americans with a new sense of humility about how much their government can influence world conditions and whether or not it should
even try. The rampant inflation of the late 1960s and early 1970s has
finally demonstrated to depression-grown liberals that government intervention into the economy and the steady expansion of the money
supply may not only not be enough but may even in some ways be
harmful to social welfare and stable economic growth. Liberal assumptions about the integration of the races, especially in the public
schools, have had to undergo painful reexamination because of stren-
uous white opposition, the realization that some blacks might even
prefer schools under their own control and with emphasis on their own
historical achievements, and the demonstrated fact that many white
families will move to other homes or send their children to private
schools rather than allow them to become guinea pigs in one more
experiment in government social engineering. Frequently, the merits
of the proposals and the good intentions of the officials are no longer
even issues. People are responding to simple and obvious failure:

America lost the war, lost control of the economy, and lost any genuine faith in many of its best-intentioned plans for racial integration. The sense of failure has affected liberals and radicals fully as much as conservatives, and indeed many of these conservatives once were the very reformers who advocated these programs in the first place.

The final disaster in this long series of government failures is, of course, the Watergate scandal. On its surface, Watergate was a conservative Republican debacle that happened to a president cordially detested by liberals. In a way it certainly was. But the real impact of Watergate on the American mind has been to introduce a pervasive skepticism about the ability of government to accomplish anything. The FBI and the CIA have turned out to have very dirty hands indeed. Government officials violated the civil liberties of American citizens from Martin Luther King to the lowliest petition signer; they invaded privacy, used confidential tax data for harassment, and circulated defamatory information about public officials. The election funds of both major parties contained money clearly improper and definitely illegal, and there has been great suspicion that the money was intended to and sometimes did lead to improper legislation favoring the wealthy. The plots to intervene abroad, and even to assassinate foreign leaders like Fidel Castro, have added to the poisonous atmosphere. Many of the ugliest events took place under liberal Democratic administrations, often with the clear cooperation of liberal presidents. The government has long been the key agent of reform in the liberal mind; the government has increasingly come to seem like an entity that cannot be trusted. In the eyes of many Americans, the government needs desperately to reform itself before attempting anything else. It needs humility, a sense of what can actually be accomplished in the world, and some notion of where and when to stop. Conservatism has long been arguing against big government and has long been insisting that private means should be found for settling social and political problems. It thus has reaped benefits even from the disaster of a seemingly conservative president.

In the eighteenth and nineteenth centuries, conservative thought played an important role in the shaping of the American republic. John Adams was a staunchly middle-class revolutionary in the 1770s, but with his later writings, especially those about the virtues necessary for democratic citizens, he in effect established conservative thought within the American nation. For the next century, the Adams family continued to contribute to the conservative tradition, reaching a kind of climax with the despairing cultural conservatism of *The Education of Henry Adams* and its vision of an exhausted democracy grown industrial and corrupt. Political figures like Henry Clay, Daniel Webster, and John C. Calhoun added ideas and acts to the sum of political conservatism before the Civil War, while Lincoln performed the task of tying conservatism to the often radical problems of war.

In the postwar atmosphere of economic expansion and political mediocrity, conservatism of any articulate sort retreated from politics and
social criticism and tended to find refuge in universities or in the independent world of arts and letters. Figures like Charles Eliot Norton,
William Graham Sumner, and William C. Brownell represented a conservatism that could no longer cope with political issues and that often
viewed contemporary life with revulsion.

Political historians have dealt in detail with the generation of Clay,
Webster, and Calhoun. Cultural historians have examined Henry
Adams from a number of angles and have not really neglected the
lesser figures of that period any more than their obscurity warrants.
But with the turn of the twentieth century, the landscape of conservative action becomes curiously unclear. Parts of it have been studied
in almost obsessive detail, especially in literature, but students can
find few works that treat conservatism as a subject worthy of study on
its own terms. Scholars who came of age in the depression and the
years that followed it found little to interest them in the subject, and
so study of it has languished while books on, say, liberal politics have
multiplied endlessly. The new emphases of the 1970s seem to indicate a revival of interest in cultural conservatism, and this book is
an attempt to provide a preliminary overview of this unjustly neglected topic.

The period from approximately 1900 to 1945 forms something of a
natural unit, in addition to being a neglected field of research. The
conservative generation that died with Henry Adams had about it a
feeling of exhaustion, a sense that little that it wrote or created really
mattered, and an obsession with nineteenth-century themes like Darwinism and political corruption that irrevocably locate this generation
in the Gilded Age. While many of these themes persist in the writings
of twentieth-century conservatives, the student immediately notices a
great invigoration, an ability often to innovate in radical and productive ways, as the new generation finds its voice. George Santayana
virtually created serious study of the philosophy of art in America;
H. L. Mencken was a tireless champion of radical European thought
of the kind associated with Nietzsche; Albert Jay Nock began as a
single taxer trying to overthrow the entire American system of taxation and the structure of government finance; T. S. Eliot was widely
regarded as the wild man of modernism in poetry. One can argue that
when these men did these things they were not conservative, or one
can argue, as I do here, that conservative beliefs neither support nor
oppose innovation in many areas of life and art. Conservatism is instead more of an assumption about which areas of life are genuinely
rewarding for the intelligent person to concentrate upon than it is a
stance in support of the status quo.

In order to examine intelligently the range of contributions made
by modern conservatives, a study including two generations seems to
me essential to form a coherent unit. These pioneer thinkers quickly

produced disciples and, especially in that area known as agrarianism, these disciples made important and widely publicized contributions of their own which shed light on conservative thinking. When these ideas flowered into the New Criticism, they produced one of the most important contributions to the cultural history of modern America, one that, as an influence on university teaching, the writing of literature, and literary criticism, persists to this day.

By the middle 1940s, the vigor of these innovations is clearly over. Santayana, Nock, Mencken, and Ralph Adams Cram are either dead or becoming silent, although Santayana continued to write almost until his death in an Italian nursing home in 1952. The younger generation often remained active as university professors, but their innovative work had been accomplished and they had little new to say that had much importance for the student of conservatism. Instead, a new and clearly different generation appeared: first with Peter Viereck and his attempts to "conserve" much of American liberalism but to reinvigorate it with a new sense of humane values; and, second, with William F. Buckley, Jr., and his attempts to organize a radical right in America that did not always have much in common with prewar conservatism. The issues of McCarthyism and the Cold War added new concerns which are simply too different from the concerns of the earlier decades to warrant their consideration in this book.

As I point out in the bibliographical essay at the end of this book, many treatments of conservatism have not been satisfactory. A number of scholars entered the field because they were specialists in the early years of the American nation, and they have tended to assess conservative thought by means of analyzing what John Adams or Alexander Hamilton wrote or what Edmund Burke in England represented. Conditions in America changed rapidly, however, and never much resembled those in England. Thus the political values which were important to the revolutionary generation became less and less relevant to their children and grandchildren. To measure a Henry Adams or a George Santayana in terms of his political stance, as if he were a John Adams, is ludicrously inappropriate; one might as well measure cream with a yardstick. Conservatives in any time period might well have political ideas, but these political ideas were rarely central to their lives, and the general conservative position has always been to *oppose* governmental activity even when a given conservative is a part of a functioning government. Religion, literature, the family, or farm life might each be more important; political activity might be a social duty but never an end in itself.

Other students of the field have bogged down in a persistent present-mindedness. Many of the anthologies and secondary sources published after World War II were clearly compiled with too much concern for current political and social issues. Some of these books overemphasized religious values, even though many of the most im-

portant conservatives had no obvious faith themselves and at times
were actively hostile to religion of any kind. Others tried to meet liberal scholars on their own ground and overemphasized political writings. But conservatives since the revolutionary generation have never
been at their sharpest in political writing, and to study closely the pronouncements of President Hoover or Senators Taft and Goldwater is
to waste time on marginal and unrewarding material. Whole areas of
conservatism, from the Gothic Revival in architecture to agrarianism
in literature, often never appeared in these books at all. It is thus no
wonder that major scholars, not to mention students, often remain
unfamiliar with much of value that conservatism has contributed to
American cultural history.

The material I have gathered together for this book is a conscious
attempt to reshape the field and to establish a more accurate geography of the contribution of conservatism to America in the recent past.
This collection is limited to work produced by men who were identifi-
ably American in some meaningful way, whether or not they were
American citizens throughout their lives. One of them lived permanently abroad for much of his adult life, and one lived frequently in
Europe while doing some of his most productive writing. All of them
received American upbringing and higher education, and even when
they were abroad they felt called upon to offer commentary on the
American scene and to use their American experiences to measure
larger principles and values. Likewise, at one time or another, they regarded themselves as conservatives and were welcomed or attacked
by opponents for their conservative views. An occasional phrase like
"old liberal" or "high tory" appears in their writings, along with more
specific terms like "agrarian" or "humanist," but the general rubric
"conservative" as defined below covers them all. Likewise, as far as
can be determined, many of these men knew each other, wrote and
talked to each other, and criticized each other's work, frequently in
published reviews. Occasionally, they disliked each other and openly
disagreed with each other. I have included some of these disagree-
ments in my selections; they seem to me without exception to be criticisms from within, not from without, the pale of the word "conservative."

Conservatism in America between 1900 and 1945, then, means
the following: The most important single doctrine in the conservative
frame of reference is that the best things in life are not political and
cannot be obtained by political means. The religion that is so often
present in a conservative mind is only a part of this larger principle.
True conservatives may value a tradition of freedom, the heritage of
an architectural form, the conventions of centuries of poetry, or the
rural life lived by their families for generations. Conservatives generally have an acute sense of what makes life worth living, and they
do not associate it with political activity. The business of politics is
to keep the larger society functioning efficiently and invisibly, so that

people may worship, write, create, cultivate, or otherwise do what gives their lives meaning. In this sense, conservatism is insistently "cultural" and demonstrably "interdisciplinary." It treasures anything that nourishes the soul, from art to religion to literature; it normally associates the greatest treasures with the past, with that which has proven most nourishing to most people over the longest time.

Because of this stance toward the past, and toward cultural concerns, conservatives remain relatively detached from everyday life, from the fads, tumults, patriotisms, and heresies of the newspaper. Others may shout for a specific reform, advocate a new art form, join a new religious, political, or social group, or demand war for some higher goal. Cultural conservatives will very rarely do this, whatever political conservatives or military conservatives might advocate. Instead, they might style themselves superfluous, as Albert Jay Nock did in his memorable autobiography of 1943, *The Memoirs of a Super-fluous Man*, because not only are conservatives detached from society and often critical of it, but they find that society really is not much interested in their ideas and that they are in a real sense superfluous to the basic concerns of their own culture. As George Santayana put it in an early poem,

> For some are born to be beatified
> By anguish, and by grievous penance done;
> And some, to furnish forth the age's pride,
> And to be praised of men beneath the sun;
> And some are born to stand perplexed aside
> From so much sorrow—of whom I am one.

Given the demands of the day, this attitude seems all too often to be negativism. The early-twentieth-century conservatives said no to modern painting, or to stream-of-consciousness fiction, or to Coolidge prosperity, or to the New Deal so often that they seemed unable to say yes to anything. When, as Irving Babbitt remarked repeatedly, the world was going wrong on first principles, it was hard not to keep telling it so. In fact, the conservatives valued many things, and these values take up much space in this book. They valued religion, the classics, church architecture, useless knowledge, beauty, and the land, and they desperately wanted the world to stop wasting time, money, and energy on destructive diversions and to get on with the really important things in life.

As a refuge from the unpleasant present, the conservatives insisted on the right to choose their own traditions. All too often, genuine American conditions included egalitarianism, civil religion, liberalism, economic individualism, and pragmatic naturalism, and to conservatives most of these elements of their heritage did not seem worth conserving. They sought instead for alternative traditions with which to identify. If they could, they found them in America, concealed under blankets of liberal misunderstanding. Jefferson, a liberal god who was so often invoked in support of egalitarianism, became instead in conservative hands the man who hated politics, who took office only because his supporters refused to allow him to retire, and whose dearest loves were architecture, his farm, his family, music, and good reading. The domestic, conservative agrarian Jefferson they developed was historically accurate, however he might differ from the equally genuine Jefferson who wrote the Kentucky Resolutions, sympathized with the French Revolution, and detested the power of the organized clergy in America. The Edmund Burke who looms so significantly in recent scholarship on American conservatism did not have one-tenth the force of Jefferson for American conservatives between 1900 and 1945, nor was Burke even as important as Hamilton, John Adams, Lincoln, Calhoun, or Henry Adams.

This eclecticism within American history likewise ruled farther afield. Many American conservatives carried on an extensive love affair with ancient Greece. Its philosophers came in for extensive analysis. They often turned out to have values compatible with or preferable to the best in Christianity. The study of Greece disciplined the mind and better equipped it to cope with modern problems. The lessons the study of Greece taught about political elites, moderation, self-control, and what qualities were most human established norms which Americans flouted to their own loss. The kind of government pioneered in Athens inspired and shaped notions of democracy and equality, in terms rather different from those associated, most insistently, with Rousseau, Locke, and other liberal heroes.

Many conservatives chose their traditions elsewhere. A few learned Sanskrit and drew solace from the study of Asian epics. Others became adept at Old French and presented evidence of their devotion to the values of the Abbey of Thélème by scholarship on Rabelais; or tried to master the principles of English Gothic architecture, thus to educate and tame the American spirit by making it contemplate the beauty of the past; or found in the poetry of John Donne or the sermons of Lancelot Andrewes principles whose value was not yet exhausted. The heritages were many, the principle one: conservatives in modern America could opt out of their culture psychologically and find another which suited them better.

Part of the reason conservatives felt so out of place in modern America was that so many half-articulate assumptions seemed to be both universally held and demonstrably untrue. Americans seemed to believe in progress from their first breath, and at no time was this more infuriating than during the placid, complacent years before 1914 or during the Coolidge prosperity of the 1920s, when the Couéism of the media told the semiliterate voters that every day, in every way, they were getting better and better. Conservatives thought otherwise. They knew that change was not reform. They knew that people were irredeemably flawed in their characters, always had been and always would be, and that under stress they were capable of enormities as yet undreamed of by liberal positivists. They knew that "better" in this context simply meant "more." They would admit that scientific insights accumulated and that engineering often contributed material improvements to human life, but they insisted that such superficial measures demeaned the best in people. They liked to drive a motorcar or listen to a good concert on the radio as well as the next person, but they never dreamed that this kind of "progress" had any close relationship with progress in human nature, religion, or the conduct of government. American voters were neither better nor worse than Athenian voters, but the level of cant about their abilities seemed to have escalated intolerably over the years.

These ideas merged almost imperceptibly into a kind of elitism. In America, elitism seemed almost absurd. Wealth seemed to be the only recognizable criterion for success. The educational system often seemed to deny that anyone was ineducable, the political system by the 1920s allowed all but the young, the criminal, the immigrant, and the illiterate to vote and hold office, and the religious system was an implicit universalism that had not kept anyone out of heaven since the withering of Calvinism in the late eighteenth and early nineteenth centuries. Yet conservatives could not help noticing that the universities seemed swamped with people who could not read intelligently or write clearly. The political system produced city, state, and federal governments that were corrupt on the most venal levels, from Boss Croker to Teapot Dome, and capable of imperialistic adventures in the name of equality and Christianity that would shame Cecil Rhodes. The religious system no longer nourished the soul or gave a sense of any transcendent meaning to life; it left people free to enjoy themselves in the most joyless fashion imaginable. The inescapable conclusion was that most people did not know what was good for them. They needed the trained and intelligent few to run institutions that would teach them morals and great ideas and instruct them in proper political behavior. Given such training, people would be happier. They would not exhaust themselves on passing fancies and enervating fads. They would then deserve the legal and religious equality which their institutions already proclaimed.

At this point, modern American conservatism has in fact joined up with conservatism elsewhere. It, too, can preach of the values of institutions, of standards, measures, and principles. Conservatives in other countries could find these traditions growing at home and simply adopt them, but in America they needed to be imported, and the tariff was often high. A more clearly orthodox church, a more rigorously classical college, a restricted voting franchise, a more intelligent group of communications media: such institutions could help teach Americans how to live and escape from the ceaseless flux of the present. Politics, economics, and pleasure were not adequate for the attainment of happiness.

Liberals, in contrast, held other values. In a sense, they possessed the whole history of the country, and so in any Burkean sense of prescriptive right, the nation was theirs and *they* were the true Conservatives. Be that as it may, the typical liberal seemed to believe that most of the good things in life could indeed be obtained by political means. Whether called the New Freedom, the New Nationalism, or the New Deal, the cult of newness always implied legislative intervention into the concerns of society to force reform on labor or capital, to redistribute income, to subsidize farmers, or to force people to contribute to their own pensions. People were politically equal; they should have equal access to the courts, to jobs, to colleges, and to the voting booth. Progress was real, and the advance of social-welfare legislation was a useful measure of how real it was. Institutions in fact only fettered a person, and an individual left free and unguided was the ideal democratic citizen. Human nature for a liberal was not static; it could be improved, and better in a democracy than in any other system.

The modern revival of interest in conservative thought is alone enough justification for a reexamination of the work of the men included in this book. However detached from everyday concerns these men seemed at the time, they did indeed have insights that have some relevance to the problems of the last quarter of the twentieth century. But conservatives could not be genuinely happy with such a justification for studying their thoughts. They would prefer a more substantial reason, related to the past, humane values, and useless knowledge, and in fact such a reason exists and gives the selections in this book far more applicability to American thought than mere contemporary relevance.

To the student of the history of American culture, the conservative mentality has given America an astonishing number of major writers: poets from Poe and Dickinson to Stevens and Lowell, and novelists from Melville and James to Faulkner and Robert Penn Warren. It has given America the majority of its major philosophers, from Jonathan Edwards to Charles Peirce and Santayana, and it has incidentally contributed more to both John Dewey and William James than most people realize. It organized the country and can rightfully claim Washington, Adams, Hamilton, and Jay and at least portions of Jefferson and Madison. It has dominated modern literary criticism since the days of William C. Brownell and has done much to inform the minds of liberals and radicals about the proper way to study literature. The conservatives are more, in other words, than the "stupid party" of John Stuart Mill or the inarticulate grumps of Lionel Trilling's famous dismissal, whose minds are merely full of "irritable mental gestures which seek to resemble ideas." The conservative mind has contributed a major portion of American culture, even when it has not called itself conservative and even when its products have been seized with enthusiastic incomprehension by the liberal intellectual majority. The men in this book, while not always or even often those contributors themselves, were in fact the men who made these conservative values articulate. One can read these men and then return to the literature, the criticism, or the philosophy with a renewed understanding of the complexity of the American experience and the fragility of easy generalizations about it.

The headnotes of the sections that follow give the basic information necessary to read the selections in context. A bibliographical essay of primary and secondary material comes at the end of the book. But certain brief editorial comments are in order.

Most conservative books for this period are either completely unavailable or obtainable only in expensive, hardcover library reprints. Even larger academic libraries do not possess many of the volumes from which I have chosen selections. I have therefore felt free to print in their entirety pieces which seem to be especially illuminative of the conservative mentality. The limitations of space have prevented me from doing this with every selection, however, and so I have had to abridge a number of pieces I would have preferred to print in their entirety. Where several pieces were available which said much the same thing, I have intentionally picked the lesser known or less obtainable piece. I have also several times chosen authors who might otherwise go unrepresented, simply to expand the focus of the book and indicate more of the breadth of conservatism. Most obvious, perhaps, is my neglect of "professional" achievements, like technical aesthetics by George Santayana or poetic analysis by T. S. Eliot or Allen Tate. I have preferred instead pieces about the writers themselves or about American life to illustrate the larger cultural context which remains the core of any genuine conservatism.

I. Growing Up Conservative in America

THE CAREER and opinions of George Santayana (1863–1952) provide an excellent introduction to some of the basic themes of cultural conservatism and its relationship to American culture. Due to the accidents of private life, he grew up within a strange mixture of the Spanish Roman Catholic and the Boston Unitarian environments, never felt at home in either, and used the tensions so created to analyze and criticize not only European and American cultures but also the many religious, philosophical, and literary ideas that grew out of them. In the process he became an eminent member of the famous Harvard University philosophy department, which also included William James and Josiah Royce, and wrote an enormous number of pages that ranged from technical philosophy to a best-selling novel.

In the following essay, Santayana himself gives the biographical details of his life and the key elements of his philosophical position. For the student of conservatism, this material needs supplementing from certain other volumes, parts of which will appear later in this book. Never an American citizen, Santayana always kept his distance from Harvard, President Charles Eliot, and Boston society. He found unpleasant the pervasive American tendency to make everything utilitarian and quantitative and to systematize knowledge. Too often, American intellectuals and artists responded to this environment with an effete gentility that was airless and that killed beauty and spontaneity. Santayana used his divided heritage to remain detached. The English language, he remarks, was more a medium than a source for him, and he found himself compelled to use it to say as many un-English things as possible. This sense of displacement and nonconformity marks a major theme of cultural conservatism in the twentieth century.

Santayana likewise gives students an extended example of the relationship between conservatism and religion. He grew up in an atmosphere suffused with religion, and yet he had no faith. In a dogmatic, institutionalized sense, he had no religion at all. Yet he found in religion, broadly understood, perhaps the greatest work of the human imagination, something of far more value than anything generated by what is so casually assumed to be the "real" world. Just as he loved great poetry and great art, Santayana loved religion; he simply could not believe in it. It was a great fairy tale of the conscience, and as a fairy tale it possessed infinite value, like any other great product of the human imagination.

The actual contribution Santayana made to philosophy is beyond the boundaries of this book. What remains important in this context is the attitude toward knowledge and professional activity which he so clearly articulates below: "My pleasure was rather in expression, in reflection, in irony: my spirit was content to intervene, in whatever world it might seem to find itself, in order to disentangle the intimate moral and intellectual echoes audible to it in that world."

This pose of detached irony, combined with a sense that such a pose is incompatible with the basic values of American culture, sets the basic tone of this volume and of cultural conservatism in America.

1. A Brief History of My Opinions

By George Santayana

How came a child born in Spain of Spanish parents to be educated in Boston and to write in the English language? The case of my family was unusual. We were not emigrants; none of us ever changed his country, his class, or his religion. But special circumstances had given us hereditary points of attachment in opposite quarters, moral and geographical; and now that we are almost extinct—I mean those of us who had these mixed associations—I may say that we proved remarkably staunch in our complex allegiances, combining them as well as logic allowed, without at heart ever disowning anything. My philosophy in particular may be regarded as a synthesis of these various traditions, or as an attempt to view them from a level from which their several deliverances may be justly understood. I do not assert that such was actually the origin of my system: in any case its truth would be another question. I propose simply to describe as best I can the influences under which I have lived, and leave it for the reader, if he cares, to consider how far my philosophy may be an expression of them.

In the first place, we must go much farther afield than Boston or Spain, into the tropics, almost to the antipodes. Both my father and my mother's father were officials in the Spanish civil service in the Philippine Islands. This was in the 1840's and 1850's, long before my birth; for my parents were not married until later in life, in Spain, when my mother was a widow. But the tradition of the many years which each of them separately had spent in the East was always alive in our household. Those had been, for both, their more romantic and prosperous days. My father had studied the country and the natives, and had written a little book about the Island of Mindanao; he had been three times round the world in the sailing-ships of the period, and had incidentally visited England and the United States, and been immensely impressed by the energy and order prevalent in those nations. His respect for material greatness was profound, yet not unmixed with a secret irony or even repulsion. He had a seasoned and incredulous mind, trained to see other sorts of excellence also: in his boyhood he had worked in the studio of a professional painter of the school of Goya, and had translated the tragedies of Seneca into

Note: Originally published in *Contemporary American Philosophy*, edited by George P. Adams and William P. Montague (New York: Macmillan, 1930), pp. 239–257. Reprinted by permission of Mrs. Margot Cory.

Spanish verse. His transmarine experiences, therefore, did not rattle, as so often happens, in an empty head. The sea itself, in those days, was still vast and blue, and the lands beyond it full of lessons and wonders. From childhood I have lived in the imaginative presence of interminable ocean spaces, coconut islands, blameless Malays, and immense continents swarming with Chinamen, polished and industrious, obscene and philosophical. It was habitual with me to think of scenes and customs pleasanter than those about me. My own travels have never carried me far from the frontiers of Christendom or of respectability, and chiefly back and forth across the North Atlantic—thirty-eight fussy voyages; but in mind I have always seen these things on an ironical background enormously empty, or breaking out in spots, like Polynesia, into nests of innocent particoloured humanity.

My mother's figure belonged to the same broad and somewhat exotic landscape; she had spent her youth in the same places; but the moral note resounding in her was somewhat different. Her father, José Borrás, of Reus in Catalonia, had been a disciple of Rousseau, an enthusiast and a wanderer; he taught her to revere pure reason and republican virtue and to abhor the vices of a corrupt world. But her own temper was cool and stoical, rather than ardent, and her disdain of corruption had in it a touch of elegance. At Manila, during the time of her first marriage, she had been rather the grand lady, in a style half Creole, half early Victorian. Virtue, beside those tropical seas, might stoop to be indolent. She had given a silver dollar every morning to her native major-domo, with which to provide for the family and the twelve servants, and keep the change for his wages. Meantime she bathed, arranged the flowers, received visits, and did embroidery. It had been a spacious life; and in our narrower circumstances in later years the sense of it never forsook her.

Her first husband, an American merchant established in Manila, had been the sixth son of Nathaniel Russell Sturgis, of Boston (1779–1856). In Boston, accordingly, her three Sturgis children had numerous relations and a little property, and there she had promised their father to bring them up in case of his death. When this occurred, in 1857, she therefore established herself in Boston; and this fact, by a sort of pre-natal or pre-established destiny, was the cause of my connection with the Sturgis family, with Boston, and with America.

It was in Madrid in 1862, where my mother had gone on a visit intended to be temporary, that my father and she were married. He had been an old friend of hers and of her first husband's, and was well aware of her settled plan to educate her children in America, and recognized the propriety of that arrangement. Various projects and combinations were mooted: but the matter eventually ended in a separation, friendly, if not altogether pleasant to either party. My mother returned with her Sturgis children to live in the United States and my father and I remained in Spain. Soon, however, this compromise proved unsatisfactory. The education and prospects which my father, in his modest retirement, could offer me in Spain were far from brilliant; and in 1872 he decided to take me to Boston, where, after remaining for one cold winter, he left me in my mother's care and went back to Spain.

I was then in my ninth year, having been born on December 16, 1863, and I did not know one word of English. Nor was I likely to learn the language at home, where the family always continued to speak a Spanish more or less pure. But by a happy thought I was sent during my first winter in Boston to a Kindergarten, among much younger children, where there were no books, so that I picked up English by ear before knowing how it was written: a circumstance to which I probably owe speaking the language without a marked foreign accent. The Brimmer School, the Boston Latin School, and Harvard College then followed in order: but apart from the taste for English poetry which I first imbibed from our excellent English master, Mr. Byron Groce, the most decisive influences over my mind in boyhood continued to come from my family, where, with my grown-up brother and sisters, I was the only child. I played no games, but sat at home all the afternoon and evening reading or drawing; especially devouring anything I could find that regarded religion, architecture, or geography.

In the summer of 1883, after my Freshman year, I returned for the first time to Spain to see my father. Then, and during many subsequent holidays which I spent in his company, we naturally discussed the various careers that might be open to me. We should both of us have liked the Spanish army or diplomatic service: but for the first I was already too old, and our means and our social relations hardly sufficed for the second. Moreover, by that time I felt like a foreigner in Spain, more acutely so than in America, although for more trivial reasons: my Yankee manners seemed outlandish there, and I could not do myself justice in the language. Nor was I inclined to overcome this handicap, as perhaps I might have done with a little effort: nothing in Spanish life or literature at that time particularly attracted me. English had become my only possible instrument, and I deliberately put away everything that might confuse me in that medium. English, and the whole Anglo-Saxon tradition in literature and philosophy, have always been a medium to me rather than a source. My natural affinities were elsewhere. Moreover, scholarship and learning of any sort seemed to me a means, not an end. I always hated to be a professor. Latin and Greek, French, Italian, and German, although I can read them, were languages which I never learned well. It seemed an accident to me if the matters which interested me came clothed in the rhetoric of one or another of these nations: I was not without a certain temperamental rhetoric of my own in which to recast what I adopted. Thus in renouncing everything else for the sake of English letters I might be said to have been guilty, quite unintentionally, of a little strategem, as if I had set out to say plausibly in English as many un-English things as possible.

This brings me to religion, which is the head and front of everything. Like my parents, I have always set myself down officially as a Catholic: but this is a matter of sympathy and traditional allegiance, not of philosophy. In my adolescence, religion on its doctrinal and emotional side occupied me much more than it does now. I was more unhappy and unsettled; but I have never had any unquestioning faith in any dogma, and have never been what is called a practising Catholic. Indeed, it would hardly have been possible. My mother, like her father before her, was a Deist: she was sure there was a God, for who else could have made the world? But God was too great to take special thought for man: sacrifices, prayers, churches, and tales of immortality were invented by rascally priests in order to dominate the foolish. My father, except for the Deism, was emphatically of the same opinion. Thus, although I learned my prayers and catechism by rote, as was then inevitable in Spain, I knew that my parents regarded all religion as a work of human imagination: and I agreed, and still agree, with them there. But this carried an implication in their minds against which every instinct in me rebelled, namely that the works of human imagination are bad. No, said I to myself even as a boy: they are good, they alone are good; and the rest—the whole real world— is ashes in the mouth. My sympathies were entirely with those other members of my family who were devout believers. I loved the Christian epic, and all those doctrines and observances which bring it down into daily life: I thought how glorious it would have been to be a Dominican friar, preaching that epic eloquently, and solving afresh all the knottiest and sublimest mysteries of theology. I was delighted with anything, like Mallock's *Is Life Worth Living?*, which seemed to rebuke the fatuity of that age. For my own part, I was quite sure that life was not worth living; for if religion was false everything was worthless, and almost everything, if religion was true. In this youthful pessimism I was hardly more foolish than so many amateur mediaevalists and religious aesthetes of my generation. I saw the same alternative between Catholicism and complete disillusion; but I was never afraid of disillusion, and I have chosen it.

Since those early years my feelings on this subject have become less strident. Does not modern philosophy teach that our idea of the so-called real world is also a work of imagination? A religion—for there are other religions than the Christian—simply offers a system of faith different from the vulgar one, or extending beyond it. The question is which imaginative system you will trust. My matured conclusion has been that no system is to be trusted, not even that of science in any literal or pictorial sense; but all systems may be used and, up to a certain point, trusted as symbols. Science expresses in human terms our dynamic relation to surrounding reality. Philosophies and religions, where they do not misrepresent these same dynamic relations and do not contradict science, express destiny in moral dimensions, in obviously mythical and poetical images: but how else should these moral truths be expressed at all in a traditional or popular fashion? Religions are the great fairy-tales of the conscience.

When I began the formal study of philosophy as an undergraduate at Harvard, I was already alive to the fundamental questions, and even had a certain dialectical nimbleness, due to familiarity with the fine points of theology: the arguments for and against free will and the proofs of the existence of God were warm and clear in my mind. I accordingly heard James and Royce with more wonder than serious agreement: my scholastic logic would have wished to reduce James at once to a materialist and Royce to a solipsist, and it seemed strangely irrational in them to resist such simplification. I had heard many Unitarian sermons (being taken to hear them lest I should become too Catholic), and had been interested in them so far as they were rationalistic and informative, or even amusingly irreligious, as I often thought them to be: but neither in those discourses nor in Harvard philosophy was it easy for me to understand the Protestant combination of earnestness with waywardness. I was used to see water flowing from fountains, architectural and above ground: it puzzled me to see it drawn painfully in bucketfuls from the subjective well, muddied, and half spilt over.

There was one lesson, however, which I was readier to learn, not only at Harvard from Professor Palmer and afterwards at Berlin from Paulsen, but from the general temper of that age well represented for me by the *Revue Des Deux Mondes* (which I habitually read from cover to cover) and by the works of Taine and of Matthew Arnold— I refer to the historical spirit of the nineteenth century, and to that splendid panorama of nations and religions, literatures and arts, which it unrolled before the imagination. These picturesque vistas into the past came to fill in circumstantially that geographical and moral vastness to which my imagination was already accustomed. Professor Palmer was especially skilful in bending the mind to a suave and sympathetic participation in the views of all philosophers in turn: were they not all great men, and must not the aspects of things which seemed persuasive to them be really persuasive? Yet even this form of romanticism, amiable as it is, could not altogether put to sleep my scholastic dogmatism. The historian of philosophy may be as sympathetic and as self-effacing as he likes: the philosopher in him must still ask whether any of those successive views were true, or whether the later ones were necessarily truer than the earlier: he cannot, unless he is a shameless sophist, rest content with a truth *pro tem.* In reality the sympathetic reconstruction of history is a literary art, and it depends for its plausibility as well as for its materials on a conventional belief in the natural world. Without this belief no history and no science would be anything but a poetic fiction, like a classification of the angelic choirs. The necessity of naturalism as a foundation for all further serious opinions was clear to me from the beginning. Naturalism might indeed be criticized—and I was myself intellectually and emotionally predisposed to criticize it, and to oscillate between supernaturalism and solipsism—but if naturalism was condemned, supernaturalism itself could have no point of application in the world of fact; and the whole edifice of human knowledge would crumble, since no perception would then be a report and no judgment would have a transcendent object. Hence historical reconstruction seemed to me more honestly and solidly practised by Taine, who was a professed naturalist, than by Hegel and his school, whose naturalism, though presupposed at every stage, was disguised and distorted by a dialectic imposed on it by the historian and useful at best only in simplifying his dramatic perspectives and lending them a false absoluteness and moralistic veneer.

The influence of Royce over me, though less important in the end than that of James, was at first much more active. Royce was the better dialectician, and traversed subjects in which I was naturally more interested. The point that particularly exercised me was Royce's Theodicy or justification for the existence of evil. It would be hard to exaggerate the ire which his arguments on this subject aroused in my youthful breast. Why that emotion? Romantic sentiment that could find happiness only in tears and virtue only in heroic agonies was something familiar to me and not unsympathetic: a poetic play of mine, called *Lucifer*, conceived in those days, is a clear proof of it. I knew Leopardi and Musset largely by heart; Schopenhauer was soon to become, for a brief period, one of my favourite authors. I carried Lucretius in my pocket: and although the spirit of the poet in that case was not romantic, the picture of human existence which he drew glorified the same vanity. Spinoza, too, whom I was reading under Royce himself, filled me with joy and enthusiasm: I gathered at once from him a doctrine which has remained axiomatic with me ever since, namely that good and evil are relative to the natures of animals, irreversible in that relation, but indifferent to the march of cosmic events, since the force of the universe infinitely exceeds the force of any one of its parts. Had I found, then, in Royce only a romantic view of life, or only pessimism, or only stoical courage and pantheistic piety, I should have taken no offence, but readily recognized the poetic truth or the moral legitimacy of those positions. Conformity with fate, as I afterwards came to see, belongs to post-rational morality, which is a normal though optional development of human sentiment: Spinoza's "intellectual love of God" was a shining instance of it.

But in Royce these attitudes, in themselves so honest and noble, seemed to be somehow embroiled and rendered sophistical: nor was he alone in this, for the same moral equivocation seemed to pervade

Hegel, Browning, and Nietzsche. That which repelled me in all these men was the survival of a sort of forced optimism and pulpit unction, by which a cruel and nasty world, painted by them in the most lurid colours, was nevertheless set up as the model and standard of what ought to be. The duty of an honest moralist would have been rather to distinguish, in this bad or mixed reality, the part, however small, that could be loved and chosen from the remainder, however large, which was to be rejected and renounced. Certainly the universe was in flux and dynamically single: but this fatal flux could very well take care of itself; and it was not so fluid that no islands of a relative permanence and beauty might not be formed in it. Ascetic conformity was itself one of these islands: a scarcely inhabitable peak from which almost all human passions and activities were excluded. And the Greeks, whose deliberate ethics was rational, never denied the vague early Gods and the environing chaos, which perhaps would return in the end: but meantime they built their cities bravely on the hill-tops, as we all carry on pleasantly our temporal affairs, although we know that to-morrow we die. Life itself exists only by a modicum of organization, achieved and transmitted through a world of change: the momentum of such organization first creates a difference between good and evil, or gives them a meaning at all. Thus the core of life is always hereditary, steadfast, and classical; the margin of barbarism and blind adventure round it may be as wide as you will, and in some wild hearts the love of this fluid margin may be keen, as might be any other loose passion. But to *preach* barbarism as the only good, in ignorance or hatred of the possible perfection of every natural thing, was a scandal: a belated Calvinism that remained fanatical after ceasing to be Christian. And there was a further circumstance which made this attitude particularly odious to me. This romantic love of evil was not thoroughgoing: wilfulness and disorder were to reign only in spiritual matters; in government and industry, even in natural science, all was to be order and mechanical progress. Thus the absence of a positive religion and of a legislation, like that of the ancients, intended to be rational and final, was very far from liberating the spirit for higher flights: on the contrary, it opened the door to the pervasive tyranny of the world over the soul. And no wonder: a soul rebellious to its moral heritage is too weak to reach any firm definition of its inner life. It will feel lost and empty unless it summons the random labours of the contemporary world to fill and to enslave it. It must let mechanical and civic achievements reconcile it to its own moral confusion and triviality.

It was in this state of mind that I went to Germany to continue the study of philosophy—interested in all religious or metaphysical systems, but sceptical about them and scornful of any romantic worship or idealization of the real world. The life of a wandering student, like those of the Middle Ages, had an immense natural attraction for me— so great, that I have never willingly led any other. When I had to choose a profession, the prospect of a quiet academic existence seemed the least of evils. I was fond of reading and observation, and I liked young men; but I have never been a diligent student either of science or art, nor at all ambitious to be learned. I have been willing to let cosmological problems and technical questions solve themselves as they would or as the authorities agreed for the moment that they should be solved. My pleasure was rather in expression, in reflection, in irony: my spirit was content to intervene, in whatever world it might seem to find itself, in order to disentangle the intimate moral and intellectual echoes audible to it in that world. My naturalism or materialism is no academic opinion: it is not a survival of the alleged materialism of the nineteenth century, when all the professors of philosophy were idealists: it is an everyday conviction which came to me, as it came to my father, from experience and observation of the world at large, and especially of my own feelings and passions. It seems to me that those who are not materialists cannot be good observers of themselves: they may hear themselves thinking, but they cannot have watched themselves acting and feeling; for feeling and action are evidently accidents of matter. If a Democritus or Lucretius or Spinoza or Darwin works within the lines of nature, and clarifies some part of that familiar object, that fact is the ground of my attachment to them: they have the savour of truth; but what the savour of truth is, I know very well without their help. Consequently there is no opposition in my mind between materialism and a Platonic or even Indian discipline of the spirit. The recognition of the material world and of the conditions of existence in it merely enlightens the spirit concerning the source of its troubles and the means to its happiness or deliverance: and it was happiness or deliverance, the supervening supreme expression of human will and imagination, that alone really concerned me. This alone was genuine philosophy: this alone was the life of reason.

Had the life of reason ever been cultivated in the world by people with a sane imagination? Yes, once, by the Greeks. Of the Greeks, however, I knew very little: the philosophical and political departments at Harvard had not yet discovered Plato and Aristotle. It was with the greater pleasure that I heard Paulsen in Berlin expounding Greek ethics with a sweet reasonableness altogether worthy of the subject: here at last was a vindication of order and beauty in the institutions of men and in their ideas. Here, through the pleasant medium of transparent myths or of summary scientific images, like the water of Thales, nature was essentially understood and honestly described; and here, for that very reason, the free mind could disentangle its true good, and could express it in art, in manners, and even in the most refined or the most austere spiritual discipline. Yet, although I knew henceforth that in the Greeks I should find the natural support and point of attachment for my own philosophy, I was not then collected or mature enough to pursue the matter; not until ten

years later, in 1896–1897, did I take the opportunity of a year's leave
of absence to go to England and begin a systematic reading of Plato
and Aristotle under Dr. Henry Jackson of Trinity College, Cambridge.
I am not conscious of any change of opinion supervening, nor of any
having occurred earlier; but by that study and change of scene my
mind was greatly enriched; and the composition of *The Life of Reason*
was the consequence.

This book was intended to be a summary history of the human
imagination, expressly distinguishing those phases of it which showed
what Herbert Spencer called an adjustment of inner to outer relations; in other words, an adaptation of fancy and habit to material
facts and opportunities. On the one hand, then, my subject being the
imagination, I was never called on to step beyond the subjective
sphere. I set out to describe, not nature or God, but the ideas of God
or nature bred in the human mind. On the other hand, I was not concerned with these ideas for their own sake, as in a work of pure poetry
or erudition, but I meant to consider them in their natural genesis
and significance; for I assumed throughout that the whole life of
reason was generated and controlled by the animal life of man in the
bosom of nature. Human ideas had, accordingly, a symptomatic, ex-
pressive, and symbolic value: they were the inner notes sounded by
man's passions and by his arts: and they became rational partly by
their vital and inward harmony—for reason is a harmony of the passions—and partly by their adjustment to external facts and possibilities—for reason is a harmony of the inner life with truth and with
fate. I was accordingly concerned to discover what wisdom is possible
to an animal whose mind, from beginning to end, is poetical: and I
found that this could not lie in discarding poetry in favour of a science
supposed to be clairvoyant and literally true. Wisdom lay rather in
taking everything good-humouredly, with a grain of salt. In science
there was an element of poetry, pervasive, inevitable, and variable:
it was strictly scientific and true only in so far as it involved a close
and prosperous adjustment to the surrounding world, at first by its
origin in observation and at last by its application in action. Science
was the mental accompaniment of art.

Here was a sort of pragmatism: the same which I have again expressed, I hope more clearly, in one of the *Dialogues in Limbo* entitled "Normal Madness." The human mind is a faculty of dreaming
awake, and its dreams are kept relevant to its environment and to its
fate only by the external control exercised over them by Punishment,
when the accompanying conduct brings ruin, or by Agreement, when
it brings prosperity. In the latter case it is possible to establish cor-
respondences between one part of a dream and another, or between
the dreams of separate minds, and so create the world of literature,
or the life of reason. I am not sure whether this notion, that thought
is a controlled and consistent madness, appears among the thirteen
pragmatisms which have been distinguished, but I have reason to

think that I came to it under the influence of William James; never-theless, when his book on *Pragmatism* appeared, about the same time as my *Life of Reason*, it gave me a rude shock. I could not stomach that way of speaking about truth; and the continual substitution of human psychology—normal madness, in my view—for the universe, in which a man is but one distracted and befuddled animal, seemed to me a confused remnant of idealism, and not serious.

The William James who had been my master was not this William James of the later years, whose pragmatism and pure empiricism and romantic metaphysics have made such a stir in the world. It was rather the puzzled but brilliant doctor, impatient of metaphysics, whom I had known in my undergraduate days, one of whose maxims was that to study the abnormal was the best way of understanding the normal; or it was the genial author of *The Principles of Psychology*, chapters of which he read from the manuscript and dis-cussed with a small class of us in 1889. Even then what I learned from him was perhaps chiefly things which explicitly he never taught, but which I imbibed from the spirit and background of his teaching. Chief of these, I should say, was a sense for the immediate: for the unadulterated, unexplained, instant fact of experience. Actual experi-ence, for William James, however varied or rich its assault might be, was always and altogether of the nature of a sensation: it possessed a vital, leaping, globular unity which made the only fact, the flying fact, of our being. Whatever continuities of quality might be traced in it, its existence was always momentary and self-warranted. A man's life or soul borrowed its reality and imputed wholeness from the in-trinsic actuality of its successive parts; existence was a perpetual re-birth, a traveling light to which the past was lost and the future uncertain. The element of indetermination which James felt so strongly in this flood of existence was precisely the pulse of fresh unpredictable sensation, summoning attention hither and thither to unexpected facts. Apprehension in him being impressionistic—that was the age of impressionism in painting too—and marvellously free from intellectual assumptions or presumptions, he felt intensely the fact of contingency, or the contingency of fact. This seemed to me not merely a peculiarity of temperament in him, but a profound in-sight into existence, in its inmost irrational essence. Existence, I learned to see, is intrinsically dispersed, seated in its distributed moments, and arbitrary not only as a whole, but in the character and place of each of its parts. Change the bits, and you change the mosaic; nor can we count or limit the elements, as in a little closed kaleido-scope, which may be shaken together into the next picture. Many of them, such as pleasure and pain, or the total picture itself, cannot possibly have pre-existed.

But, said I to myself, were these novelties for that reason uncon-ditioned? Was not sensation, by continually surprising us, a continual warning to us of fatal conjunctions occurring outside? And would not

the same conjunctions, but for memory and habit, always produce
the same surprises? Experience of indetermination was no proof of
indeterminism; and when James proceeded to turn immediate experience into ultimate physics, his thought seemed to me to lose itself in
words or in confused superstitions. Free will, a deep moral power
contrary to a romantic indetermination in being, he endeavoured to
pack into the bias of attention—the most temperamental of accidents.
He insisted passionately on the efficacy of consciousness, and invoked
Darwinian arguments for its utility—arguments which assumed that
consciousness was a material engine absorbing and transmitting
energy: so that it was no wonder that presently he doubted whether
consciousness existed at all. He suggested a new physics or metaphysics in which the essences given in immediate experience should
be deployed and hypostatized into the constituents of nature: but this
pictorial cosmology had the disadvantage of abolishing the human
imagination, with all the pathos and poetry of its animal status.
James thus renounced that gift for literary psychology, that romantic
insight, in which alone he excelled; and indeed his followers are
without it. I pride myself on remaining a disciple of his earlier un-
sophisticated self, when he was an agnostic about the universe, but
in his diagnosis of the heart an impulsive poet: a master in the art
of recording or divining the lyric quality of experience as it actually
came to him or to me.

Lyric experience and literary psychology, as I have learned to conceive them, are chapters in the life of one race of animals, in one
corner of the natural world. But before relegating them to that modest
station (which takes nothing away from their spiritual prerogatives)
I was compelled to face the terrible problem which arises when, as in
modern philosophy, literary psychology and lyric experience are made
the fulcrum or the stuff of the universe. Has this experience any external conditions? If it has, are they knowable? And if it has not, on
what principle are its qualities generated or its episodes distributed?
Nay, how can literary psychology or universal experience have any
seat save the present fancy of the psychologist or the historian? Although James had been bothered and confused by these questions,
and Royce had enthroned his philosophy upon them, neither of these
my principal teachers seemed to have come to clearness on the subject: it was only afterwards, when I read Fichte and Schopenhauer,
that I began to see my way to a solution. We must oscillate between a
radical transcendentalism, frankly reduced to a solipsism of the living
moment, and a materialism posited as a presupposition of conventional sanity. There was no contradiction in joining together a scepticism
which was not a dogmatic negation of anything and an animal faith
which avowedly was a mere assumption in action and description.
Yet such oscillation, if it was to be justified and rendered coherent,
still demanded some understanding of two further points: what,
starting from immediate experience, was the *causa cognoscendi* of the

natural world; and what, starting from the natural world, was the *causa fiendi* of immediate experience?

On this second point (in spite of the speculations of my friend Strong) I have not seen much new light. I am constrained merely to register as a brute fact the emergence of consciousness in animal bodies. A psyche, or nucleus of hereditary organization, gathers and governs these bodies, and at the same time breeds within them a dreaming, suffering, and watching mind. Such investigations as those of Fraser and of Freud have shown how rich and how mad a thing the mind is fundamentally, how pervasively it plays about animal life, and how remote its first and deepest intuitions are from any understanding of their true occasions. An interesting and consistent complement to these discoveries is furnished by behaviourism, which I heartily accept on its positive biological side: the hereditary life of the body, modified by accident or training, forms a closed cycle of habits and actions. Of this the mind is a concomitant spiritual expression, invisible, imponderable, and epiphenomenal, or, as I prefer to say, hypostatic: for in it the moving unities and tensions of animal life are synthesized on quite another plane of being, into actual intuitions and feelings. This spiritual fertility in living bodies is the most natural of things. It is unintelligible only as all existence, change, or genesis is unintelligible; but it might be better understood, that is, better assimilated to other natural miracles, if we understood better the life of matter everywhere, and that of its different aggregates.

On the other point raised by my naturalism, namely on the grounds of faith in the natural world, I have reached more positive conclusions. Criticism, I think, must first be invited to do its worst: nothing is more dangerous here than timidity or convention. A pure and radical transcendentalism will disclaim all knowledge of fact. Nature, history, the self become ghostly presences, mere notions of such things; and the being of these images becomes purely internal to them; they exist in no environing space or time; they possess no substance or hidden parts, but are all surface, all appearance. Such a being, or quality of being, I call an essence; and to the consideration of essences, composing of themselves an eternal and infinite realm, I have lately devoted much attention. To that sphere I transpose the familiar pictures painted by the senses, or by traditional science and religion. Taken as essences, all ideas are compatible and supplementary to one another, like the various arts of expression; it is possible to perceive, up to a certain point, the symbolic burden of each of them, and to profit by the spiritual criticism of experience which it may embody. In particular, I recognize this spiritual truth in the Neo-Platonic and Indian systems, without admitting their fabulous side; after all, it is an old maxim with me that many ideas may be convergent as poetry which would be divergent as dogmas. This applies, in quite another quarter, to that revolution in physics which is now loudly announced, sometimes as the bankruptcy of science, sometimes as the breakdown of materialism. This revolution becomes, in my view, simply a change in notation. Matter may be called gravity or an electric charge or a tension in an ether; mathematics may readjust its equations to more accurate observations; any fresh description of nature which may result will still be a product of human wit, like the Ptolemaic and the Newtonian systems, and nothing but an intellectual symbol for man's contacts with matter, in so far as they have gone or as he has become distinctly sensitive to them. The real matter, within him and without, will meantime continue to rejoice in its ancient ways, or to adopt new ones, and incidentally to create these successive notions of it in his head.

When all the data of immediate experience and all the constructions of thought have thus been purified and reduced to what they are intrinsically, that is, to eternal essences, by a sort of counterblast the sense of existence, of action, of ambushed reality everywhere about us, becomes all the clearer and more imperious. This assurance of the not-given is involved in action, in expectation, in fear, hope, or want: I call it animal faith. The object of this faith is the substantial energetic thing encountered in action, whatever this thing may be in itself; by moving, devouring, or transforming this thing I assure myself of its existence; and at the same time my respect for it becomes enlightened and proportionate to its definite powers. But throughout, for the description of it in fancy, I have only the essences which my senses or thought may evoke in its presence; these are my inevitable signs and names for that object. Thus the whole sensuous and intellectual furniture of the mind becomes a store whence I may fetch terms for the description of nature, and may compose the silly home-poetry in which I talk to myself about everything. All is a tale told, if not by an idiot, at least by a dreamer; but it is far from signifying nothing. Sensations are rapid dreams: perceptions are dreams sustained and developed at will; sciences are dreams abstracted, controlled, measured, and rendered scrupulously proportional to their occasions. Knowledge accordingly always remains a part of imagination in its terms and in its seat; yet by virtue of its origin and intent it becomes a memorial and a guide to the fortunes of man in nature.

In the foregoing I have said nothing about my sentiments concerning aesthetics or the fine arts; yet I have devoted two volumes to those subjects, and I believe that to some people my whole philosophy seems to be little but rhetoric or prose poetry. I must frankly confess that I have written some verses; and at one time I had thoughts of becoming an architect or even a painter. The decorative and poetic aspects of art and nature have always fascinated me and held my attention above everything else. But in philosophy I recognize no separable thing called aesthetics; and what has gone by the name of the philosophy of art, like the so-called philosophy of history, seems to me sheer verbiage. There is in art nothing but manual knack and professional tradition on the practical side, and on the contemplative side pure intuition of essence, with the inevitable intellectual or luxurious pleasure which pure intuition involves. I can draw no distinction—save for academic programmes—between moral and aesthetic values: beauty, being a good, is a moral good; and the practice and enjoyment of art, like all practice and all enjoyment, fall within the sphere of morals—at least if by morals we understand moral economy and not moral superstition. On the other hand, the good, when actually realized and not merely pursued from afar, is a joy in the immediate; it is possessed with wonder and is in that sense aesthetic. Such pure joy when blind is called pleasure, when centred in some sensible image is called beauty, and when diffused over the thought of ulterior propitious things is called happiness, love, or religious rapture. But where all is manifest, as it is in intuition, classifications are pedantic. Harmony, which might be called an aesthetic principle, is also the principle of health, of justice, and of happiness. Every impulse, not the aesthetic mood alone, is innocent and irresponsible in its origin and precious in its own eyes; but every impulse or indulgence, including the aesthetic, is evil in its effect, when it renders harmony impossible in the general tenor of life, or produces in the soul division and ruin. There is no lack of folly in the arts; they are full of inertia and affectation and of what must seem ugliness to a cultivated taste; yet there is no need of bringing the catapult of criticism against it: indifference is enough. A society will breed the art which it is capable of, and which it deserves; but even in its own eyes this art will hardly be important or beautiful unless it engages deeply the resources of the soul. The arts may die of triviality, as they were born of enthusiasm. On the other hand, there will always be beauty, or a transport akin to the sense of beauty, in any high contemplative moment. And it is only in contemplative moments that life is truly vital, when routine gives place to intuition, and experience is synthesized and brought before the spirit in its sweep and truth. The intention of my philosophy has certainly been to attain, if possible, such wide intuitions, and to celebrate the emotions with which they fill the mind. If this object be aesthetic and merely poetical, well and good: but it is a poetry or aestheticism which shines by disillusion and is simply intent on the unvarnished truth.

RALPH ADAMS CRAM (1863–1942) was born into a New England family typical in its intellectual devotion to the writings of Emerson and the religion of Unitarianism. He vacillated for a while between journalism and architecture, and he proved to be especially interested in some of the newer currents in the fine arts, like Pre-Raphaelite painting and Wagnerian opera. A brief stint as a private tutor took him to Europe in 1888, and while there he experienced the religious and vocational conversion described below. He returned to Boston to join the first in a series of notable architectural firms and in time combined his interests to specialize in church architecture and Gothic designs in general. He also became an outspoken communicant of the high church wing of the Protestant Episcopal church.

Throughout his life he wrote prolifically, ranging from ghost stories to studies of Japanese architecture, and was responsible for an impressive series of architectural projects: much of West Point and Princeton, Rice University, and a major reorganization of the plan for the Cathedral of St. John the Divine in New York City. He was probably the preeminent conservative architect in the country and the most able of those involved in the craze for collegiate Gothic.

The autobiographical passage below gives us a picture of a rather decadent young man, using John Ruskin, Aubrey Beardsley, and Oscar Wilde to throw off the dull Unitarianism of Cram's minister father to replace it with ideas that are sensuous, aesthetic, and mysterious. Cram here provides a fruitful comparison to Santayana within conservatism—Cram devoutly religious, Santayana completely skeptical, yet both intensely aesthetic, loving beauty, scarcely aware of political or economic realities, and basically hostile to and ignored by American culture. Cram's professed monarchism and socialism quite obviously are imaginative constructs here, not responses to social need, in no danger of any possible application.

2. My Life in Architecture

By Ralph Adams Cram

I suppose that to everyone there comes a moment when a certain definite thing, not necessarily in itself of major importance or even appositeness, acts as the precipitant on a fluid and amorphous personality, bringing some sort of order out of the chaos and dark night of immaturity, and in a way lifting self-consciousness out of the unconscious. With me, I know, it was music,—particularly that of Richard Wagner, though all operas, and the Symphony Concerts in the old Music Hall in Hamilton Place, and the piano-playing of my first human associates in Boston were fish to my net,—even though I could never learn to read music or play any musical instrument. Just why Wagner, and especially his Ring cycle, should have made—and still makes—a more personal and poignant appeal than even Bach or Brahms or Beethoven, I do not know, unless it is because, from the time of Louis le Débonnaire to that of Henry VIII, my forebears in direct line were Teutonic *Freiherrn* in the Grand Duchy of Brunswick, and some inherited racial inclination persisted in my subconscious personality. In any case, the impulse and the call were there, and the first time I went to Europe in the year 1886 was primarily for the purpose of attending the Wagner Festival in Bayreuth. Here three performances of "Parsifal" and three of "Tristan" in the space of two weeks—with Richter conducting and Materna, Winckleman, and Scaria singing, together with others personally trained by Wagner himself—were enough to make or mar any youth of twenty-three who had just begun to open his eyes on a world of wonder and enchantment.

Almost simultaneously came the Pre-Raphaelites' revelation, through the small showing at the old Art Museum, and the appearance of the Rossetti poems; and these three things—music, painting, and poetry—will always remain associated in my mind as a dynamic unit of inspiration. The ground had already been measurably prepared for the pictorial seed, for by that time I had read everything that Ruskin had written; my father's small library contained all these books, as well as Emerson, Matthew Arnold, and Carlyle, admirably—and providentially—balancing the scientific side, consisting of a full

Note: Originally published in *My Life in Architecture* (Boston: Little, Brown, 1936), pp. 8–11, 18–22, 55–60. Reprinted by permission of the Estate of Ralph Adams Cram.

assortment of the works of Herbert Spencer, Darwin, Tyndall, Huxley, and the other evolutionists of all sorts. Most of this I had devoured by the time of the Wagner-Rossetti revelation (with Walter Scott, Dickens, Thackeray, Dumas, and the "Arabian Nights" for added literary and emotional stimulus); and so the balance between speculative and philosophical science on the one hand, and aesthetics of every sort on the other, was definitely inclined in the latter direction.

Indeed it was these same Pre-Raphaelite pictures that were responsible for my first literary effort, which won me away from architecture for a few years and gave me that newspaper experience that I would not have missed for anything. "First" is not quite true: the very first appearance I ever made in print was a passionate appeal to the people of Boston to preserve Trinity Church (then the object of contemporary architectural idolatry) from a peril that had suddenly revealed itself. Some real estate operator or other had acquired title to the little triangle of land in front of the church (the façade of which was still unfinished), and announced his intention of building thereon a four-story triangular apartment house. I saw red, and in a fury of indignation wrote a passionate appeal (of course to the *Transcript*) for all good citizens to rise in their might and avert this shocking act of vandalism. I remember that E. H. Clement, who was then the editor, printed my effusion with the caption "Have We a Ruskin among Us?" Whether this, my first advent into public affairs, had anything to do with the issue I know not; but in any case the result was that "Trinity Triangle" was taken over by the City and the peril passed.

As soon as one begins writing letters to the Editor—whether in the London *Times* or the *Boston Evening Transcript*—the die is cast, and so one continues to the end. *Cacoëthes scribendi* has seized upon its victim, and nevermore may he escape its subtle and persistent virus. The Pre-Raphaelite pictures gave the next incentive, and with much purple phraseology I begged leave again to appeal to the citizens of Boston to recognize the apocalyptic glory of this work and its revelation of new worlds opening in a new radiance. I have never dared to turn back into the files of the *Transcript*, searching out the issues for—I think—the years eighty-five and eighty-six. I fear the worst; and yet, whatever they were, they must have struck some chord in the heart of E. H. Clement, for he incontinently sent for me to call on him, and forthwith offered me the position of art critic.

.   .   .   .

Of course it was quite the thing, at this time, to proclaim the era as one of decadence; indeed, the word was capitalized and widely used as a sufficient characterization of the age. This did not disturb us in the least or blur our optimism. Instead we rather gloated over the fact. If the world was indeed decadent, so much louder was the call for crusading. Besides, it was rather fun to envisage a crumbling society in which we could look on ourselves as superior beings. We rather revelled in Oscar Wilde and the brilliant and epicene drawings of Aubrey Beardsley. We accented our optimism with the vivacious but really most mistaken idea that we were quite wicked and, to use another tag of the day, *fin de siècle*. We savoured the varied flavours of the cultural menu with relish, and altogether thought of ourselves as monstrously clever fellows—a conception notably lacking in validity.

All this was very superficial, impinging only on the skin. Fundamentally we had, I think, a genuine seriousness both of outlook and of purpose. Religion and sociology made a real appeal. Father Hall was preaching Anglo-Catholicism in the old church on Bowdoin Street, and Father Frisby at the Church of the Advent was doing the same, so the anti-Protestant crusade was in full swing. Christian socialism came over from England and some of us even hired a vacant shop on Boylston Street and tried to start a "Church of the Carpenter" that was to follow the Catholic religion but combine with it a socialism that could but appeal to the working classes—which it conspicuously did not. Those of us who recognized religion as a part of the general scheme of things were *very* High Church, attaching ourselves to the Catholic congregations in Bowdoin and Brimmer Streets. We were, however, in the minority, for already the abandonment of formal religion was well under way. On the other hand, we were pretty generally monarchist in our political sympathies, for, again, that abandonment of the democratic theory and practice, which has since gone to such lengths, was well begun, though it was still, so to speak, in the Catacombs. Indeed, for a time there was a fully organized local branch of the English Jacobite society, "The Order of the White Rose," and we had our services of mourning and expiation on the Feast of Charles the Martyr and on other Loyalist days, drank our seditious toasts, sang our Jacobite songs, and even indulged in complimentary (but limited) correspondence with Queen Mary of Bavaria (the "legitimist" English Sovereign), Don Carlos (the "legitimist" King of Spain), and other deposed monarchs. I still treasure my parchment Charter as "Prior" in those American territories lying between the Canadian border and the Rio Grande.

If we were monarchists, we were also, by and large, socialists—at least theoretically and in a bookish sense. This connection is not so anomalous as it might seem, for just as it is said (and I think with truth) that democracy is possible only where there is a king on his throne, so, as we seem to be discovering to-day, socialism is safe, both in itself and in its operations, only under substantially similar conditions; otherwise, it degenerates into communism which, in its turn, always leads to dictatorships. Of this—I mean communism—happily we knew nothing. I doubt if any one of us had ever read a line of Karl

Marx, and the most of us had not even heard his name. We were
socialists because we were young enough to have generous impulses.
We were William Morris enough to hate industrialism, and were rebellious enough to want to attach ourselves to something new and not
as yet accorded that popular favour that was so soon to follow in
more fashionable circles.

Altogether it was a great moment in history, not only for our own
small group in Boston, but in actuality. High hopes, definite ambitions, certainty of achievement, and lightness of heart created an
atmosphere of which one could breathe deeply. There was no sign, no
cloud, even the smallest, on the horizon of destiny; no indication
(and fortunately) of the coming era of big business, mass production,
and high finance, of labour wars, racketeering, gangsterism and
wholesale kidnapping. A war in which America would be involved—
even a little one like that with Spain, then coming close—was un-
thinkable. As for a World War, exceeding in magnitude and devastation any of those in the past—the money-madness and gamblers'
paradise—the complete breakdown of our social, moral, and economic system—the disintegration of Europe under the red light of a
new Terror, communist interludes of anarchy and massacre, with
kings hurled from their thrones only to be followed by dictators in
half the States of the world—an American President taking, or accepting, such powers over men and things as none other had ever held
or dreamed of holding—as for such a farrago of lunatic impossibili-
ties, the maddest of us all would never have conceived of anything of
the kind, or, if in some delirium inventing such devastating absurdities, wouldn't have mentioned them aloud for fear of the process,
"De lunatico inquirendo."

Yes, a great age, and one that should have furnished fertile
ground for the germination of great personalities. Why it did not is a
cosmic mystery, the solution of which is still to seek.

I wonder if, perhaps, the theory that goes back even to Egypt and
Babylonia, and has haunted the imaginations of speculative philosophers ever since, may give the solution? I mean the doctrine that
there is an implacable rhythm in life, a periodical rise and fall like
the waves of the sea, that, measured by nodal points fixed at intervals
of five hundred years, guarantees an ascent at the beginning of each
measured era that is inevitably followed by a corresponding fall. If
this is so, then our own age—which began with the year fifteen
hundred—must come to its end by the year two thousand; and, however ardent and aspiring the individuals that come to birth during the
last century or so of the five-hundred-year period, they must fail of
fruition, since they ride on the sweep of the declining wave. Certainly
the record of the elapsed years of the present century would seem to
give colour to such a theory, while it would explain the abortive results of so many of those lives that opened with high hopes during

the half-century of which I am now recovering the fast-fading memory.

.   .   .   .

We found ourselves in Rome late in the autumn—none of us, by that time, in very good spirits. Rome received us in most surly fashion: it rained all the time, was bitterly cold; the pension on the Pincio was dreary, human relationships were being strained to the utmost, and, incidentally, I was, I suppose, the most ineffectual tutor at large. On the other hand I was seeing Rome (I had stopped short of this universal bourne when in Italy a year and a half before), and finding out a lot about architecture I had never suspected, even if the knowledge was gained in the midst of rain and snow and sleet. This was much; but the great thing was that here I made a new friend who was to play a vital part, though only too brief, in my life. This was one T. Henry Randall, a young architectural student from Maryland. I do not remember how I first met him, but I am persuaded it could have been the result of no accident.

I have lived long enough to learn that it is these personal contacts that count. For sixty years I have read incessantly and, while I have traveled over the world so widely that I have seen pretty much all the good architecture and most of the other art of Western Europe, never have I been taught anything of lasting value by a school or a professional teacher; while I had seven years' experience in trying, in my turn, to teach others. There is no reason to disparage the results of contact with the great art of the past, or of such as has been mercifully preserved to us out of the wreckage of war and fanaticism and complacent ignorance; none to discount the subconscious results of book-reading. Both have their place and do their work; but I am firmly persuaded that for the stimulating of inner potential, for the building up of any sort of personal entity, it is the association with dynamic personalities, the interplay of minds and characters, that bring concrete results. There are men and there are women who for a time enter one's life who, so to speak, become the "enacting clause" that makes operative the latent power that otherwise would remain without effect or realization.

I could name four or five people who have done this for me, and I imagine anyone else could do the same. If not, I am sorry for him: he has missed one of the essential elements in life. Amongst these personalities that have been an evocative and formative influence in my life, I must place Henry Randall high in the list. Representing the best social tradition of the Old South, he had a personality of singular charm and a passion for good architecture that did much to rebuild the fabric of my vision and set me on the way of architecture again. Also, though unconsciously, he helped me to find a definite religion for myself—not the least of the counts in my indebtedness to him. When I first met him in Rome, I was of the ordinary type of bumptious and self-satisfied youth that, in his mental superiority, scorns all religions other than the ethical culture and the respectful deism of the "liberal" Protestant denominations. Randall was an Episcopalian of the sound Southern sort, vitalized by Catholic tendencies; and when the matter of religion came up, as of course it was sure to do sooner or later, I found my rationalistic self-sufficiency showing rather thin in the light of his definiteness and certainty.

By this time I discovered I could not argue with any deep confidence, because all the art of a thousand years, in which I was fast becoming immersed, was getting in its deadly work, and I was beginning to realize that if it had validity, if it related itself to life, it was not the life of rationalism and physical science and liberal Unitarianism, but very specifically the life of the Catholic Church. Furthermore, what I had seen of desecration and destruction in England and France during the era of the Protestant Revolution, not to speak of the sort of "art" that had followed after this upheaval, had demonstrated rather clearly that this sort of thing—from Luther, Calvin, Knox, and Cromwell to the latest phases of so-called religious thought—had produced nothing whatever with which I could have anything to do. It was all to lead one to think furiously, and when I tried to meet Randall on his own ground it was with no firm basis on which to stand and even, increasingly, without conviction.

Two years before, when I was wandering through North Italy, I had come to Assisi and there, in the Lower Church, before the tomb of Saint Francis, by some unaccountable impulse I had found myself on my knees and trying to say something in the way of prayers. I did not make out very well, for it was actually the first time in my life when anything of the sort had happened. With a mystical philosopher for a father and a mother of keen rationalistic convictions (albeit a poet), prayer, or indeed anything approaching formal religious action, was out of the question, and I had been allowed to go my own way. The sudden impulse, there before the tomb of the Saint, was, I think, genuine, but for the time without lasting results, and it soon passed out of mind.

Now it happened (is that the word, I wonder?) that Randall had obtained two tickets for the midnight Mass on Christmas Eve in the Church of San Luigi dei Francesi, and he asked me, casually enough, if I should like to go. Quite willing to try anything once, I assented. Architecturally the church is not one that appealed to me then or appeals to me now, being Rococo of a most elaborate sort, but that night it was blazing with hundreds of candles, crowded with worshippers and instinct with a certain atmosphere of devotion and of ardent waiting. For the half-hour after we arrived it was quite still except for the subdued rustle of men and women on their knees and the delicate click of rosaries. Then, in their white and gold vestments, the sacred ministers came silently to the high altar, attended by crucifers, thurifers and acolytes, and stood silently waiting. Suddenly came the bells striking the hour of midnight, and with the last clang the great organs and choir burst into a melodious thunder of sound; the incense rose in clouds, filling the church with a veil of pale smoke; and the Mass proceeded to its climax with the offering of the Holy Sacrifice of the Body and Blood of Christ. I did not understand all of this with my mind, but *I understood.*

On the way home, through the dark Roman streets, Randall remarked that he was going next morning to an early service of Holy Communion at the English Church. I told him, somewhat to my own surprise, and to his, that I would go with him, which I did, though only of course to "assist" at the Mass, not to receive. As soon as I got back to Boston, I went over to the Church of St. John the Evangelist and placed myself in the hands of Father Hall for instruction, and shortly after was baptized, young Mr. Brent, later Bishop of the Philippines, being my sponsor; and in due course I received the Sacrament of Confirmation in the Anglican Communion of the Catholic Church.

ALBERT JAY NOCK (1870–1945) *provides us with another example of a conservative coming of age, one that offers rather sharp contrasts to Santayana and Cram. Gone are the exotic elements of Santayana's Spanish Catholic background and Cram's aesthetic high Anglican revolt against the aridities of New England culture. Nock's background and upbringing were far more typically American, and his experience with American government and society was more direct. Much of his life does not even appear in the sketch that follows. He was for many years an Episcopal minister, but he left the church to pursue a career in radical journalism. He was an active supporter of Henry George's single tax theories and was active in liberal and radical circles until his disillusionment with Woodrow Wilson's war policies propelled him to the "anarchism" he describes below. In the two decades of life that remained for him after writing this essay, he became a distinguished man of letters. He wrote many essays on topical subjects and published scholarship on Jefferson and Rabelais. He also translated his antistatist views into a conscious cultural conservatism militantly critical of the New Deal and American culture in general.*

The central message of Nock's essay is clearly his growing contempt for the entire subject of American politics. Politics involves the lowest kind of person and brings out the worst qualities of everyone associated with it, yet such is the democratic cant of the day that Americans overlook all the evidence and regard its legal and social consequences with respect and even awe. The state monopolizes crime and enables individuals to commit acts as public officials that they would be ashamed to do as private citizens. Politics originated in conquest and confiscation and persists in order that one class of people can exploit the others.

Nock had no room in the essay to dwell on the valuable aspects of life, but they are nevertheless implicit and occasionally explicit. A useless liberal education, good breeding and manners, detached analysis, tolerance—these are valuable. People need more sound and disinterested thinking and less action, or they are doomed to life in a meanly corrupt environment.

3. Anarchist's Progress

By Albert Jay Nock

I

When I was seven years old, playing in front of our house on the outskirts of Brooklyn one morning, a policeman stopped and chatted with me for a few moments. He was a kindly man, of a Scandinavian blonde type with pleasant blue eyes, and I took to him at once. He sealed our acquaintance permanently by telling me a story that I thought was immensely funny; I laughed over it at intervals all day. I do not remember what it was, but it had to do with the antics of a drove of geese in our neighborhood. He impressed me as the most entertaining and delightful person that I had seen in a long time, and I spoke of him to my parents with great pride.

At this time I did not know what policemen were. No doubt I had seen them, but not to notice them. Now, naturally, after meeting this highly prepossessing specimen, I wished to find out all I could about them, so I took the matter up with our old colored cook. I learned from her that my fine new friend represented something that was called the law; that the law was very good and great, and that everyone should obey and respect it. This was reasonable; if it were so, then my admirable friend just fitted his place, and was even more highly to be thought of, if possible. I asked where the law came from, and it was explained to me that men from all over the country got together on what was called election day, and chose certain persons to make the law and others to see that it was carried out; and that the sum-total of all this mechanism was called our government. This again was as it should be; the men I knew, such as my father, my uncle George, and Messrs. So-and-so among the neighbours (running them over rapidly in my mind), could do this sort of thing handsomely, and there was probably a good deal in the idea. But what was it all for? Why did we have law and government, anyway? Then I learned that there were persons called criminals; some of them stole, some hurt or killed people or set fire to houses; and it was the duty of men like my friend the policeman to protect us from them. If he saw any he would catch them and lock them up, and they could be punished according to the law.

A year or so later we moved to another house in the same neighbourhood, only a short distance away. On the corner of the block—rather a long block—behind our house stood a large one-story wooden building, very dirty and shabby, called the Wigwam. While getting the lie of my new surroundings, I considered this structure and remarked with disfavour the kind of people who seemed to be making themselves at home there. Some one told me it was a "political headquarters," but I did not know what that meant, and therefore did not connect it with my recent researches into law and government. I had little curiosity about the Wigwam. My parents never forbade my going there, but my mother once casually told me that it was a pretty good place to keep away from, and I agreed with her.

Two months later I heard some one say that election day was shortly coming on, and I sparked up at once; this, then, was the day when the lawmakers were to be chosen. There had been great doings at the Wigwam lately; in the evenings, too, I had seen noisy processions of drunken loafers passing our house, carrying transparencies, and tin torches that sent up clouds of kerosene-smoke. When I had asked what these meant, I was answered in one word "politics," uttered in a disparaging tone, but this signified nothing to me. The fact is that my attention had been attracted by a steam-calliope that went along with one of the first of these processions, and I took it to mean that there was a circus going on; and when I found that there was no circus, I was disappointed and did not care what else might be taking place.

On hearing of election day, however, the light broke in on me. I was really witnessing the august performances that I had heard of from our cook. All these processions of yelling hoodlums who sweat and stank in the parboiling humidity of the Indian-summer evenings—all the squalid goings-on in the Wigwam—all these, it seemed, were part and parcel of an election. I noticed that the men whom I knew in the neighbourhood were not prominent in this election; my uncle George voted, I remember, and when he dropped in at our house that evening, I overheard him say that going to the polls was a filthy business. I could not make it out. Nothing could be clearer than that the leading spirits in the whole affair were most dreadful swine; and I wondered by what kind of magic they could bring forth anything so majestic, good and venerable as the law. But I kept my questionings to myself for some reason, though, as a rule, I was quite a hand for pestering older people about matters that seemed anomalous. Finally, I gave it up as hopeless, and thought no more about the subject for three years.

An incident of that election night, however, stuck in my memory.

Some devoted brother, very far gone in whisky, fell by the wayside in
a vacant lot just back of our house, on his way to the Wigwam to
await the returns. He lay there all night, mostly in a comatose state.
At intervals of something like half an hour he roused himself up in
the darkness, apparently aware that he was not doing his duty by the
occasion, and tried to sing the chorus of "Marching Through Georgia,"
but he could never get quite through three measures of the first bar
before relapsing into somnolence. It was very funny; he always began
so bravely and earnestly, and always petered out so lamentably. I
often think of him. His general sense of political duty, I must say,
still seems to me as intelligent and as competent as that of any man
I have met in the many, many years that have gone by since then, and
his mode of expressing it still seems about as effective as any I could
suggest.

II

When I was just past my tenth birthday we left Brooklyn and went to
live in a pleasant town of ten thousand population. An orphaned
cousin made her home with us, a pretty girl, who soon began to cut a
fair swath among the young men of the town. One of these was an
extraordinary person, difficult to describe. My father, a great tease, at
once detected his resemblance to a chimpanzee, and bored my cousin
abominably by always speaking of him as Chim. The young man was
not a popular idol by any means, yet no one thought badly of him.
He was accepted everywhere as a source of legitimate diversion, and
in the graduated, popular scale of local speech was invariably designated as a fool—a born fool, for which there was no help. When I
heard he was a lawyer, I was so astonished that I actually went into
the chicken court one day to hear him plead some trifling case, out of
sheer curiosity to see him in action; and I must say I got my money's
worth. Presently the word went around that he was going to run for
Congress, and stood a good chance of being elected; and what amazed
me above all was that no one seemed to see anything out of the way
about it.

My tottering faith in law and government got a hard jolt from this.
Here was a man, a very good fellow indeed—he had nothing in common with the crew who herded around the Wigwam—who was regarded by the unanimous judgment of the community, without doubt,
peradventure, or exception, as having barely sense enough to come in
when it rained; and this was the man whom his party was sending
to Washington as contentedly as if he were some Draco or Solon. At
this point my sense of humour forged to the front and took permanent charge of the situation, which was fortunate for me, since otherwise my education would have been aborted, and I would perhaps,

like so many who have missed this great blessing, have gone in with
the reformers and up-lifters; and such a close shave as this, in the
words of Rabelais, is a terrible thing to think upon. How many reformers there have been in my day; how nobly and absurdly busy they
were, and how dismally unhumorous! I can dimly remember Pingree
and Altgeld in the Middle West, and Godkin, Strong, and Seth Low
in New York. During the 'nineties, the goodly fellowship of the prophets buzzed about the whole country like flies around a tar-barrel—
and, Lord! where be they now?

III

It will easily be seen, I think, that the only unusual thing about all
this was that my mind was perfectly unprepossessed and blank
throughout. My experiences were surely not uncommon, and my rea-
sonings and inferences were no more than any child, who was more
than half-witted, could have made without trouble. But my mind had
never been perverted or sophisticated; it was left to itself. I never
went to school, so I was never indoctrinated with pseudo-patriotic fustian of any kind, and the plain, natural truth of such matters as I
have been describing, therefore, found its way to my mind without
encountering any artificial obstacle.

This freedom continued, happily, until my mind had matured and
toughened. When I went to college I had the great good luck to hit on
probably the only one in the country (there certainly is none now)
where all such subjects were so remote and unconsidered that one
would not know they existed. I had Greek, Latin, and mathematics,
and nothing else, but I had these until the cows came home; then I
had them all over again (or so it seemed) to make sure nothing was
left out; then I was given a bachelor's degree in the liberal arts, and
turned adrift. The idea was that if one wished to go in for some special branch of learning, one should do it afterward, on the foundation
laid at college. The college's business was to lay the foundation, and
the authorities saw to it that we were kept plentifully busy with the
job. Therefore, all such subjects as political history, political science,
and political economy were closed to me throughout my youth and
early manhood; and when the time came that I wished to look into
them, I did it on my own, without the interference of instructors, as
any person who has gone through a course of training similar to mine
at college is quite competent to do.

That time, however, came much later, and meanwhile I thought
little about law and government, as I had other fish to fry; I was living more or less out of the world, occupied with literary studies. Occasionally some incident happened that set my mind perhaps a little
farther along in the old sequences, but not often. Once, I remember,

I ran across the case of a boy who had been sentenced to prison, a poor, scared little brat, who had intended something no worse than mischief, and it turned out to be a crime. The judge said he disliked to sentence the lad; it seemed the wrong thing to do; but the law left him no option. I was struck by this. The judge, then, was doing something as an official that he would not dream of doing as a man; and could do it without any sense of responsibility, or discomfort, simply because he was acting as an official and not as a man. On this principle of action, it seemed to me that one could commit almost any kind of crime without getting into trouble with one's conscience. Clearly, a great crime had been committed against this boy; yet nobody who had had a hand in it—the judge, the jury, the prosecutor, the complaining witness, the policemen and jailers—felt any responsibility about it, because they were not acting as men, but as officials. Clearly, too, the public did not regard them as criminals, but rather as upright and conscientious men.

The idea came to me then, vaguely but unmistakably, that if the primary intention of government was not to abolish crime but merely to monopolize crime, no better device could be found for doing it than the inculcation of precisely this frame of mind in the officials and in the public; for the effect of this was to exempt both from any allegiance to those sanctions of humanity or decency which anyone of either class, acting as an individual, would have felt himself bound to respect—nay, would have wished to respect. This idea was vague at the moment, as I say, and I did not work it out for some years, but I think I never quite lost track of it from that time.

Presently I got acquainted in a casual way with some officeholders, becoming quite friendly with one in particular, who held a high elective office. One day he happened to ask me how I would reply to a letter that bothered him; it was a query about the fitness of a certain man for an appointive job. His recommendation would have weight; he liked the man, and really wanted to recommend him—moreover, he was under great political pressure to recommend him—but he did not think the man was qualified. Well, then, I suggested offhand, why not put it just that way?—it seemed all fair and straightforward. "Ah yes," he said, "but if I wrote such a letter as that, you see, I wouldn't be reëlected." This took me aback a bit, and I demurred somewhat. "That's all very well," he kept insisting, "but I wouldn't be reëlected." Thinking to give the discussion a semi-humorous turn, I told him that the public, after all, had rights in the matter; he was their hired servant, and if he were not reëlected it would mean merely that the public did not want him to work for them any more, which was quite within their competence. Moreover, if they threw him out on any such issue as this, he ought to take it as a compliment; indeed, if he were reëlected, would it not tend to show in some measure that he and the people did not fully understand each other? He did not like my tone of levity, and dismissed the subject with the remark that I knew nothing of practical politics, which was no doubt true.

IV

Perhaps a year after this I had my first view of a legislative body in action. I visited the capital of a certain country, and listened attentively to the legislative proceedings. What I wished to observe, first of all, was the kind of business that was mostly under discussion; and next, I wished to get as good a general idea as I could of the kind of men who were entrusted with this business. I had a friend on the spot, formerly a newspaper reporter who had been in the press gallery for years; he guided me over the government buildings, taking me everywhere and showing me everything I asked to see.

As we walked through some corridors in the basement of the Capitol, I remarked the resonance of the stonework. "Yes," he said, thoughtfully, "these walls, in their time, have echoed to the uncertain footsteps of many a drunken statesman." His words were made good in a few moments when we heard a spirited commotion ahead, which we found to proceed from a good-sized room, perhaps a committee room, opening off the corridor. The door being open, we stopped, and looked in on a strange sight

In the centre of the room, a florid, square-built, portly man was dancing an extraordinary kind of break-down, or *kazák* dance. He leaped straight up to an incredible height, spun around like a teetotum, stamped his feet, then suddenly squatted and hopped through several measures in a squatting position, his hands on his knees, and then leaped up in the air and spun around again. He blew like a turkey-cock, and occasionally uttered hoarse cries; his protruding and fiery eyes were suffused with blood, and the veins stood out on his neck and forehead like the strings of a bass-viol. He was drunk.

About a dozen others, also very drunk, stood around him in crouching postures, some clapping their hands and some slapping their knees, keeping time to the dance. One of them caught sight of us in the doorway, came up, and began to talk to me in a maundering fashion about his constituents. He was a loathsome human being; I have seldom seen one so repulsive. I could make nothing of what he said; he was almost inarticulate; and in pronouncing certain syllables he would slaver and spit, so that I was more occupied with keeping out of his range than with listening to him. He kept trying to buttonhole me, and I kept moving backward; he had backed me thirty feet down the corridor when my friend came along and dis-engaged me; and as we resumed our way, my friend observed for my consolation that "you pretty well need a mackintosh when X talks to you, even when he is sober."

This man, I learned, was interested in the looting of certain valuable public lands; nobody had heard of his ever being interested in any other legislative measures. The florid man who was dancing was interested in nothing but a high tariff on certain manufactures; he shortly became a Cabinet officer. Throughout my stay I was struck by seeing how much of the real business of legislation was in this category—how much, that is, had to do with putting unearned money in the pockets of beneficiaries—and what fitful and perfunctory attention the legislators gave to any other kind of business. I was even more impressed by the prevalent air of cynicism; by the frankness with which everyone seemed to acquiesce in the view of Voltaire, that government is merely a device for taking money out of one person's pocket and putting it into another's.

V

These experiences, commonplace as they were, prepared me to pause over and question certain sayings of famous men, when subsequently I ran across them, which otherwise I would perhaps have passed by without thinking about them. When I came upon the saying of Lincoln, that the way of the politician is "a long step removed from common honesty," it set a problem for me. I wondered just why this should be generally true, if it were true. When I read the remark of Mr. Jefferson, that "whenever a man has cast a longing eye on office, a rottenness begins in his conduct," I remembered the judge who had sentenced the boy, and my officeholding acquaintance who was so worried about reëlection. I tried to re-examine their position, as far as possible putting myself in their place, and made a great effort to understand it favorably. My first view of a parliamentary body came back to me vividly when I read the despondent observation of John Bright, that he had sometimes known the British Parliament to do a good thing, but never just because it was a good thing. In the meantime I had observed many legislatures, and their principal occupations and preoccupations seemed to me precisely like those of the first one I ever saw; and while their personnel was not by any means composed throughout of noisy and disgusting scoundrels (neither, I hasten to say, was the first one), it was so unimaginably inept that it would really have to be seen to be believed. I cannot think of a more powerful stimulus to one's intellectual curiosity, for instance, than to sit in the galleries of the last Congress, contemplate its general run of membership, and then recall these sayings of Lincoln, Mr. Jefferson, and John Bright.[1]

1. As indicating the impression made on a more sophisticated mind, I may mention an amusing incident that happened to me in London two years ago. Having an engagement with a member of the House of Com-

It struck me as strange that these phenomena seemed never to stir any intellectual curiosity in anybody. As far as I know, there is no record of its ever having occurred to Lincoln that the fact he had remarked was striking enough to need accounting for; nor yet to Mr. Jefferson, whose intellectual curiosity was almost boundless; nor yet to John Bright. As for the people around me, their attitudes seemed strangest of all. They all disparaged politics. Their common saying, "Oh, that's politics," always pointed to something that in any other sphere of action they would call shabby and disreputable. But they never asked themselves why it was that in this one sphere of action alone they took shabby and disreputable conduct as a matter of course. It was all the more strange because these same people still somehow assumed that politics existed for the promotion of the highest social purposes. They assumed that the State's primary purpose was to promote through appropriate institutions the general welfare of its members. This assumption, whatever it amounted to, furnished the rationale of their patriotism, and they held to it with a tenacity that on slight provocation became vindictive and fanatical. Yet all of them were aware, and if pressed, could not help acknowledging, that more than 90 per cent of the State's energy was employed directly against the general welfare. Thus one might say that they seemed to have one set of credenda for week-days and another for Sundays, and never to ask themselves what actual reasons they had for holding either.

I did not know how to take this, nor do I now. Let me draw a rough parallel. Suppose vast numbers of people to be contemplating a machine that they had been told was a plough, and very valuable—indeed, that they could not get on without it—some even saying that its design came down in some way from on high. They have great feelings of pride and jealousy about this machine, and will give up their lives for it if they are told it is in danger. Yet they all see that it will not plough well, no matter what hands are put to manage it, and in fact does hardly any ploughing at all; sometimes only, with enormous difficulty and continual tinkering and adjustment can it be got to scratch a sort of furrow, very poor and short, hardly practicable, and ludicrously disproportionate to the cost and pains of cutting it. On the other hand, the machine harrows perfectly, almost automatically. It looks like a harrow, has the history of a harrow, and even when the most enlightened effort is expended on it to make it act like a

---

mons, I filled out a card and gave it to an attendant. By mistake I had written my name where the member's should be, and his where mine should be. The attendant handed the card back, saying, "I'm afraid this will 'ardly do, sir. I see you've been making yourself a member. It doesn't go quite as easy as that, sir—though from some of what you see around 'ere, I wouldn't say as 'ow you mightn't think so."

plough, it persists, except for an occasional six or eight per cent of efficiency, in acting like a harrow.

Surely such a spectacle would make an intelligent being raise some enquiry about the nature and original intention of that machine. Was it really a plough? Was it ever meant to plough with? Was it not designed and constructed for harrowing? Yet none of the anomalies that I had been observing ever raised any enquiry about the nature and original intention of the State. They were merely acquiesced in. At most, they were put down feebly to the imperfections of human nature which render mismanagement and perversion of every good institution to some extent inevitable; and this is absurd, for these anomalies do not appear in the conduct of any other human institution. It is no matter of opinion, but of open and notorious fact, that they do not. There are anomalies in the church and family that are significantly analogous; they will bear investigation, and are getting it; but the analogies are by no means complete, and are mostly due to the historical connection of these two institutions with the State.

Everyone knows that the State claims and exercises the monopoly of crime that I spoke of a moment ago, and that it makes this monopoly as strict as it can. It forbids private murder, but itself organizes murder on a colossal scale. It punishes private theft, but itself lays unscrupulous hands on anything it wants, whether the property of citizen or of alien. There is, for example, no human right, natural or Constitutional, that we have not seen nullified by the United States Government. Of all the crimes that are committed for gain or revenge, there is not one that we have not seen it commit—murder, mayhem, arson, robbery, fraud, criminal collusion and connivance. On the other hand, we have all remarked the enormous relative difficulty of getting the State to effect any measure for the general welfare. Compare the difficulty of securing conviction in cases of notorious malfeasance, and in cases of petty private crime. Compare the smooth and easy going of the Teapot Dome transactions with the obstructionist behaviour of the State toward a national child-labour law. Suppose one should try to get the State to put the same safeguards (no stronger) around service-income that with no pressure at all it puts around capital-income: what chance would one have? It must not be understood that I bring these matters forward to complain of them. I am not concerned with complaints or reforms, but only with the exhibition of anomalies that seem to me to need accounting for.

VI

In the course of some desultory reading I noticed that the historian Parkman, at the outset of his volume on the conspiracy of Pontiac, dwells with some puzzlement, apparently, upon the fact that the Indians had not formed a State. Mr. Jefferson, also, who knew the Indians well, remarked the same fact—that they lived in a rather highly organized society, but had never formed a State. Bicknell, the historian of Rhode Island, has some interesting passages that bear upon the same point, hinting that the collisions between the Indians and the whites may have been largely due to a misunderstanding about the nature of land-tenure; that the Indians, knowing nothing of the British system of land-tenure, understood their land-sales and land-grants as merely an admission of the whites to the same communal use of land that they themselves enjoyed. I noticed, too, that Marx devotes a good deal of space in *Das Kapital* to proving that economic exploitation cannot take place in any society until the exploited class has been expropriated from the land. These observations attracted my attention as possibly throwing a strong side light upon the nature of the State and the primary purpose of government, and I made note of them accordingly.

At this time I was a good deal in Europe. I was in England and Germany during the Tangier incident, studying the circumstances and conditions that led up to the late war. My facilities for this were exceptional, and I used them diligently. Here I saw the State behaving just as I had seen it behave at home. Moreover, remembering the political theories of the eighteenth century, and the expectations put upon them, I was struck with the fact that the republican, constitutional-monarchical and autocratic States behaved exactly alike. This has never been sufficiently remarked. There was no practical distinction to be drawn among England, France, Germany, and Russia; in all these countries the State acted with unvarying consistency and unfailing regularity against the interests of the immense, the overwhelming majority of its people. So flagrant and flagitious, indeed, was the action of the State in all these countries, that its administrative officials, especially its diplomats, would immediately, in any other sphere of action, be put down as a professional-criminal class; just as would the corresponding officials in my own country, as I had already remarked. It is a noteworthy fact, indeed, concerning all that has happened since then, that if in any given circumstances one went on the assumption that they were a professional-criminal class, one could predict with accuracy what they would do and what would happen; while on any other assumption one could predict almost nothing. The accuracy of my own predictions during the war and throughout the Peace Conference was due to nothing but their being based on this assumption.

The Liberal party was in power in England in 1911, and my attention became attracted to its tenets. I had already seen something of Liberalism in America as a kind of glorified mugwumpery. The Cleveland Administration had long before proved what everybody already knew, that there was no essential difference between the Republican and Democratic parties; an election meant merely that one was in office and wished to stay in, and the other was out and wished to get in. I saw precisely the same relation prevailing between the two major parties in England, and I was to see later the same relation sustained by the Labour Administration of Mr. Ramsay MacDonald. All these political permutations resulted only in what John Adams admirably called " a change of impostors." But I was chiefly interested in the basic theory of Liberalism. This seemed to be that the State is no worse than a degenerate or perverted institution, beneficent in its original intention, and susceptible of restoration by the simple expedient of "putting good men in office."

I had already seen this experiment tried on several scales of magnitude, and observed that it came to nothing commensurate with the expectations put upon it or the enormous difficulty of arranging it. Later I was to see it tried on an unprecedented scale, for almost all the Governments engaged in the war were Liberal, notably the English and our own. Its disastrous results in the case of the Wilson Administration are too well known to need comment; though I do not wish to escape the responsibility of saying that of all forms of political impostorship, Liberalism always seemed to me the most vicious, because the most pretentious and specious. The general upshot of my observations, however, was to show me that whether in the hands of Liberal or Conservative, Republican or Democrat, and whether under nominal constitutionalism, republicanism or autocracy, the mechanism of the State would work freely and naturally in but one direction, namely: against the general welfare of the people.

VII

So I set about finding out what I could about the origin of the State, to see whether its mechanism was ever really meant to work in any other direction; and here I came upon a very odd fact. All the current popular assumptions about the origin of the State rest upon sheer guesswork; none of them upon actual investigation. The treatises and textbooks that came into my hands were also based, finally, upon guesswork. Some authorities guessed that the State was originally formed by this-or-that mode of social agreement; others, by a kind of muddling empiricism; others, by the will of God; and so on. Apparently none of these, however, had taken the plain course of going back upon the record as far as possible to ascertain how it actually had been formed, and for what purpose. It seemed that enough information must be available; the formation of the State in America, for example, was a matter of relatively recent history, and one must be able to find out a great deal about it. Consequently I began to look around to see whether anyone had ever anywhere made any such investigation, and if so, what it amounted to.

I then discovered that the matter had, indeed, been investigated by scientific methods, and that all the scholars of the Continent knew about it, not as something new or startling, but as a sheer common-place. The State did not originate in any form of social agreement, or with any disinterested view of promoting order and justice. Far otherwise. The State originated in conquest and confiscation, as a device for maintaining the stratification of society permanently into two classes —an owning and exploiting class, relatively small, and a propertyless dependent class. Such measures of order and justice as it established were incidental and ancillary to this purpose; it was not interested in any that did not serve this purpose; and it resisted the establishment of any that were contrary to it. No State known to history originated in any other manner, or for any other purpose than to enable the continuous economic exploitation of one class by another.[2]

This at once cleared up all the anomalies which I had found so troublesome. One could see immediately, for instance, why the hunting tribes and primitive peasants never formed a State. Primitive peasants never made enough of an economic accumulation to be worth stealing; they lived from hand to mouth. The hunting tribes of North America never formed a State, because the hunter was not exploitable. There was no way to make another man hunt for you; he would go off in the woods and forget to come back; and if he were expropriated from certain hunting-grounds, he would merely move on beyond them, the territory being so large and the population so sparse. Similarly, since the State's own primary intention was essentially criminal, one could see why it cares only to monopolize crime, and not to suppress it; this explained the anomalous behaviour of officials, and showed why it is that in their public capacity, whatever their private character, they appear necessarily as a professional-criminal class; and it further accounted for the fact that the State never moves disinterestedly for the general welfare, except grudgingly and under great pressure.

Again, one could perceive at once the basic misapprehension which forever nullifies the labors of Liberalism and Reform. It was once quite seriously suggested to me by some neighbours that I should go to Congress. I asked them why they wished me to do that, and they replied with some complimentary phrases about the satisfaction of having some one of a somewhat different type "amongst those damned rascals down there." "Yes, but," I said, "don't you see that it would be only a matter of a month or so—a very short time, anyway—before I should be a damned rascal, too?" No, they did not see this; they were rather taken aback; would I explain? "Suppose," I said, "that you put

2. There is a considerable literature on this subject, largely untranslated. As a beginning, the reader may be conveniently referred to Mr. Charles A. Beard's *Rise of American Civilization* and his work on the Constitution of the United States. After these he should study closely—for it is hard reading—a small volume called *The State* by Professor Franz Oppenheimer, of the University of Frankfort. It has been well translated and is easily available.

in a Sunday-school superintendent or a Y.M.C.A. secretary to run an assignation-house on Broadway. He might trim off some of the coarser fringes of the job, such as the badger game and the panel game, and put things in what Mayor Gaynor used to call a state of 'outward order and decency,' but he *must* run an assignation-house, or he would promptly hear from the owners." This was a new view to them, and they went away thoughtful.

Finally, one could perceive the reason for the matter that most puzzled me when I first observed a legislature in action, namely, the almost exclusive concern of legislative bodies with such measures as tend to take money out of one set of pockets and put it into another —the preoccupation with converting labour-made property into law-made property, and redistributing its ownership. The moment one becomes aware that just this, over and above a purely legal distribution of the ownership of natural resources, is what the State came into being for, and what it yet exists for, one immediately sees that the legislative bodies are acting altogether in character, and otherwise one cannot possibly give oneself an intelligent account of their behaviour.[3]

Speaking for a moment in the technical terms of economics, there are two general means whereby human beings can satisfy their needs and desires. One is by work—*i.e.*, by applying labour and capital to natural resources for the production of wealth, or to facilitating the exchange of labour-products. This is called the economic means. The other is by robbery—*i.e.*, the appropriation of the labour-products of others without compensation. This is called the political means. The State, considered functionally, may be described as *the organization of the political means*, enabling a comparatively small class of beneficiaries to satisfy their needs and desires through various delegations of the taxing power, which have no vestige of support in natural right, such as private land-ownership, tariffs, franchises, and the like.

It is a primary instinct of human nature to satisfy one's needs and desires with the least possible exertion; everyone tends by instinctive preference to use the political means rather than the economic means, if he can do so. The great desideratum in a tariff, for instance, is its license to rob the domestic consumer of the difference between the price of an article in a competitive and a non-competitive market. Every manufacturer would like this privilege of robbery if he could get it, and he takes steps to get it if he can, thus illustrating the pow-

3. When the Republican convention which nominated Mr. Harding was almost over, one of the party leaders met a man who was managing a kind of dark-horse, or one-horse, candidate, and said to him, "You can pack up that candidate of yours, and take him home now. I can't tell you who the next President will be; it will be one of three men, and I don't just yet know which. But I can tell you who the next Secretary of the Interior will be, and that is the important question, because there are still a few little things lying around loose that the boys want." I had this from a United States Senator, a Republican, who told it to me merely as a good story.

erful instinctive tendency to climb out of the exploited class, which lives by the economic means (exploited, because the cost of this privilege must finally come out of production, there being nowhere else for it to come from), and into the class which lives, wholly or partially, by the political means.

This instinct—and this alone—is what gives the State its almost impregnable strength. The moment one discerns this, one understands the almost universal disposition to glorify and magnify the State, and to insist upon the pretence that it is something which it is not—something, in fact, the direct opposite of what it is. One understands the complacent acceptance of one set of standards for the State's conduct, and another for private organizations; of one set for officials, and another for private persons. One understands at once the attitude of the press, the Church and educational institutions, their careful inculcations of a specious patriotism, their nervous and vindictive proscriptions of opinion, doubt or even of question. One sees why purely fictitious theories of the State and its activities are strongly, often fiercely and violently, insisted on; why the simple fundamentals of the very simple science of economics are shirked or veiled; and why, finally, those who really know what kind of thing they are promulgating, are loth to say so.

VIII

The outbreak of the war in 1914 found me entertaining the convictions that I have here outlined. In the succeeding decade nothing has taken place to attenuate them, but quite the contrary. Having set out only to tell the story of how I came by them, and not to expound them or indulge in any polemic for them, I may now bring this narrative to an end, with a word about their practical outcome.

It has sometimes been remarked as strange that I never joined in any agitation, or took the part of a propagandist for any movement against the State, especially at a time when I had an unexampled opportunity to do so. To do anything of the sort successfully, one must have more faith in such processes than I have, and one must also have a certain dogmatic turn of temperament, which I do not possess. To be quite candid, I was never much for evangelization; I am not sure enough that my opinions are right, and even if they were, a second-hand opinion is a poor possession. Reason and experience, I repeat, are all that determine our true beliefs. So I never greatly cared that people should think my way, or tried much to get them to do so. I should be glad if they *thought*—if their general turn, that is, were a little more for disinterested thinking, and a little less for impetuous action motivated by mere unconsidered prepossession; and what little I could ever do to promote disinterested thinking has, I believe, been done.

According to my observations (for which I claim nothing but that they are all I have to go by) inaction is better than wrong action or premature right action, and effective right action can only follow right thinking. "If a great change is to take place," said Edmund Burke, in his last words on the French Revolution, "the minds of men *will be fitted to it.*" Otherwise the thing does not turn out well; and the processes by which men's minds are fitted seem to me untraceable and imponderable, the only certainty about them being that the share of any one person, or any one movement, in determining them is extremely small. Various social superstitions, such as magic, the divine right of kings, the Calvinist teleology, and so on, have stood out against many a vigorous frontal attack, and thrived on it; and when they finally disappeared, it was not under attack. People simply stopped thinking in those terms; no one knew just when or why, and no one even was much aware that they had stopped. So I think it very possible that while we are saying, "Lo, here!" and "Lo, there!" with our eye on this or that revolution, usurpation, seizure of power, or what not, the superstitions that surround the State are quietly disappearing in the same way.[4]

My opinion of my own government and those who administer it can probably be inferred from what I have written. Mr. Jefferson said that if a centralization of power were ever effected at Washington, the United States would have the most corrupt government on earth. Comparisons are difficult, but I believe it has one that is thoroughly corrupt, flagitious, tyrannical, oppressive. Yet if it were in my power to pull down its whole structure overnight and set up another of my own devising—to abolish the State out of hand, and replace it by an organization of the economic means—I would not do it, for the minds of Americans are far from fitted to any such great change as this, and the effect would be only to lay open the way for the worse enormities of usurpation—possibly, who knows? with myself as the usurper! After the French Revolution, Napoleon!

Great and salutary social transformations, such as in the end do not cost more than they come to, are not effected by political shifts, by movements, by programs and platforms, least of all by violent revolutions, but by sound and disinterested thinking. The believers in action are numerous, their gospel is widely preached, they have many followers. Perhaps among those who will see what I have here written, there are two or three who will agree with me that the believers in action do not need us—indeed, that if we joined them, we should be rather a dead weight for them to carry. We need not deny that

4. The most valuable result of the Russian Revolution is in its liberation of the idea of the State as an engine of economic exploitation. In Denmark, according to a recent article in *The English Review*, there is a considerable movement for a complete separation of politics from economics, which, if effected, would of course mean the disappearance of the State.

their work is educative, or pinch pennies when we could up its cost in
the inevitable reactions against it. We need only remark that our
place and function in it are not apparent, and then proceed on our
own way, first with the more obscure and extremely difficult work of
clearing and illuminating our own minds, and second, with what
occasional help we may offer to others whose faith, like our own, is
set more on the regenerative power of thought than on the uncertain
achievements of premature action.

II. The Critique of Modern American Culture

AT LEAST *in part because of his detachment from the dominant concerns of American culture, George Santayana became one of the most perceptive commentators on it. His insights are scattered among many sources, including his three-volume autobiography, but his major contribution to the subject was his book* Character and Opinion in the United States. *Scholars will forever disagree about whether or not there is such a thing as a typical American, but for Santayana the issue was not one of genuine differences between peoples and races but rather one of a moral atmosphere which dominated the tone of discourse in the world he knew. The typical American was thus a symbol of the uniformity he sensed while teaching and living in the Boston area. Americans were adventurous social radicals living in a perpetual present, with their eyes always on the future. They were always moving and had no time for the arts, the social graces, and the niceties of civilized existence. They remained forever young, while Santayana always felt old among them, displaced, superfluous, and out of step.*

A man like himself born into such an environment, he says, is "luckless," as is anyone "who is drawn to poetic subtlety, pious retreats, or gay passions." He has "the categorical excellence of work, growth, enterprise, reform, and prosperity dinned into his ears," and as a result "he either folds up his heart and withers in a corner," or else "he flies to Oxford or Florence or Montmartre to save his soul—or perhaps not to save it."

4. Materialism and Idealism

By George Santayana

I speak of the American in the singular, as if there were not millions of them, north and south, east and west, of both sexes, of all ages, and of various races, professions, and religions. Of course the one American I speak of is mythical; but to speak in parables is inevitable in such a subject, and it is perhaps as well to do so frankly. There is a sort of poetic ineptitude in all human discourse when it tries to deal with natural and existing things. Practical men may not notice it, but in fact human discourse is intrinsically addressed not to natural existing things but to ideal essences, poetic or logical terms which thought may define and play with. When fortune or necessity diverts our attention from this congenial ideal sport to crude facts and pressing issues, we turn our frail poetic ideas into symbols for those terrible irruptive things. In that paper money of our own stamping, the legal tender of the mind, we are obliged to reckon all the movements and values of the world. The universal American I speak of is one of these symbols; and I should be still speaking in symbols and creating moral units and a false simplicity, if I spoke of classes pedantically subdivided, or individuals ideally integrated and defined. As it happens, the symbolic American can be made largely adequate to the facts; because, if there are immense differences between individual Americans—for some Americans are black—yet there is a great uniformity in their environment, customs, temper, and thoughts. They have all been uprooted from their several soils and ancestries and plunged together into one vortex, whirling irresistibly in a space otherwise quite empty. To be an American is of itself almost a moral condition, an education, and a career. Hence a single ideal figment can cover a large part of what each American is in his character, and almost the whole of what most Americans are in their social outlook and political judgements.

The discovery of the new world exercised a sort of selection among the inhabitants of Europe. All the colonists, except the negroes, were voluntary exiles. The fortunate, the deeply rooted, and the lazy remained at home; the wilder instincts or dissatisfaction of others tempted them beyond the horizon. The American is accordingly the

Note: Originally published in *Character and Opinion in the United States* (New York: Scribner's, 1920; reprint, New York: W. W. Norton, n.d.), pp. 167–187.

most adventurous, or the descendant of the most adventurous of Europeans. It is in his blood to be socially a radical, though perhaps not intellectually. What has existed in the past, especially in the remote past, seems to him not only not authoritative, but irrelevant, inferior, and outworn. He finds it rather a sorry waste of time to think about the past at all. But his enthusiasm for the future is profound; he can conceive of no more decisive way of recommending an opinion or a practice than to say that it is what everybody is coming to adopt. This expectation of what he approves, or approval of what he expects, makes up his optimism. It is the necessary faith of the pioneer.

Such a temperament is, of course, not maintained in the nation merely by inheritance. Inheritance notoriously tends to restore the average of a race, and plays incidentally many a trick of atavism. What maintains this temperament and makes it national is social contagion or pressure—something immensely strong in democracies. The luckless American who is born a conservative, or who is drawn to poetic subtlety, pious retreats, or gay passions, nevertheless has the categorical excellence of work, growth, enterprise, reform, and prosperity dinned into his ears: every door is open in this direction and shut in the other; so that he either folds up his heart and withers in a corner—in remote places you sometimes find such a solitary gaunt idealist—or else he flies to Oxford or Florence or Montmartre to save his soul—or perhaps not to save it.

The optimism of the pioneer is not limited to his view of himself and his own future: it starts from that; but feeling assured, safe, and cheery within, he looks with smiling and most kindly eyes on everything and everybody about him. Individualism, roughness, and self-trust are supposed to go with selfishness and a cold heart; but I suspect that is a prejudice. It is rather dependence, insecurity, and mutual jostling that poison our placid gregarious brotherhood; and fanciful passionate demands upon people's affections, when they are disappointed, as they soon must be, breed illwill and a final meanness. The milk of human kindness is less apt to turn sour if the vessel that holds it stands steady, cool, and separate, and is not too often uncorked. In his affections the American is seldom passionate, often deep, and always kindly. If it were given me to look into the depths of a man's heart, and I did not find goodwill at the bottom, I should say without any hesitation, You are not an American. But as the American is an individualist his goodwill is not officious. His instinct is to think well of everybody, and to wish everybody well, but in a spirit of rough comradeship, expecting every man to stand on his own legs and to be helpful in his turn. When he has given his neighbour a chance he thinks he has done enough for him; but he feels it is an absolute duty to do that. It will take some hammering to drive a coddling socialism into America.

As self-trust may pass into self-sufficiency, so optimism, kindness, and goodwill may grow into a habit of doting on everything. To the good American many subjects are sacred: sex is sacred, women are sacred, children are sacred, business is sacred, America is sacred, Masonic lodges and college clubs are sacred. This feeling grows out of the good opinion he wishes to have of these things, and serves to maintain it. If he did not regard all these things as sacred he might come to doubt sometimes if they were wholly good. Of this kind, too, is the idealism of single ladies in reduced circumstances who can see the soul of beauty in ugly things, and are perfectly happy because their old dog has such pathetic eyes, their minister is so eloquent, their garden with its three sunflowers is so pleasant, their dead friends were so devoted, and their distant relations are so rich.

Consider now the great emptiness of America: not merely the primitive physical emptiness, surviving in some regions, and the continental spacing of the chief natural features, but also the moral emptiness of a settlement where men and even houses are easily moved about, and no one, almost, lives where he was born or believes what he has been taught. Not that the American has jettisoned these impedimenta in anger; they have simply slipped from him as he moves. Great empty spaces bring a sort of freedom to both soul and body. You may pitch your tent where you will; or if ever you decide to build anything, it can be in a style of your own devising. You have room, fresh materials, few models, and no critics. You trust your own experience, not only because you must, but because you find you may do so safely and prosperously; the forces that determine fortune are not yet too complicated for one man to explore. Your detachable condition makes you lavish with money and cheerfully experimental; you lose little if you lose all, since you remain completely yourself. At the same time your absolute initiative gives you practice in coping with novel situations, and in being original; it teaches you shrewd management. Your life and mind will become dry and direct, with few decorative flourishes. In your works everything will be stark and pragmatic; you will not understand why anybody should make those little sacrifices to instinct or custom which we call grace. The fine arts will seem to you academic luxuries, fit to amuse the ladies, like Greek and Sanskrit; for while you will perfectly appreciate generosity in men's purposes, you will not admit that the execution of these purposes can be anything but business. Unfortunately the essence of the fine arts is that the execution should be generous too, and delightful in itself; therefore the fine arts will suffer, not so much in their express professional pursuit—for then they become practical tasks and a kind of business—as in that diffused charm which qualifies all human action when men are artists by nature. Elaboration, which is something to accomplish, will be preferred to simplicity, which is something to rest in; manners will suffer somewhat; speech will suffer horribly. For the American the urgency of his novel attack upon matter, his zeal in gathering its fruits, precludes meanderings in primrose paths; devices must be short cuts, and symbols must be mere symbols. If his wife wants luxuries, of course she may have them; and if he has vices, that can be provided for too; but they must all be set down under those headings in his ledgers.

At the same time, the American is imaginative; for where life is intense, imagination is intense also. Were he not imaginative he would not live so much in the future. But his imagination is practical, and the future it forecasts is immediate; it works with the clearest and least ambiguous terms known to his experience, in terms of number, measure, contrivance, economy, and speed. He is an idealist working on matter. Understanding as he does the material potentialities of things, he is successful in invention, conservative in reform, and quick in emergencies. All his life he jumps into the train after it has started and jumps out before it has stopped; and he never once gets left behind, or breaks a leg. There is an enthusiasm in his sympathetic handling of material forces which goes far to cancel the illiberal character which it might otherwise assume. The good workman hardly distinguishes his artistic intention from the potency in himself and in things which is about to realise that intention. Accordingly his ideals fall into the form of premonitions and prophecies; and his studious prophecies often come true. So do the happy workmanlike ideals of the American. When a poor boy, perhaps, he dreams of an education, and presently he gets an education, or at least a degree; he dreams of growing rich, and he grows rich—only more slowly and modestly, perhaps, than he expected; he dreams of marrying his Rachel and, even if he marries a Leah instead, he ultimately finds in Leah his Rachel after all. He dreams of helping to carry on and to accelerate the movement of a vast, seething, progressive society, and he actually does so. Ideals clinging so close to nature are almost sure of fulfillment; the American beams with a certain self-confidence and sense of mastery; he feels that God and nature are working with him.

Idealism in the American accordingly goes hand in hand with present contentment and with foresight of what the future very likely will actually bring. He is not a revolutionist; he believes he is already on the right track and moving towards an excellent destiny. In revolutionists, on the contrary, idealism is founded on dissatisfaction and expresses it. What exists seems to them an absurd jumble of irrational accidents and bad habits, and they want the future to be based on reason and to be the pellucid embodiment of all their maxims. All their zeal is for something radically different from the actual and (if they only knew it) from the possible; it is ideally simple, and they love it and believe in it because their nature craves it. They think life would be set free by the destruction of all its organs. They are therefore extreme idealists in the region of hope, but not at all, as poets and artists are, in the region of perception and memory. In the atmosphere of civilised life they miss all the refraction and all the fragrance;

so that in their conception of actual things they are apt to be crude realists; and their ignorance and inexperience of the moral world, unless it comes of ill-luck, indicates their incapacity for education. Now incapacity for education, when united with great inner vitality, is one root of idealism. It is what condemns us all, in the region of sense, to substitute perpetually what we are capable of imagining for what things may be in themselves; it is what condemns us, wherever it extends, to think *a priori*; it is what keeps us bravely and incorrigibly pursuing what we call the good—that is, what would fulfill the demands of our nature—however little provision the fates may have made for it. But the want of insight on the part of revolutionists touching the past and the present infects in an important particular their idealism about the future; it renders their dreams of the future unrealisable. For in human beings—this may not be true of other animals, more perfectly preformed—experience is necessary to pertinent and concrete thinking; even our primitive instincts are blind until they stumble upon some occasion that solicits them; and they can be much transformed or deranged by their first partial satisfactions. Therefore a man who does not idealise his experience, but idealises *a priori*, is incapable of true prophecy; when he dreams he raves, and the more he criticises the less he helps. American idealism, on the contrary, is nothing if not helpful, nothing if not pertinent to practicable transformations; and when the American frets, it is because whatever is useless and impertinent, be it idealism or inertia, irritates him; for it frustrates the good results which he sees might so easily have been obtained.

The American is wonderfully alive; and his vitality, not having often found a suitable outlet, makes him appear agitated on the surface; he is always letting off an unnecessarily loud blast of incidental steam. Yet his vitality is not superficial; it is inwardly prompted, and as sensitive and quick as a magnetic needle. He is inquisitive, and ready with an answer to any question that he may put to himself of his own accord; but if you try to pour instruction into him, on matters that do not touch his own spontaneous life, he shows the most extraordinary powers of resistance and oblivescence; so that he often is remarkably expert in some directions and surprisingly obtuse in others. He seems to bear lightly the sorrowful burden of human knowledge. In a word, he is young.

What sense is there in this feeling, which we all have, that the American is young? His country is blessed with as many elderly people as any other, and his descent from Adam, or the Darwinian rival of Adam, cannot be shorter than that of his European cousins. Nor are his ideas always very fresh. Trite and rigid bits of morality and religion, with much seemly and antique political lore, remain axiomatic in him, as in the mind of a child; he may carry all this about with an unquestioning familiarity which does not comport understanding. To keep traditional sentiments in this way insulated and un-

criticised is itself a sign of youth. A good young man is naturally
conservative and loyal on all those subjects which his experience has
not brought to a test; advanced opinions on politics, marriage, or literature are comparatively rare in America; they are left for the ladies
to discuss, and usually to condemn, while the men get on with their
work. In spite of what is old-fashioned in his more general ideas, the
American is unmistakably young; and this, I should say, for two reasons: one, that he is chiefly occupied with his immediate environment, and the other, that his reactions upon it are inwardly prompted,
spontaneous, and full of vivacity and self-trust. His views are not yet
lengthened; his will is not yet broken or transformed. The present moment, however, in this, as in other things, may mark a great change
in him; he is perhaps now reaching his majority, and all I say may
hardly apply to-day, and may not apply at all to-morrow. I speak of
him as I have known him; and whatever moral strength may accrue
to him later, I am not sorry to have known him in his youth. The
charm of youth, even when it is a little boisterous, lies in nearness
to the impulses of nature, in a quicker and more obvious obedience
to that pure, seminal principle which, having formed the body and
its organs, always directs their movements, unless it is forced by vice
or necessity to make them crooked, or to suspend them. Even under
the inevitable crust of age the soul remains young, and, wherever it
is able to break through, sprouts into something green and tender.
We are all as young at heart as the most youthful American, but the
seed in his case has fallen upon virgin soil, where it may spring up
more bravely and with less respect for the giants of the wood. Peoples
seem older when their perennial natural youth is encumbered with
more possessions and prepossessions, and they are mindful of the
many things they have lost or missed. The American is not mindful
of them.

. . . .

The circumstances of his life hitherto have necessarily driven the
American into moral materalism; for in his dealings with material
things he can hardly stop to enjoy their sensible aspects, which are
ideal, nor proceed at once to their ultimate uses, which are ideal too.
He is practical as against the poet, and worldly as against the clear
philosopher or the saint. The most striking expression of this materialism is usually supposed to be his love of the almighty dollar; but
that is a foreign and unintelligent view. The American talks about
money, because that is the symbol and measure he has at hand for
success, intelligence, and power; but as to money itself he makes,
loses, spends, and gives it away with a very light heart. To my mind
the most striking expression of his materialism is his singular preoccupation with quantity. If, for instance, you visit Niagara Falls, you
may expect to hear how many cubic feet or metric tons of water are
precipitated per second over the cataract; how many cities and towns

(with the number of their inhabitants) derive light and motive power from it; and the annual value of the further industries that might very well be carried on by the same means, without visibly depleting the world's greatest wonder or injuring the tourist trade. That is what I confidently expected to hear on arriving at the adjoining town of Buffalo; but I was deceived. The first thing I heard instead was that there are more miles of asphalt pavement in Buffalo than in any city in the world. Nor is this insistence on quantity confined to men of business. The President of Harvard College, seeing me once by chance soon after the beginning of a term, inquired how my classes were getting on; and when I replied that I thought they were getting on well, that my men seemed to be keen and intelligent, he stopped me as if I was about to waste his time. "I meant," said he, "*what is the number* of students in your classes."

Here I think we may perceive that this love of quantity often has a silent partner, which is diffidence as to quality. The democratic conscience recoils before anything that savours of privilege; and lest it should concede an unmerited privilege to any pursuit or person, it reduces all things as far as possible to the common denominator of quantity. Numbers cannot lie: but if it came to comparing the ideal beauties of philosophy with those of Anglo-Saxon, who should decide? All studies are good—why else have universities?—but those must be most encouraged which attract the greatest number of students. Hence the President's question. Democratic faith, in its diffidence about quality, throws the reins of education upon the pupil's neck, as Don Quixote threw the reins on the neck of Rocinante, and bids his divine instinct choose its own way.

GEORGE SANTAYANA'S *published material is a strong enough critique of the American environment as a kind of prosperous philistia populated by vigorous young animals, but it sometimes pales beside what Santayana could say to his friends in private. Three excerpts from published letters quickly demonstrate this acerbity. They have been taken from Santayana to William James, Easter 1900; to Susana Sturgis De Sastre, December 7, 1911; and to Logan Pearsall Smith, December 2, 1921.*

5. Excerpts from Three Letters

By George Santayana

You tax me several times with impertinence and superior airs. I wonder if you realize the years of suppressed irritation which I have past in the midst of an unintelligible sanctimonious and often disingenuous Protestantism, which is thoroughly alien and repulsive to me, and the need I have of joining hands with something far away from it and far above it. My Catholic sympathies didn't justify me in speaking out because I felt them to be merely sympathies and not to have a rational and human backing: but the study of Plato and Aristotle has given me confidence and, backed by such an authority as they and all who have accepted them represent, I have the right to be sincere, to be absolutely objective and unapologetic, because it is not I that speak but human reason that speaks in me. Truly the Babel in which we live has nothing in it so respectable as to put on the defensive the highest traditions of the human mind. No doubt, as you say, Latinity is moribund, as Greece itself was when it transmitted to the rest of the world the seeds of its own rationalism; and for that reason there is the more need of transplanting and propagating straight thinking among the peoples who hope to be masters of the world in the immediate future. Otherwise they will be its physical masters only, and the Muses will fly over them to alight among some future race that may understand the Gods better. . . .

.   .   .   .

I am very sorry if you have been *debanandote los sesos* about what I could have meant by saying that I thought you were not in sympathy with my present mood. What I meant was (chiefly) that I am very sick of America and of professors and professoresses, and that I am pining for a sunny, quiet, remote, friendly, intellectual, obscure existence, with large horizons and no empty noise in the foreground. What I have seen in California and Canada—apart from the geography of those regions—has left no impression on my mind whatever. They are intellectually emptier than the Sahara, where I understand the Arabs have some idea of God or of Fate. Where did you get the impression that anything in California could have affected my opin-

Note: Originally published in *The Letters of George Santayana*, edited by Daniel Cory (New York: Scribner's, 1955), pp. 62, 110, 192–194. Reprinted by permission of Mrs. Margot Cory.

ions or sentiments? When there, in my Italian restaurant, or in Montreal among the ultra-British Scotch-Canadians I saw, I felt almost out of America, so much so that I once said inadvertently to someone in San Francisco that I soon had to go back *to America*. That is why, from those places, I felt like expressing myself: because when I am here in the midst of the dull round, a sort of instinct of courtesy makes me take it for granted, and I become almost unconscious of how much I hate it all: otherwise I couldn't have stood it for *forty years!*

.   .   .   .

This taste of mine for living in the midst of a noisy, vulgar rush of people, most of them ugly, with whom I have nothing to do, will perhaps hint to you why I am not altogether in sympathy with your judgement on America. Not that I disagree with your characterization of it; they say it has changed even in these last ten years, but not essentially. I could perfectly recognize, though the genteel tradition may then have been stronger, that America had "no interest for the life of the mind," was "without a head," and "alien." But why do you call this condition "lying fallow" and "deterioration"? Isn't the judgement of the American people rather the opposite, namely that its condition is constantly improving, and its labours splendidly fruitful? Not for the "mind," which in our lips means, I suppose, the liberal or aristocratic life, the mind turned to pure reflection and pure expression and pure pleasure. But why need all the tribes of men sacrifice at our altar? I agree that it is barbarous and tragic to strain after merely conventional ends, by attaining which nobody is the happier, but everyone is sacrificed to some fetish. But isn't America happy? The old genteel America was not happy; it was eager to know the truth, and to be "cultured" and to love "art," and to miss nothing that made other nations interesting or distinguished; and it was terribly and constitutionally unhappy, because with its handicap and its meagreness of soul and its thinness of temper and its paucity of talent, it *could* not attain, nor even approach, any of those ideals. But is the new America unhappy? Does it feel that it is living in a desert, and thirsting for the gardens and the treasure-houses of the Arabian Nights? I think not: it wants simply the sort of life it has, only more of it. It wants comfort and speed and good cheer; it wants health and spirits, and a round of weddings, foot-ball games, campaigns, outings, and cheerful funerals; and it is getting them. In the midst of this, as a sort of joke (and you may make a business of joking) there is a patter of sophomoric art and lady-like religion—never mind what, if only it is new and funny. Why not? When I was at Harvard, from my Freshman days on, I "belonged" to the Lampoon: and that seems to me a sort of symbol or oracle: I belonged to the Lampoon just as much in the philosophical faculty, as I did in the Lampoon "sanctum." It was all a pleasant hard-working exuberance *by the way*; there was not, and could not be anything serious or substantial in it. But notice: *all* learning and all "mind" in America is not of this ineffectual Sophomoric sort. There is your doctor at Baltimore who is a great expert, and *really knows how to do things:* and you will find that, in the service of material life, all the arts and sciences are prosperous in America. But it must be in the service of material life; because it is material life (of course with the hygiene, morality, and international good order that can minister to material life) that America has and wants to have and may perhaps bring to perfection. Think of that! If material life could be made perfect, as (in a very small way) it was perhaps for a moment among the Greeks, would not that of itself be a most admirable achievement, like the creation of a new and superior mammal, who would instinctively suck only the bottle? Imagine a race perfectly adapted to elevated railroads and aeroplanes and submarines, with a regular percentage of a neutral sex to serve as "schoolmarms," and not the least dissatisfaction with the extremes of the weather, the pains of childbirth or toothache (all pains being eliminated) or English as she is spoke by three hundred million Americans! I submit that such a race would be as well worth having and as precious in its own eyes (and any other criterion is irrelevant) as ever were the Chinese or the Egyptians or the Jews. And possibly on that basis of perfected material life, a new art and philosophy would grow unawares, not similar to what we call by those names, but having the same relation to the life beneath which art and philosophy amongst us ought to have had, but never have had actually. You see I am content to let the past bury its dead. It does not seem to me that we can impose on America the task of imitating Europe. The more different it can come to be, the better; and we must let it take its own course, going a long way round, perhaps, before it can shake off the last trammels of alien tradition, and learn to express itself simply, not apologetically, after its own heart. Of course, I don't mean that I feel confident that America will ever produce a true civilisation of a new sort; it may all come to nothing, as almost all experiments in nature do; but while the experiment is going on it seems only fair to give it a chance, and to watch it sympathetically.

ALBERT JAY NOCK *carried many of the themes of Santayana's analysis into his acute and often amusing comments on American education. The American emphasis on large schools, on educating everyone who arrived, and on producing vocationally trained workers bothered many conservatives and cheapened the schools in which many of them taught. Of these, Nock was probably the most prolific on the subject: it crops up in his study of Jefferson, in* The Theory of Education in the United States, *and in his memoirs, as well as in numerous essays. American education, for someone of Nock's outlook, was another preposterous example of liberal political theory, ignoring the abilities of the voters and flattering them with the assumption that each of them was as educable as anyone else. Average democratic citizens were no more qualified for the university than for public office, and it demeaned the institution to admit them at all. For Nock as for his beloved Jefferson, education at least as a public enterprise ought to be formative, classical, and for the very few. Instrumental, vocational, or utilitarian knowledge should have no place in it.*

Nock's own preference appears chiefly at the end of the essay, where he defends in all seriousness the old-fashioned classical curriculum on the grounds that it disciplined and experienced the mind and thus educated students in the proper sense of the term, so that when they did deal with life's problems they had a sense of distance and perspective. Needless to say, his view was not popular and had little direct impact. The essay remains an excellent brief example of a cultural conservative trying to deal with education in a liberal democratic society.

6. American Education

By Albert Jay Nock

Complaint within the teaching profession about the quality of education in America has lately taken an interesting turn. For forty years, to my knowledge,—I do not know how much longer,—professional criticism has confined itself pretty strictly to matters that went on under the general system, and has not questioned the system itself. It has run to questions of pedagogic method and curricular content; to the *what* and the *how*. One notices with satisfaction, however, that within the past year some of our educators have gone beyond these matters and touched the system's structural principles. The presidents of Brown, Haverford and St. Stephen's have spoken out plainly. Professor Giddings, of Columbia, has been very explicit, and even the president of Columbia has made some observations that might be construed as disparaging. These gentlemen have spoken informally, mostly by implication, and not pretending to present anything like a complete thesis on the subject; nevertheless their implications are clear.

One wishes they had gone further; one hopes they may yet do so. My own reason for writing is that perhaps a layman's view of the situation may call out additional professional comment on it. One need make no apology for the intervention, for the subject is quite within the layman's competence. Matters of content and method (the *what* and the *how*) are primarily a professional concern, and the layman speaks of them under correction. But the system itself is not a technical affair, and its points of strength and weakness lie as properly under lay review as under professional review. In any kind of fairness, in deed, if professional opinion takes responsibility for correctness in technical matters it has enough on its shoulders, and lay opinion may well take the lead on matters which are not technical.

I

On its moral and social side, our educational system is indeed a noble experiment—none more so. In all the history of noble experiments I

know of none to match it. There is every evidence of its being purely
an expression—no, one may put it even stronger than that, an organization—of a truly noble, selfless and affectionate desire. The representative American, whatever his faults, has been notably character-
ized by the wish that his children might do better by themselves than
he could do by himself. He wished them to have all the advantages
that he had been obliged to get on without, all the "opportunities,"
not only for material well-being but also for self-advancement in the
realm of the spirit. I quite believe that in its essence and intention
our system may be fairly called no less than an organization of this
desire; and as such it can not be too much admired or too highly
praised.

But unfortunately Nature recks little of the nobleness prompting
any human enterprise. Perhaps it is rather a hard thing to say, but
the truth is that Nature seems much more solicitous about her repu-
tation for order than she is about keeping up her character for morals.
Apparently no pressure of noble and unselfish moral earnestness will
cozen the sharp old lady into countenancing a breach of order. Hence
any enterprise, however nobly and disinterestedly conceived, will fail
if it be not also organized intelligently. We are having a fine illustration of this great truth in the fate of the other noble experiment
which Mr. Hoover commended on moral grounds in one of his campaign speeches; and an equally conspicuous illustration of it is furnished by the current output of our educational institutions.

Our educational pot has always been sufficiently astir; there can be
no doubt of that. It would seem that there is no possible permutation
or combination in pedagogic theory and practice that we have not
tried. The roster of our undergraduate and secondary courses reads
like the advertisement of a bargain-counter. One of our pioneer wom-
en's colleges offers, among other curious odds-and-ends, some sort of
"course" in baby-tending! Our floundering ventures in university-
training have long been fair game for our cartoonists. Only this morning I saw a capital cartoon in a New York paper, prompted by a news-
item on some new variant of a cafeteria or serve-self educational
scheme vamped up in one of our top-heavy state universities. But
now, after all this feverish and hopeful fiddling with the mechanics
of education, the current product seems to be, if anything, a little
poorer than any that has gone before it.

This statement may rest as it lies. I see no point in a digression to
define education or to describe the marks that set off an educated
person. If I were writing on oyster-culture, I should consider it a waste
of space to define an oyster, because everyone likely to read my paper
would know well enough what an oyster is; at least, he would know
very well what it is not. Similarly, everyone likely to read this essay
may be presumed to know an educated person from an uneducated
person. But if this seems a cavalier way of dealing with one's readers,
one may establish a perfect understanding by a reference to Mr.

James Truslow Adams's paper in the November 1929 issue of the *Atlantic Monthly*. It is enough to say that one who, by whatever means, has compassed just the discipline intimated by Mr. Adams,— a discipline directed as steadily towards *being* and *becoming* as towards *doing* and *getting*,—and who in all his works and ways reflects that discipline, is an educated person. One who has not compassed it, and whose works and ways do not reflect it, may not properly be called an educated person, no matter what his training, learning, aptitudes and accomplishments may be.

Mr. Adams's paper makes it clear that the educated American is not often to be met with; and there is a pretty complete consensus that he is at present much scarcer than he was, say, twenty-five years ago. An Italian nobleman of high culture, who has seen a great deal of our college and university life, lately told me that he had made a curious observation while here, and asked me whether I thought it was a fair one, and if so, how I should account for it. He said he had now and then met Americans who were extremely well educated, but they were all in the neighbourhood of sixty years old; he had not seen a single person below that age who impressed him as having been even respectably educated, although interest in the matter had led him to look everywhere. It is unsafe to generalize from a single opinion, but it may be worth remembering that this reference is the judgment of one foreign observer of experience and distinction.

This state of things is obviously not due to any deficiency in our mechanical equipment. What impresses one most, I think, at sight of the Continental school, is the very moderate character of its plant and general apparatus of learning, as compared with ours. I have elsewhere remarked that no live-wire, up-to-date, go-getting American college president would look twice at the University of Poitiers or the old university at Brussels. Even Bonn, the aristocrat of German universities, is a very modest and plain affair in its physical aspects. The secondary schools of France and Belgium have in our eyes an appearance of simplicity almost primitive. Yet see what comes out of them. Compare the order of disciplined intelligence that somehow manages to squeeze itself out of Poitiers and Brussels with that which floats through one of our universities. With every imaginable accessory and externality in his favour, the American simply makes no comparison. Put a cost-accounting system on education in France and America, with reference to the quality of the product,—if such a thing were possible,—and the result would be, I think, a most disquieting surprise.

Nor have the French and Belgians any natural advantage over us in respect of raw material. I firmly believe that the run-of-mine American is just as intelligent as the run-of-mine Frenchman, and the picked American as the picked Frenchman. The trouble is not there, nor can I see that it lies anywhere in the technique of pedagogy; I must needs be shown wherein our pedagogy is not entitled to a clean bill. Yet the fact is that with relatively poor equipment, with no better raw material and no better pedagogy than ours, French institutions turn out extremely well-educated men, and ours do not.

The whole trouble is that the American system from beginning to end is gauged to the run-of-mine American rather than to the picked American. The run-of-mine Frenchman does not get any nearer the university than the adjacent woodpile. He does not get into the French equivalent of our undergraduate college. If he gets through the French equivalent of our secondary school, he does so by what our ancestors called the uncovenanted mercies of Providence, and every step of his progress is larded with bitter sweat. The chief reason why my Italian friend found no educated American under sixty years of age is that forty years ago the run-of-mine American did not, as a rule, get much nearer the founts of the higher learning than the run-of-mine French-man does to-day, and for the same reason—he could not, speaking strictly, "make the grade." The newspapers some time ago quoted the president of Columbia as saying that during the past half-century the changes in school and college instruction, as to both form and con-tent, have been so complete that it is probably safe to say that to-day no student in Columbia College, and perhaps no professor on its fac-ulty, could pass satisfactorily the examination-tests that were set for admission to Columbia College fifty years ago.

The root-idea, or ideal, of our system is the very fine one that edu-cational opportunity should be open to all. The practical approach to this ideal, however, was not planned intelligently, but, on the con-trary, very stupidly; it was planned on the official assumption that everybody is educable, and this assumption still remains official. In-stead of firmly establishing the natural limit to opportunity—the abil-ity to make any kind of use of it—and then making opportunity as free as possible within that limit, our system says, let them all come, and we will scratch up some sort of brummagem opportunity for each of them. What they do not learn at school, the college will teach them; the university will go through some motions for them on what the college failed to get into their heads. This is no jaunty exaggeration. I have a friend who has spent years in a mid-Western state university, trying to teach elementary English composition to adult illiterates. I have visited his classes, seen what they were about, seen his pupils, examined their work, and speak whereof I know. A short time ago in another enormous university,—a university, mind; not a grade school, but a university dealing with adult persons,—two instructors pub-lished samples of the kind of thing produced for them by their stu-dents. Here are a few:

Being a tough hunk of meat, I passed up the steak.
Lincoln's mind grew as his country kneaded it.
The camel carries a water tank with him; he is also a rough rider and has four gates.

As soon as music starts, silence rains, but as soon as it stops it gets worse than ever.

College students as a general rule like such readings that will take the least mental inertia.

Modern dress is extreme and ought to be checked.

Although the Irish are usually content with small jobs, they have won a niche in the backbone of the country.

At the hands of some upper-classmen and second-year men, Shakespeare fared as follows:

Edmund, in *King Lear*, "committed a base act and allowed his illegitimate father to see a forged letter." Cordelia's death "was the straw that broke the camel's back and killed the king." Lear's fool "was prostrated on the neck of the king." "Hotspur," averred a sophomore, "was a wild, irresolute man. He loved honor above all. He would go out and kill twenty Scotchmen before breakfast." Kate was "a woman who had something to do with hot spurs."

Also Milton:

"Diabetes was Milton's Italian friend," one student explained. Another said, "Satan had all the emotions of a woman, and was a sort of trustee in heaven, so to speak." The theme of *Comus* was given as "purity protestriate." Mammon, in *Paradise Lost*, suggests that the best way "to endure hell is to raise hell and build a pavilion."

Would it be unfair to ask the reader how long he thinks that order of intelligence would be permitted to display itself at the University of Brussels or the University of Poitiers?

II

The history of our system shows a significant interplay between the sentiment for an indiscriminate and prodigal distribution of "opportunity" and certain popular ideas or pseudo-ideas that flourished beside it. One of these was the popular conception of democracy. It is an interesting fact that this originally got its currency through the use of the word by politicians as a talking-point. Practically all publicists now quite arbitrarily use the word "democratic" as a synonym for "republican"—as when, for instance, they speak of the United States and France as "great democracies." The proper antithesis of democracy is not autocracy, monarchy, or oligarchy, but absolutism; and, as we all know, absolutism is much deeper entrenched in these republican countries than in monarchical Denmark, say. The term, too, became debased in its more special uses. In the America which Dickens visited, a democratic society meant one in which "one man was just as good as another, or a little better"; this phrase itself is of sound American coinage current with the merchant. Democratic manners to-day, as a rule, mean merely coarse manners; for instance, the ostentatiously "democratic" luncheon-etiquette of our booster clubs means that all hands shall, under some sort of penalty, call each fellow member by his given name, regardless of previous acquaintance or the lack of it.

Thus the educational free-for-all sentiment got a very powerful endorsement. It was democratic. Poverty-stricken Tom, from the slashes, should go through school, college and university hand in hand with Dick the scion of Wall Street, and toplofty Harry of the Back Bay. Democracy so willed it, in spite of Nature's insuperable differentiations whereby Tom had no first-rate school-ability, Harry had excellent ability in other directions but no school-ability, and Dick was a *Dummkopf* with no ability of any kind. Privately these differentiations might be recognized, indeed must be, but it was of the essence of democracy that there should be no official or institutional recognition of them. The unspeakable silliness of our truant laws, which make compulsory attendance a matter purely of school-age instead of school-ability, appropriately expresses this limitation.

The very human but rather ignoble tendency to self-assertion which led us to put the label of democracy on what was merely indiscriminate or vulgar led us also to put the label of greatness on what was merely big. With a whole civilization groveling in the unintelligent worship of bigness, a great school must be a big school. The thing to notice is how admirably this fell in with pseudo-democratic doctrine and also with the noble but ill-starred sentiment pervading our system. To make a big school, students must be got; to get them, standards of eligibility must be brought down to a common denominator of intelligence, aptitude and interest. Then, when they are got, something has to be found for them to do that they can do, or at least upon which they are able to mark time,—such as "courses in English," the number of which exhibited annually by our institutions will amaze the reader, if he has curiosity enough about it to look it up,—and this means a profound sophistication of requirements. It can be seen at once how solidly sentiment and pseudo-democratic doctrine stood behind these developments and encouraged them.

By another interesting coincidence—these coincidences in the history of our system are really remarkable—these developments also met, as if made to order, the great and sudden expansion of the nation's industrial life, the glorification of profit-making, and the implied disparagement of all intellectual, aesthetic, and even moral processes which did not tend directly or indirectly to profit-making. It was promptly perceived that the ineducable person might become a successful banker, industrialist, broker, bond-salesman or what not; plenty such there were who could manage no more than to read the stock-quotations and write their own signatures—Daniel Drew, for instance, and Cornelius Vanderbilt. Thus vocationalism came at once to the burdened system's aid. Circumstances were created whereby the ineducable person might bear directly on the business of banking, brokerage, industry, and so on, with the prestige of a college or university career thrown in. The elective bargain-counter was extended all over the academic floor-space; its limit was only at the line where imaginative ingenuity broke down and ceased to work; and certain fragile windflowers, such as "courses in English," were distributed over it here and there, partly by way of garnishment, partly as camouflage. Thus everything was made satisfactory all round. The ineducable person was taken care of with an academic career to all appearances as respectable as anybody's; sentiment was assuaged; democratic doctrine was satisfied; the general regard for size was satisfied, and so was the general preoccupation with profit.

III

In discussing the effect of all this, I wish to make it as clear as possible that I am not laying the slightest blame upon our educators. They had to take the system as they found it; its faults were none of their making. They had to meet measurably the egregious demands of a noble but undiscriminating sentiment, a preposterous misconception of the democratic principle, a childish reverence for bigness, and an exclusive preoccupation with profit-making. It is a large order; if in practice they were able to meet these demands by ever so little obliquely, one might reasonably ask no more. With this clearly understood, we may observe that one immediate effect is a calamitous overlapping of effort, whereby the lines marking off the school from the college and the college from the university have been obliterated. As in the case I cited, the university is doing work that by the handsomest possible concession one would say should be done in the eighth grade. The secondary school and the undergraduate college, again, are overlapping on the university in their furtherance of vocationalism. Hence, whatever may be done for sentiment or democracy or the promotion of profit-making, none of them are doing anything for education. An institution, like an individual, has only twenty-four hours a day, and only a limited amount of attention at its disposal; and so much of time and attention as it devotes to one pursuit must be taken from another.

This overlapping, indeed, gives rise to a great deal of justifiable avoidance on the part of educators, or what I understand is better known as "passing the buck." In looking over an undergraduate college last year, I remarked to the president that, on the one hand, he seemed to be doing a good deal of rather elementary school-work, and at the same time trespassing pretty heavily on the university, especially in his science courses; so that on the whole his college made me think of the small boy's objection to some asparagus that his mother offered him—it tasted raw at one end and rotten at the other. He said this was so; he had to give way to vocationalism somewhat—much more than he wished; he was doing his best against it. As for the other matter, it was the fault of the schools; they left ragged holes in the boys' preparation. "Don't you think we should do something for the poor fellows who come to us with these deficiencies?"

"Certainly," I replied. "Fire them."

"Ah, but then we should have no students, and should be obliged to shut up shop."

"Well, but at that," I suggested, "would it really be such a killing misfortune?"

"Possibly so, I think," he answered, after a moment's reflection. "My ideas are the same as yours precisely, but needs must when the devil drives. We are doing only half a job, I know,—perhaps not that,—but we are doing it better than any other college, and perhaps that justifies us in keeping on."

There may be something in this,—I personally doubt it,—but that is another matter. The point is that we can see clearly just what it is to which this lamentable situation runs back. The secondary school must take in all the shaky material sent up from the grade-school, for of such is the kingdom of democracy. In its turn the grade-school must take in all the enormous masses of human ineptitude that are dumped on it by the truant laws; and thus from one end of our system to the other do we see the ramification of the four social principles that our civilization has foisted on it as fundamental.

A second immediate effect is the loss, in practice, of any functional distinction between formative knowledge and instrumental knowledge. Formerly a student gave up, in round numbers, the first twenty years of his life to formative knowledge; his pursuits during this time were directed exclusively toward the *being* and *becoming*. This was the stated business of the school and college, and they kept him so busy at it that he hardly knew there was such a thing as instrumental knowledge in the world. He got his introduction to that later, at the university or technical school, where first he began to concern himself with the *doing* and *getting*. I have not space to discuss this aspect of our system at length,—done properly, it would take many pages,—but I think the reader will have no trouble about perceiving it in all its relation with what has been said already.

A third effect is the grotesque and monstrous shift of responsibility from the student to the teacher. Formerly the teacher had none of it; now he has practically all of it. The student who formerly presented himself was capable of learning; that was what he was there for; it was "up to" him to do it, and he did it. The teacher directed him, perhaps helped him a little,—precious little, in my experience,—but took no responsibility whatever for the student's progress. The run-of-mine student now arrives, incapable of anything, usually indifferent and incurious toward everything. Well, what is to be done? He may be relied on to do nothing particularly striking for himself,—Nature has attended to that,—therefore what is done must be done either for him or with him; and thus the burden of responsibility immediately passes to the teacher, and there it remains.

IV

For some reason that I have never been able to discover, Mr. Jefferson seems to be regarded as a great democrat; on public occasions he is regularly invoked as such by gentlemen who have some sort of political axe to grind, so possibly that view of him arose in this way. The fact is that he was not even a doctrinaire republican, as his relation to the French Revolution clearly shows. When Mr. Jefferson was revising the Virginia Statutes in 1797, he drew up a comprehensive plan for public education. Each ward should have a primary school for the three R's, open to all. Each year the best pupil in each school should be sent to the grade-school, of which there were to be twenty, conveniently situated in various parts of the state. They should be kept there one year or two years, according to results shown, and then all dismissed but one, who should be continued six years. "By this means," said the good old man, "twenty of the best geniuses will be raked from the rubbish annually"—a most unfortunate expression for a democrat to use! At the end of six years, the best ten out of the twenty were to be sent to college, and the rest turned adrift.

As an expression of sound public policy, this plan has never been improved upon. Professor Chinard, who has lately put us all under great obligations by his superb study—by far the best ever made—of Mr. Jefferson's public life, thinks it quite possible that those who formed the French system had this plan before them. Whether so or not, the French system is wholly in accord with Mr. Jefferson's hard good sense in accepting the fact that the vast majority of his countrymen were ineducable, and with his equally hard realism in permitting this fact to determine the fundamentals of his plan. The Faculty of Literature at the University of Poitiers is domiciled in the Hôtel Fumée, an exquisitely beautiful family mansion, built about 1510 by a rich lawyer. From an outside view, which is all I ever had of either property, I should say the Hôtel Fumée carries about as much floorspace as Mr. James Speyer's residence on Fifth Avenue. I venture to say that if Columbia University cleared out all of its ineducable students, root and branch, its Faculty of Literature could do a land-office business in a house the size of Mr. James Speyer's, with maybe a room or two to rent.

From what Professor Giddings and the presidents of Brown, Haver-

ford, and St. Stephen's have said, I infer that this is the season of repentance. Whether or not it will lead to a season of good works is
another matter; I think it highly improbable. Nevertheless it seems
useful at the present time that the situation should be diagnosed, and
its "indications," as the doctors say, taken into account. Artemus Ward
once said the trouble with Napoleon was that he tried to do too much
and did it. Just this is the trouble with American education. In my
judgment, the indications are simply that the whole school-population
of the country, above the primary grade, should be cut down by ninety per cent. If anyone thinks that this proportion is too high, let him
take it out on Mr. Jefferson, who is much bigger than I am; my figures
are fairly liberal as compared with his. With him on my side I make
bold to believe that nine-tenths of our student population, in university, college, grade schools and secondary schools, have no more justification for being where they are than they would have for an intru-
sion upon the French Academy or the Royal Society; and that unless
and until this mass is cut adrift, the prospects for American education will show no improvement worth considering.

Professional criticism has already suggested that the college and
university—and I believe there has been some similar hint about the
secondary school—should slough off the otiose bulk of those brought
to them by the mere *vis inertiae*, and those who present themselves
because it is the thing to do, or as a liberation from home or a fur-
lough for parents; likewise those who are going in for contacts, ath-
letics, husbands, the atmosphere and flavour of college life, or for
what I understand the authorities now delicately call "extra-curricular
activities," whereof the coonskin coat and pocket-flask are said to be
the symbols. At present this would no doubt account for sixty per cent
of Mr. Jefferson's "rubbish," probably seventy, but that is not enough.
The intention of Mr. Jefferson's plan was to off-load all ineducable
persons, no matter what their disposition, and to have this relief applied continuously at every point in the system above the primary
school.

This reform seems unlikely to be carried out, and I do not urge it or
even recommend it. Conversance with human history begets a deal of
respect for Nature's well-established policy of progress by trial and
error, and a profound circumspection about trying to anticipate it.
The experienced person regards root-and-branch reforms, even good
ones, with justifiable doubt. One may be by no means sure—far from
it—that it would be a good thing "by and large" and in the long run
for the United States to produce any educated people, or that in its
present summary sacrifice of its educable individuals it is not taking
precisely the right way with them. I am not disposed to dogmatize
either way, and hence I do not recommend this reform, or, indeed,
any reform. I am merely recording observations of certain social phenomena, placing them in their right relations and drawing the con-

clusions that seem warranted in the premises. As to the final desirability of the state of things contemplated by these conclusions, I have nothing to say.

V

Still, education seems as yet to be a subject of experiment with us, and I observe with interest that, according to some educators, the next experiment will be with the revival of the small college. There is obviously no more saving grace in smallness than in bigness; everything depends upon what the small college is like. The forecast, however, sets one's fancy going. Perhaps—one must have one's doubts about it, but perhaps—without too much infringement on Nature's policy, or deflection of our great moral and social mission to the world at large, one small laboratory experiment might be tried, such as has never yet been tried by us. I mean an experiment in educating educable persons only. It would be interesting and possibly useful to set up two small institutions, a school and an undergraduate college, both so well endowed as not to care a straw whether a student came near them or not, and both committed wholly to the pursuit of formative knowledge; the school's attendance limited, say, to sixty, and the college's to two hundred. The school should take pupils at the age of eight, and carry them on until they could meet the college's requirements. Neither institution should take any account whatever of bogus democratic doctrine, the idolatry of mass, vocationalism or the pretended rights of ineducable persons. If such persons presented themselves they should be turned away, and if anyone got in and afterward was found for any reason or to any degree ineducable, he should be forthwith bounced out.

These institutions should be largely a reversion to type, their distinction being that of representing the pure type, without a trace of hybridization. Requirements for entrance to the college should be the ability to read and write Latin and Greek prose with such ease and correctness as to show that language-difficulties were forever left behind; knowledge of arithmetic and of algebra up to quadratics; nothing more. The four years' course in college should cover the whole range of Greek and Latin literature from Homer's time to that of Erasmus, mathematics as far as the differential calculus, a compendium of formal logic, and one of the history of the English language (not literature), and nothing more; and this should lead to the degree of Bachelor of Arts, the only degree that the college should confer.

My notion is that the instructors in these institutions could pretty well follow their own devices for five years, having no students to teach, but that in ten years things would look up a little, and that in fifty years a review of the experiment would be interesting. One could then make the observations and comparisons necessary to determine what it was worth. I can not say flatly that I recommend this experiment; I merely say that it would be interesting, might be useful enough to be worth its cost, and incidentally some poor few, at least, of our educable fry would lay up out of it a treasure more to be desired than gold—yea, than much fine gold. Yet it is nothing that I would urge, for quite possibly the Larger Good requires that things should go on as they are now going.

Probably, however, I should give (though in all diffidence) some decorous hint about the sort of thing I should look for from it, if it were carried out under strictly aseptic experimental conditions. The literature of Greece and Rome represents the longest continuous record available to us,—a matter of some twenty-five hundred years or more, if mediaeval and Renaissance literature were included, as it should be,—as well as the fullest and most diversified record, of what the human mind has ever been busy about. Therefore the one great benefit of the "grand old fortifying classical curriculum," as far as it went, was that on one's way through it one saw by centuries instead of weeks, by whole periods instead of years, the operation of the human mind upon every aspect of collective human life, every department of spiritual, industrial, commercial and social activity; one touched the theory and practice of every science and every art. Hence a person came out from this discipline with not only a trained mind but an experienced mind. He was like one who had had a profound and weighty experience. He was habituated to the long-time point of view, and instinctively brought it to bear on current affairs and happenings. In short, he was mature.

"*Sobald er reflektirt,*" said Goethe of Lord Byron, "*ist er ein Kind.*" Byron was one of the great natural forces in literature,—all praise to him for that,—but of maturity, the best assurance of a right interpretation and right use of personal experience of the world and its affairs, he had none. So too, the composite American is one of the greatest natural forces that have ever appeared in human society. Perhaps it is as such, and such only, that Nature proposes to use him, and she may intend to fade him out and supersede him when this function in her inscrutable economy is fulfilled,—she has never been any too scrupulous about turning such tricks,—and, if so, it would be hazardous to tamper with the fundamentals of a training that fits him for her purpose. Our system seems to have been constructed in anticipation of just this purpose on the part of Nature; it confirms him in a perpetual adolescence, permits his inner adjustment to the world and its affairs to proceed by a series of juvenile, casual and disorderly improvisations—*sobald er reflektirt ist er ein Kind.*

HENRY LOUIS MENCKEN (1880–1956) *was in many ways the best known of all the cultural conservatives. He was an enormously prolific editor and writer for both newspapers and magazines, and he habitually collected his briefer pieces into hardcover books that had great impact on college students and the educated young adults of the first three decades of the twentieth century. He developed a prose style that was the envy and despair of many imitators, as well as a habit of overstatement, grotesquely vivid imagery, and allusive playfulness of discourse that make all his work provocative. Behind the verbal fireworks, however, lay a reasonably consistent body of knowledge that touched all aspects of human life from politics to literature to morals.*

In the passage that follows, Mencken takes many of the ideas already expressed by Santayana and Nock into social life. For him, American life was a comedy of conformity, envy, and plutocracy, in large part because no responsible aristocracy set an example for the masses to emulate. A genuine aristocracy had "interior security," a sense of inner freedom that enabled it to be "autonomous, curious, venturesome, courageous," and the "custodian of the qualities that make for change and experiment." Unless America recognized the need for such a group, it was doomed to have shameful national orgies like the Red Scare of 1919 and to pursue ludicrous statist experiments like prohibition. The result would be a deadening conformity which would make "the free functioning of personality into a capital crime against society."

7. The Need for an Aristocracy

By Henry Louis Mencken

So far, the disease. As to the cause, I have delivered a few hints. I now describe it particularly. It is, in brief, a defect in the general culture of the country—one reflected, not only in the national literature, but also in the national political theory, the national attitude toward religion and morals, the national habit in all departments of thinking. It is the lack of a civilized aristocracy, secure in its position, animated by an intelligent curiosity, skeptical of all facile generalizations, superior to the sentimentality of the mob, and delighting in the battle of ideas for its own sake.

The word I use, despite the qualifying adjective, has got itself meanings, of course, that I by no means intend to convey. Any mention of an aristocracy, to a public fed upon democratic fustian, is bound to bring up images of stockbrokers' wives lolling obscenely in opera boxes, or of haughty Englishmen slaughtering whole generations of grouse in an inordinate and incomprehensible manner, or of Junkers with tight waists elbowing American schoolmarms off the sidewalks of German beer towns, or of perfumed Italians coming over to work their abominable magic upon the daughters of breakfast-food and bathtub kings. Part of this misconception, I suppose, has its roots in the gaudy imbecilities of the yellow press, but there is also a part that belongs to the general American tradition, along with the oppression of minorities and the belief in political panaceas. Its depth and extent are constantly revealed by the naïve assumption that the so-called fashionable folk of the large cities—chiefly wealthy industrials in the interior-decorator and country-club stage of culture—constitute an aristocracy, and by the scarcely less remarkable assumption that the peerage of England is identical with the gentry—that is, that such men as Lord Northcliffe, Lord Iveagh and even Lord Reading are English gentlemen, and of the ancient line of the Percys.

Here, as always, the worshiper is the father of the gods, and no less when they are evil than when they are benign. The inferior man must find himself superiors, that he may marvel at his political equality with them, and in the absence of recognizable superiors *de facto* he creates superiors *de jure*. The sublime principle of one man, one vote must be translated into terms of dollars, diamonds, fashionable intelligence; the equality of all men before the law must have clear

Note: Originally published in "The Cultural Background," in *Prejudices: Second Series* (New York, 1920), pp. 65–78.

and dramatic proofs. Sometimes, perhaps, the thing goes further and is more subtle. The inferior man needs an aristocracy to demonstrate, not only his mere equality, but also his actual superiority. The society columns in the newspapers may have some such origin: they may visualize once more the accomplished journalist's understanding of the mob mind that he plays upon so skillfully, as upon some immense and cacophonous organ, always going *fortissimo*. What the inferior man and his wife see in the sinister revels of those amazing first families, I suspect, is often a massive witness to their own higher rectitude —to their relative innocence of cigarette-smoking, poodle-coddling, child-farming and the more abstruse branches of adultery—in brief, to their firmer grasp upon the immutable axioms of Christian virtue, the one sound boast of the nether nine-tenths of humanity in every land under the cross.

But this bugaboo aristocracy, as I hint, is actually bogus, and the evidence of its bogusness lies in the fact that it is insecure. One gets into it only onerously, but out of it very easily. Entrance is effected by dint of a long and bitter struggle, and the chief incidents of that struggle are almost intolerable humiliations. The aspirant must school and steel himself to sniffs and sneers; he must see the door slammed upon him a hundred times before ever it is thrown open to him. To get in at all he must show a talent for abasement—and abasement makes him timorous. Worse, that timorousness is not cured when he succeeds at last. On the contrary, it is made even more tremulous, for what he faces within the gates is a scheme of things made up almost wholly of harsh and often unintelligible taboos, and the penalty for violating even the least of them is swift and disastrous. He must exhibit exactly the right social habits, appetites and prejudices, public and private. He must harbor exactly the right political enthusiasms and indignations. He must have a hearty taste for exactly the right sports. His attitude toward the fine arts must be properly tolerant and yet not a shade too eager. He must read and like exactly the right books, pamphlets and public journals. He must put up at the right hotels when he travels. His wife must patronize the right milliners. He himself must stick to the right haberdashery. He must live in the right neighborhood. He must even embrace the right doctrines of religion. It would ruin him, for all opera box and society column purposes, to set up a plea for justice to the Bolsheviki, or even for ordinary decency. It would ruin him equally to wear celluloid collars, or to move to Union Hill, N. J., or to serve ham and cabbage at his table. And it would ruin him, too, to drink coffee from his saucer, or to marry a chambermaid with a gold tooth, or to join the Seventh Day Adventists. Within the boundaries of his curious order he is worse fettered than a monk in a cell. Its obscure conception of propriety, its nebulous notion that this or that is honorable, hampers him in every direction, and very narrowly. What he resigns when he enters, even when he makes his first deprecating knock at the door, is every right to attack the ideas that happen to prevail within. Such as they are, he must accept them without question. And as they shift and change in response to great instinctive movements (or perhaps, now and then, to the punished but not to be forgotten revolts of extraordinary rebels) he must shift and change with them, silently and quickly. To hang back, to challenge and dispute, to preach reforms and revolutions—these are crimes against the brummagem Holy Ghost of the order.

Obviously, that order cannot constitute a genuine aristocracy, in any rational sense. A genuine aristocracy is grounded upon very much different principles. Its first and most salient character is its interior security, and the chief visible evidence of that security is the freedom that goes with it—not only freedom in act, the divine right of the aristocrat to do what he jolly well pleases, so long as he does not violate the primary guarantees and obligations of his class, but also and more importantly freedom in thought, the liberty to try and err, the right to be his own man. It is the instinct of a true aristocracy, not to punish eccentricity by expulsion, but to throw a mantle of protection about it—to safeguard it from the suspicions and resentments of the lower orders. Those lower orders are inert, timid, inhospitable to ideas, hostile to changes, faithful to a few maudlin superstitions. All progress goes on on the higher levels. It is there that salient personalities, made secure by artificial immunities, may oscillate most widely from the normal track. It is within that entrenched fold, out of reach of the immemorial certainties of the mob, that extraordinary men of the lower orders may find their city of refuge, and breathe a clear air. This, indeed, is at once the hall-mark and the justification of an aristocracy —that it is beyond responsibility to the general masses of men, and hence superior to both their degraded longings and their no less degraded aversions. It is nothing if it is not autonomous, curious, venturesome, courageous, and everything if it is. It is the custodian of the qualities that make for change and experiment; it is the class that organizes danger to the service of the race; it pays for its high prerogatives by standing in the forefront of the fray.

No such aristocracy, it must be plain, is now on view in the United States. The makings of one were visible in the Virginia of the later eighteenth century, but with Jefferson and Washington the promise died. In New England, it seems to me, there was never an aristocracy, either in being or in nascency: there was only a theocracy that degenerated very quickly into a plutocracy on the one hand and a caste of sterile *Gelehrten* on the other—the passion for God splitting into a lust for dollars and a weakness for mere words. Despite the common notion to the contrary—a notion generated by confusing literacy with intelligence—New England has never shown the slightest sign of a genuine enthusiasm for ideas. It began its history as a slaughter-house of ideas, and it is to-day not easily distinguishable from a cold-storage plant. Its celebrated adventures in mysticism, once apparently so bold and significant, are now seen to have been little more than an elaborate hocus-pocus—respectable Unitarians shocking the peasantry and scaring the horned cattle in the fields by masquerading in the robes of Rosicrucians. The ideas that it embraced in those austere and far-off days were stale, and when it had finished with them they were dead: to-day one hears of Jakob Böhme almost as rarely as one hears of Allen G. Thurman. So in politics. Its glory is Abolition—an English invention, long under the interdict of the native plutocracy. Since the Civil War its six states have produced fewer political ideas, as political ideas run in the Republic, than any average county in Kansas or Nebraska. Appomattox seemed to be a victory for New England idealism. It was actually a victory for the New England plutocracy, and that plutocracy has dominated thought above the Housatonic ever since. The sect of professional idealists has so far dwindled that it has ceased to be of any importance, even as an opposition. When the plutocracy is challenged now, it is challenged by the proletariat.

Well, what is on view in New England is on view in all other parts of the nation, sometimes with ameliorations, but usually with the colors merely exaggerated. What one beholds, sweeping the eye over the land, is a culture that, like the national literature, is in three layers—the plutocracy on top, a vast mass of undifferentiated human blanks at the bottom, and a forlorn *intelligentsia* gasping out a precarious life between. I need not set out at any length, I hope, the intellectual deficiencies of the plutocracy—its utter failure to show anything even remotely resembling the makings of an aristocracy. It is badly educated, it is stupid, it is full of low-caste superstitions and indignations, it is without decent traditions or informing vision; above all, it is extraordinarily lacking in the most elemental independence and courage. Out of this class comes the grotesque fashionable society of our big towns, already described. Imagine a horde of peasants incredibly enriched and with almost infinite power thrust into their hands, and you will have a fair picture of its habitual state of mind. It shows all the stigmata of inferiority—moral certainty, cruelty, suspicion of ideas, fear. Never did it function more revealingly than in the late *pogrom* against the so-called Reds, *i. e.*, against humorless idealists who, like Andrew Jackson, took the platitudes of democracy quite seriously. The machinery brought to bear upon these feeble and scattered fanatics would have almost sufficed to repel an invasion by the united powers of Europe. They were hunted out of their sweat-shops and coffee-houses as if they were so many Carranzas or Ludendorffs, dragged to jail to the tooting of horns, arraigned before quaking judges on unintelligible charges, condemned to deportation without the slightest chance to defend themselves, torn from their dependent families, herded into prison-ships, and then finally dumped in a snow waste, to be rescued and fed by the Bolsheviki. And what was the theory at the bottom of all these astounding proceedings? So far as it can be reduced to comprehensible terms it was much less a theory than a fear—a shivering, idiotic, discreditable fear of a mere banshee—an overpowering, paralyzing dread that some extra-eloquent Red, permitted to emit his balderdash unwhipped, might eventually convert a couple of courageous men, and that the courageous men, filled with indignation against the plutocracy, might take to the highroad, burn down a nail-factory or two, and slit the throat of some virtuous profiteer. In order to lay this fear, in order to ease the jangled nerves of the American successors to the Hapsburgs and Hohenzollerns, all the constitutional guarantees of the citizen were suspended, the statute-books were burdened with laws that surpass anything heard of in the Austria of Maria Theresa, the country was handed over to a frenzied mob of detectives, informers and *agents provocateurs*—and the Reds departed laughing loudly, and were hailed by the Bolsheviki as innocents escaped from an asylum for the criminally insane.

Obviously, it is out of reason to look for any hospitality to ideas in a class so extravagantly fearful of even the most palpably absurd of them. Its philosophy is firmly grounded upon the thesis that the existing order must stand forever free from attack, and not only from attack, but also from mere academic criticism, and its ethics are as firmly grounded upon the thesis that every attempt at any such criticism is a proof of moral turpitude. Within its own ranks, protected by what may be regarded as the privilege of the order, there is nothing to take the place of this criticism. A few feeble platitudes by Andrew Carnegie and a book of moderate merit by John D. Rockefeller's press-agent constitute almost the whole of the interior literature of ideas. In other countries the plutocracy has often produced men of reflective and analytical habit, eager to rationalize its instincts and to bring it into some sort of relationship to the main streams of human thought. The case of David Ricardo at once comes to mind. There have been many others: John Bright, Richard Cobden, George Grote, and, in our own time, Walther von Rathenau. But in the United States no such phenomenon has been visible. There was a day, not long ago, when certain young men of wealth gave signs of an unaccustomed interest in ideas on the political side, but the most they managed to achieve was a banal sort of Socialism, and even this was abandoned in sudden terror when the war came, and Socialism fell under suspicion of being genuinely international—in brief, of being honest under the skin. Nor has the plutocracy of the country ever fostered an inquiring spirit among its intellectual valets and footmen, which is to say, among the gentlemen who compose headlines and leading articles for its newspapers. What chiefly distinguishes the daily press of the United States from the press of all other countries pretending to culture is not its lack of truthfulness or even its lack of dignity and honor, for these deficiencies are common to the newspapers everywhere, but its incurable fear of ideas, its constant effort to evade the discussion of fundamentals by translating all issues into a few elemental fears, its incessant reduction of all reflection to mere emotion. It is, in the true sense, never well-informed. It is seldom intelligent, save in the arts of the mob-master. It is never courageously honest. Held harshly to a rigid correctness of opinion by the plutocracy that controls it with less and less attempt at disguise, and menaced on all sides by censorships that it dare not flout, it sinks rapidly into formalism and feebleness. Its yellow section is perhaps its most respectable section, for there the only vestige of the old free journalist survives. In the more conservative papers one finds only a timid and petulant animosity to all questioning of the existing order, however urbane and sincere—a pervasive and ill-concealed dread that the mob now heated up against the orthodox hobgoblins may suddenly begin to unearth hobgoblins of its own, and so run amok. For it is upon the emotions of the mob, of course, that the whole comedy is played. Theoretically the mob is the repository of all political wisdom and virtue; actually it is the ultimate source of all political power. Even the plutocracy cannot make war upon it openly, or forget the least of its weaknesses. The business of keeping it in order must be done discreetly, warily, with delicate technique. In the main that business consists of keeping alive its deep-seated fears—of strange faces, of unfamiliar ideas, of unhackneyed gestures, of untested liberties and responsibilities. The one permanent emotion of the inferior man, as of all the simpler mammals, is fear—fear of the unknown, the complex, the inexplicable. What he wants beyond everything else is safety. His instincts incline him toward a society so organized that it will protect him at all hazards, and not only against perils to his hide but also against assaults upon his mind—against the need to grapple with unaccustomed problems, to weigh ideas, to think things out for himself, to scrutinize the platitudes upon which his everyday thinking is based. Content under kaiserism so long as it functions efficiently, he turns, when kaiserism falls, to some other and perhaps worse form of paternalism, bringing to its benign tyranny only the docile tribute of his pathetic allegiance. In America it is the newspaper that is his boss. From it he gets support for his elemental illusions. In it he sees a visible embodiment of his own wisdom and consequence. Out of it he draws fuel for his simple moral passion, his congenital suspicion of heresy, his dread of the unknown. And behind the newspaper stands the plutocracy, ignorant, unimaginative and timorous.

Thus at the top and at the bottom. Obviously, there is no aristocracy here. One finds only one of the necessary elements, and that only in the plutocracy, to wit, a truculent egoism. But where is intelligence? Where are ease and surety of manner? Where are enterprise and curiosity? Where, above all, is courage, and in particular, moral courage—the capacity for independent thinking, for difficult problems, for what Nietzsche called the joys of the labyrinth? As well look for these things in a society of half-wits. Democracy, obliterating the old aristocracy, has left only a vacuum in its place; in a century

and a half it has failed either to lift up the mob to intellectual autonomy and dignity or to purge the plutocracy of its inherent stupidity
and swinishness. It is precisely here, the first and favorite scene of the
Great Experiment, that the culture of the individual has been reduced
to the most rigid and absurd regimentation. It is precisely here, of all
civilized countries, that eccentricity in demeanor and opinion has
come to bear the heaviest penalties. The whole drift of our law is toward the absolute prohibition of all ideas that diverge in the slightest
from the accepted platitudes, and behind that drift of law there is a
far more potent force of growing custom, and under that custom
there is a national philosophy which erects conformity into the
noblest of virtues and the free functioning of personality into a capital crime against society.

DONALD DAVIDSON (1893–1968) *was a key figure in the southern agrarian movement that developed largely at Vanderbilt during the 1920s and that had considerable influence in the South and even in the North. A man much beloved by many who knew and worked with him, Davidson contributed to the movement chiefly through the force of his personality; his writings now often seem derivative and repetitious, and he made no permanent professional contributions comparable to John Crowe Ransom's critical theories or Robert Penn Warren's novels. Yet on occasion he was capable of compressing key ideas and attitudes into a brief compass, thus leaving posterity with small gems of conservative discourse. His book review column in the* Nashville Tennessean, *for some years a regular feature, gave him an ideal platform for this kind of writing.*

In the discussion of Henry Ford that follows, Davidson quickly demonstrates his distaste for the mechanical, materialistic, and capitalistic side of life. The ideals of Henry Ford and the Americans who admired him were those of quantity, production, and efficiency, and they did not take into account the basic human need to find meaningful labor and take personal pride in its result. The agrarians on occasion were capable of excessive lyricism about the glories of laboring on the farm, but when criticizing the industrial economy they had many acute things to say. Davidson's remarks here clearly indicate a conservative economic position that was as critical of Coolidge prosperity as it would be of New Deal statism.

8. The World As Ford Factory

By Donald Davidson

There is magnificence in this new book of Henry Ford's—this book of the splendid title, *Moving Forward*, which comes to us with the additional signature of Samuel Crowther as a kind of shrewd Boswellian collaborator. The title itself is a magnificent rebuke to Mr. Ford's fellow-industrialists, now wallowing sadly in the trough of business depression. And with what magnificent gall does Mr. Ford advise us, at this time of all times, that "the day when we can actually have overproduction is far distant"; that the five-day week and the eight-hour day must be still further curtailed; and that the familiar Ford doctrine of raising wages and lowering prices must go on indefinitely. Whether these pronouncements are wise or foolhardy, I am not enough of an economist to say. I can well imagine that they may seem almost wicked to some merchants and manufacturers. I am more concerned with the theories of industry and of human life that lie back of the Ford-ideas, and that perhaps have never before been so persuasively stated as in this book.

Yet since Mr. Ford's book is not all doctrine, let me first pay tribute to the part which is not. The middle chapters of the book, such as "Changing Over an Industry," "Flexible Mass Production," "A Millionth of an Inch," give us rather full glimpses into the workings of the Ford plants. Here Mr. Ford appears as the honest mechanic—or factory manager—who has an all-consuming zeal for his work. Herein, who will say that Ford is not a genius—a genius who scraps overnight "the largest automobile plant in the world," in order to replace Model T with Model A; who founds rubber plantations in Brazil, against an evil day; who commands the services of the admirable Johansson, measurer of measurers, in order to gauge to the millionth of an inch the delicate operations upon which the quantity production of Ford cars must finally depend? One cannot but admire the gusto and the not immodest pride of this Henry Ford. Yes, even though one is obliged to reflect that the fruit of these stupendous operations is nothing more magnificent than a Ford car, buzzing along the highways and no doubt transporting quite as many fools as wise men. It is comforting, too, to have Mr. Ford's insistence that it is the excellence of the product which should come first in the manufacturer's mind—and not the disposal thereof, or the profit, which will result

Note: Originally published in the *Nashville Tennessean*, November 9, 1930. Reprinted by permission of the *Nashville Tennessean*.

necessarily. Let us give Mr. Ford all the credit we can in the fields where he may speak with some authority. It is only as Mr. Ford may be taken as an oracle on other matters that he is dangerous—in fact, very dangerous indeed, and subversive of the better part of life as I conceive it.

In the first place, Mr. Ford sees the world as a gigantic Ford factory, or as some kind of factory, in which people manufacture Ford cars, or other articles, for the sole reason of getting the money to buy the articles that they manufacture. This is a very pinched and narrow view of life to begin with. It leaves out the vastly interesting departments of human life that can hardly ever be expected to submit themselves to a factory regime. Of that life and of professional life, of politics and government, of housekeeping, lovemaking, motherhood, fatherhood, literature, history (to say nothing of philosophy and religion and such pleasant trivialities as conversation and good digestion), Henry Ford takes no account. And we may presume, from his childish comments on Prohibition and his naive views of leisure, that he has no thoughts on these various subjects and no valid information about them.

If Mr. Ford's book were merely a book on economics or on methods of manufacture, I would not raise this point at all. But his theories of manufacture are all tied up with his views of life, which have the simplicity of fanaticism. Furthermore, Mr. Ford has the impertinence to suggest, at least implicitly, that we had better give up our shabby ideas of life and adopt his glittering ones; and he ludicrously puts himself forward as a missionary to Europe, who is now prepared to confer on little agricultural Denmark and disturbed England and stable France the questionable benefits of a Ford regime.

Let me now examine rather hastily some of the principal Ford-ideas.

Of the greatest importance, perhaps, is his distinction between "labor-saving and labor-serving" as applied to machines. Mr. Ford thinks that we are nowhere near the end of our ingenuity in devising machines that will substitute machine work for human work. There will be more and more machines, always more efficient ones, which will be manned by skilled technicians and made by even more skilled technicians, so that unskilled labor will eventually be quite unwanted. That this development of machines will therefore displace workers even Mr. Ford is obliged to concede; but he holds that the displaced workers (now known as the "technologically unemployed") will be taken care of by the new industries that must continuously arise, to meet the eternal new demands for new products.

Meanwhile, the skilled laborers who are retained in the factory have their tasks made physically easier; that is the meaning of "labor-serving." Their hours are short, and their pay is high—in 20 years it may reach $27 a day. They are given more leisure, which they are supposed to use in consuming the surplus products ingeniously devised for them; and for this purpose, too, they are paid high wages. And all of this must go on forever, more and more, with no limit at all in sight.

Now this is all very clever, and one cannot deny that, to some extent, the scheme has worked for Henry Ford, who has profited not only by his own genius but by the circumstances of a war-fattened, expansive period distinctly favorable to his independent experiments.

But there are serious implications behind these ideas.

What is the result for the laborer? The "labor-serving" idea is a mere quibble. Actually, Henry Ford's machines are labor-saving. This means that they are operated under the theory that labor is bad and men ought to do as little of it as possible. It implies that enjoyment is not connected with labor but must be pursued apart from it. One can only conclude that the introduction of more and more labor-saving machines signifies that labor will be held in more and more contempt. Or, still worse, that our lives are to be severely split between work and play, when as a matter of fact the two ought not to be put into opposition. In the ideal life work and play are not at odds, but harmoniously blend and interchange. God save us from the day when we may become convinced that work is an evil.

What is the result for the laborer who is thrown out of a job by the newly created machine? Mr. Ford passes lightly over this feature, in the face of a "technological unemployment" that is now giving thoughtful persons the gravest concern. Presumably, the laborer may get into some other industry, also newly created. Again, he may not. The prospect is one of fairly continuous unemployment, of both skilled and unskilled hordes milling painfully around our industrial centers. That this is already the case we know very well. And such a sharp and distressing study of unemployment as Clinch Calkins's *Some Folks Won't Work* is in severe contradiction to Mr. Ford's glib assurance.

What is the effect on industry itself? It is one of continual disadjustment and change. The manufacturer must always be scrapping his old plant and building a new one. He must put away his old machines and install better ones. This, says Mr. Ford, must be the normal procedure. There must be eternal experiment, eternal change. And what does this mean but a condition of furious uncertainty and instability, with the industrial structure always in a rickety and perilous shape?

And what, above all, is the effect on the consumers—the largest class of all, including not only laborers and capitalists, but all the immense public not engaged in factory production?

Under the Ford economy, it will be their duty to be even more thriftless than they are at present. They must spend and spend unceasingly, in order to consume the never-ending stream of new products that industry hurls upon them. They will be encouraged to make a necessity of every luxury that the clever industrialists may devise.

For industry of the Ford type has no regard for actual and fundamental needs! It seeks to create two or even twenty demands where none at all existed before.

The result of all this, almost inevitably, will not only be a terrifying expansion of the abstract money economy, now already puzzling in its weird ramifications. It will be to corrupt the public life, throughout its entire body, by persuading people to believe that life is made up of material satisfactions only, and that there are no satisfactions that cannot be purchased. On the one hand, we shall have financial chaos; on the other, a degraded citizenry, who have been taught under the inhumane principles of Fordism always to spend more than they have, and to want more than they get.

Mr. Ford means well, of course. So did old John Brown of Osawatomie, when he proposed to arm the Negro slaves with pikes and guns. But Mr. Ford (who has exactly the John Brown type of mind, applied to mechanics and money) is more dangerous than John Brown, for he proposes to disrupt a whole nation by offering to its citizens precisely the same temptation that Satan offered Christ.

No ANTHOLOGY of conservatism would be quite complete without at least one example of emotional extremism masked as cultural analysis. The same could also be said for a similar book on liberalism or radicalism. The essay I have chosen to fulfill this function was well known at the time of its publication and was occasionally reprinted during the succeeding years, but it has been ignored for the past two generations. Ralph Adams Cram was capable of quite beautiful architecture and competent discussions of any number of related topics, but he came somewhat unglued on subjects like science, anthropology, the democratic masses, war, and the future. American history supplied him with many precedents for pseudoscientific analysis, most obviously in the Henry Adams whose work he had promoted so vigorously. He carried these precedents to the extreme reprinted below. Hating doctrines of evolution and progress, since they seemed to lead to mass democracy, statism, vulgarity, and war, he took refuge in the idea of "catastrophic" genetic leaps voiced by the eminent Dutch botanist Hugo de Vries (1848–1935). For Cram, human nature remained always the same, capable of suddenly generating genius as a kind of scientific sport, yet itself always animal and incapable of higher achievements. People, he concludes with a kind of grim joy, do not behave like human beings, because they are not human beings; the term refers only to the Platos and the Jeffersons of human history. The masses are simply not up to the standard.

9. Why We Do Not Behave Like Human Beings

By Ralph Adams Cram

The ancient doctrine of progressive evolution which became dominant during the last half of the nineteenth century, was, I suggest, next to the religious and philosophical dogmas of Dr. Calvin and the political and social doctrines of M. Rousseau, the most calamitous happening of the last millennium. In union with Protestantism and democracy, and apparently justified in its works by the amazing technological civilization fostered by coal, iron, steam and electricity, it is responsible for the present estate of society, from which there is no escape, it would seem, except through comprehensive calamity.

I state my thesis thus bluntly in order to get it over with. Its justification as well as its implications I shall now expound as best I can.

Let me say that I was born and bred in the briar-patch of this same progressive evolution. By the time I was of age I had read all of Spenser's "Synthetic Philosophy" as well as the greater part of the writings of Darwin, Tyndal and Huxley, though, fortunately I believe, with a strong admixture of Ruskin, Emerson, Matthew Arnold and Carlyle, the latter group acting as a counter-agent that became operative and dominant after the passage of years.

Now the point I make is that the entire scheme was based on what was then a very partial and limited knowledge of geological, biological and anthropological facts and on a particularly faulty deductive process, whereby the nature of man, his period of existence in time and space, his relationship to other forms of life, his inherent potency and his ultimate destiny were gravely misinterpreted, with the result that during the last century he has been possessed by "delusions of grandeur" that have made it impossible for him justly to estimate his own acts, to acquire a right standard of values, or consciously to provide against the issue of his own follies and parlous courses.

According to the old doctrines of my youth, now showing so thin and thread-bare, man was the crown of an immemorial sequence of inevitable and even mechanical development from lower to higher, engineered by myriads of small upward steps from primeval slime through one vertebrate to another, through lemur and anthropoid ape to *homo sapiens*, Paleolithic and Neolithic man, to the Babylonian, Egyptian, Greek and Roman and their successors, ever in an ascend-

Note: Originally published in *Convictions and Controversies* (Boston: Marshall Jones, 1936), pp. 137–154.

ing line, to the glorious product of the Victorian era. As there had always been a constant, though intermittent upward progress to this delectable event, so, logically, this must continue indefinitely with an ever extending horizon of ever increasing glory and honour.

The prospect was alluring and it is no wonder that it was accepted with avidity. Coming in the midst of a bewildering epoch of discovery, invention and material aggrandizement, almost, though by no means quite, equal to that that we now know, occurred between 4000 and 3500 B.C., it gave a cachet of sublimity to events then transpiring and fixed the assurance that, as it was then most erroneously assumed, the Greeks were greater than the Egyptians, the Romans than the Greeks, the Renaissance than Hellenism. (They naïvely slurred over the thousand years of Christian civilization as an anomalous retrogression made amends for by the sixteenth century recovery.) Therefore, and inevitably, the new era of Protestantism, democracy and industrialism must be better than the Renaissance, with God knew what of glory in the proximate future if only all those things going strong were pushed to the limit and the old and outworn things relentlessly cast aside.

As I say then, this erroneous attitude gave an entirely wrong scheme of evolution. If man was driven irresistibly along an opened course then as Protestantism must have been better than Catholicism, so an agnostic rationalism must be better still, because it came later in time. Democracy must be better than monarchy, feudalism or aristocracy, for all men having been created free and equal (the word *created* was abandoned for the more evolutionary word *born*), there were no longer degrees of capacity, and, the human race now being emancipated, the just plain man was equal to, if not better than the great few of past ages. The intellectual, spiritual and aesthetic fields offered some difficulties. Greece was assumed to have surpassed Egypt—of which then little was known and that quite misunderstood—but Rome was disturbing and Mediaevalism calamitously retrograde. However, the Renaissance made certain amends, and after all the difficulty was got rid of by the simple expedient of disregarding these intangible values as of slight or secondary importance, which they must have been since they bore no relationship to current material values which, again being latest in time, must necessarily be of higher importance.

During the first decade of this century these ideas were in the ascendent. It was the great climacteric of our era of modernism, which actually began not about 1775 with the first mechanical discoveries and technological inventions, but with the emergence of the three R's of the turn of the fifteenth century: Renaissance, Reformation and Revolution. By some mysterious law of terrestrial life, the rhythm of history beats in great throbs of five centuries. You may trace this back in time as far as the Old Kingdom of Egypt. Each era describes a curve, varying in trajectory but inevitable; rise, culmination and fall, to be followed by another, the line of which is rising hiddenly while the precedent curve is declining to its end and ultimate disappearance. As the trajectory of our own epoch rose as hissingly as a rocket about fifteen hundred to its apogee about nineteen hundred, so its fall begins as again a rocket falls, and the first overt showing of this change of direction was the Great War.

Since then, and markedly since the Armistice, there has been a very striking transformation in the attitude of thinking men towards their own time. Where once was an irrational over-riding confidence in the destiny of man and the methods and devices by which it was ultimately to be achieved, there is now a growing doubt as to the validity of pretty much anything. The industrial age has fallen into chaos. The machine has become a Frankenstein monster, nationalism a menace of further and final war. Both domestic and foreign politics come close to being a riot of incapacity, while crime increases and becomes more widespread and intimate, the domestic and social organisms more perilously poised on the rim of dissolution. The intellectual life, compared even to the last half of the nineteenth century, is arid and sterile, while art has achieved its nemesis in the movies, jazz, modernist architecture, the "comic strip" and the subway magazines. As for religion of the Protestant sort, it is fairly well represented by the Methodist and Baptist gymnastics recorded in Mr. Mencken's "Americana."

One good sign is that physical science has lost its cock-sureness of fifty years ago and no longer thinks it knows all about everything or even very much about anything except the more obvious phenomena. Most encouraging of all, however, is the fact that at last we are beginning to reconsider our standard of values, analyze institutions and achievements, and above all to draw comparisons between men, rediscovering the great figures of our historic past of six thousand years, evaluating them anew, rating their times in terms of their own quality, and placing against them for contrast what we today have to offer.

It is a salutary proceeding that has issue in manifold revelations, while its implications are singularly valuable in the light they throw on the dissolving dream of progressive evolution. As we go back in time we find, during this same period (which, but for the baffling Cro Magnon episode, is all we know of man as man) no weakening of character and power due to a greater nearness to barbarism, but actually an increase. And the same is true of cultures. There is nothing in certain eras in Egypt, Crete, and archaic Greece inferior to more recent civilizations; indeed, as I have said before, the inventions, discoveries and accomplishments of man during the five centuries subsequent to the year 4000 B.C. cast quite into the shade our own achievements since the year 1500 A.D. From Imhotep, the Leonardo da Vinci of five thousand years ago, Rameses III and Akhenaten, those great Pharaohs, there has been an unbroken and endless list of great

men shining in great cultures, that we cannot match today nor could
have for some centuries. Judged by the character, capacity and
achievements of outstanding individuals (and there is no other way of
estimating the quality of any culture) man, five thousand years ago,
stood on as high a level as he has at any time since. Judged by the
character, capacity and achievements of the remainder of mankind,
whether the undifferentiated mob or those of its component parts that
through contemporary opportunity have found themselves in high
places, the standard of today is no whit higher than that which obtained in the Middle Kingdom of Egypt, Periclean Athens, the Byzan-
tium of Justinian or the Europe of St. Louis.

The situation would seem to be something like this. Disregarding
for the moment the Magdalenian culture, we find such thousands of
years as elapsed between the last ice age and four or five thousand
B.C. practically barren not only of the slightest signs of human evolution but also of any vestiges of anything that can rightly be called
human. Certain mammals of unpleasant habits, indifferently covered
with hair and apparently walking about as erect as some of the larger
apes, dwelt untidily in caves and fashioned, as their only mechanical
device, arrow-heads out of flint. They were less ingenious than birds
or beavers or bees. They were by no means as attractive or highly developed as the deer or the eagle, and they were most clumsily and in-
effectively adapted to environment. They were, in a word, an exceed-
ingly nasty tribe and they made no progress whatever so far as their
artifacts or interments show, for that space of ten or fifteen thousand
years which geologists tell us lasted from the extinction of the Cro
Magnons down to the opening of the Neolithic Age. I contend that
these unhandsome and inferior creatures were not men at all, and
that if man had existed before, as he undoubtedly had if the Magdalenian culture was really an event of some twenty thousand years
ago, then man is the product of recurrent intervals of creative vigour
in the *élan vital*, episodes of brief duration with long periods between
when man, as man, is non-existent. In a word, then, our own human
era had its beginnings in the Neolithic period, say eight or ten thousand years ago, and after a period of accumulating energy, suddenly
burst into complete achievement within a space of a very few hundred
years, no more perhaps, than has elapsed in our own case since the
landing of the Pilgrim Fathers. And before that, as far back as the last
occupancy of the caves of Altamira, there simply was nothing human,
just a repulsive type of animal, very inferior to pretty much all the
rest of creation.

In my youth, the leading parlor amusement was the search for the
"missing link," *i.e.*, the intermediate stage between man and the anthropoid ape. The frenzied search still goes on with the discovery now
and then of a very incomplete skull or, better still a small fragment
thereof that can be ingeniously extended according to the taste of the
restorer, into the semblance of a proof. It will be perceived that I have

no confidence in these ingenious inventions. I remember too well the hilarious episode (a year or two ago) when one tooth was discovered somewhere in the wide open spaces of the West, and was officially pronounced by one or more of the most eminent anthropologists, to be the long-sought intermediate stage. Shortly thereafter it developed that the precious tooth came from the jaw of a common or barn-yard pig, to the confusion of the savants but not to their discouragement, for the pathetic search still goes on.

Recently, however, the pursuit of the missing cultural link has become as ardent and, if progressive evolution is not to go into the discard, as important as that for the skeletal connection. Thus far the search is equally vain. In Egypt, Mesopotamia, Chaldea, Crete, excavations and discoveries reveal evidences of the highest culture that goes back, in its completeness, and a completeness that in no essential particular falls short of our own, to the solid wall of about 4000 B.C. Back of that there is nothing, and between the New Stone Age and the culture of the Egyptian Old Kingdom or of Ur of the Chaldees, there are no intermediate stages of moment as there are none between the former and the post-glacial animals that preceded them.

It would seem, then, that after all Dr. de Vries is probably right when he claims that the process of evolution and the development of new species is not after the Darwinian fashion, always from lower to higher and by the constant accretion of minute differences, but by what de Vries calls the "catastrophic" process: the periodical and unaccountable appearance, in the midst of many type forms, of one that is entirely new. In some cases this new thing reproduces itself true to form, and indefinitely; in others there is an ultimate reversion to type.

One more point in my assembling of raw material and I will proceed to my deduction which may, or may not, answer my question as to why we do not behave like human beings.

In a special cable despatch recently transmitted from England, Sir James Jeans and Sir Arthur Eddington, physicists of unquestioned authority, join in the opinion that recent astronomical discoveries indicate the strong probability that the old time-scale must be scrapped and that, whereas not so long ago the age of the universe was counted in probable billions or even trillions of years, now it must be reduced to hundreds of thousands, or at the most millions of years. This is a startling statement and its implications are obvious and significant. Such a reduction in scale, if proportional, would give the earth but a brief day of life, the animal kingdom one still more restricted in time, and man himself—well, shall we say, and with due allowance for that older civilization or culture the last vestiges of which are afforded by the Magdalenian survival of which the provenance may have been Atlantis—not millions but some tens of thousands of years.

And now what has the bearing of all this tenuous speculation (mine, not that of our distinguished scientists) to do with the question I have posited? *Why* do we not behave like human beings? for by and large we certainly do not. Regard dispassionately the history of what we call "civilization." So far as we know, which is not far, it was not so bad in Egypt, Mesopotamia, Crete, but as history becomes clearer so does the evidence of a pretty invincible beastliness. It is a farrago of cruelty, slaughter and injustice. I have no intention of rehearsing old records. Nero and Ghengis Khan and the gangs they led may rest in their unquiet graves for all me, but come down to what are, comparatively, our own times and call to mind the barbarian invasions of Italy, of northern France and of England; the wars of religion with the slaughters of Catholics and Protestants; the Inquisition with its *auto da fé*; the Thirty Years' War and the Hundred Years' War; the witchcraft insanity; the beastliness of the "Peasants' War" in Germany and of the French Revolution; the horrors of the so-called "Reformation" in England and on the Continent; the African slave trade; the debauching of the Negro tribes; the Spanish record in Mexico, Central and South America, with the blasting of Maya and Inca and Aztec civilization; the piracy and brigandage of the seventeenth century; our own treatment of the Indians; the gross evils accomplished in the South Seas by traders, adventurers and evangelical missionaries; the ruthless barbarity of the new industrialism in England from 1780 on for fifty years; the record of the Turks in Macedonia and Armenia; the Russian Revolution; gas warfare; and the blind selfishness of advancing technological and capitalist civilization.

These are only a few salient headings in one category of human activity, a few amongst the many that continue without pause or break for some three thousand years. I might match and rival this record were I to dilate on the follies and miscarriages of justice and the evidences of invincible ignorance and superstition that follow man in what was once termed his "evolutionary" progress. But this is unnecessary. We have but to regard our present estate when, at the summit of our Darwinian advance, natural selection and the survival of the fittest and the development of species have resulted in a condition where, with all the resources of a century and a half of unparalleled scientific and mechanical development, we confront a situation so irrational and apparently hopeless of solution, that there is not a scientist, a politician, an industrialist, a financier, a philosopher or a parson who has the faintest idea how we got that way or how we are to get out of it.

Yes, but there is another side to the question. However repulsive and degrading the general condition of any period in the past, there never has been a time when out of the darkness did not flame into light bright figures of men and women who in character and capacity were a glory to the human race. Nor were they only those whose names we know and whose fame is immortal. We know from the evidences that there were more whose identity is not determined, men and women lost in the great mass of the underlying mob, who in purity and honour and charity were co-equal with the great figures of history. Between them and the basic mass there was a difference greater than that which separates, shall we say, the obscene mob of the November Revolution in Russia, and the anthropoid apes. They fall into two absolutely different categories, the which is precisely the point I wish to make.

We do not behave like human beings because most of us do not fall within that classification as we have determined it for ourselves, since we do not measure up to standard. And thus:

With our invincible—and most honourable but perilous—optimism we gauge humanity by the best it has to show. From the bloody riot of cruelty, greed and lust we cull the bright figures of real men and women. Pharaoh Akhenaten, King David, Pericles and Plato, Buddha and Confucius and Lao Tse, Seneca and Marcus Aurelius and Virgil, Abd-er-Rahman of Cordoba, Charlemagne and Roland; St. Benedict, St. Francis, St. Louis; Godfrey de Bouillon, Saladin, Richard Coeur de Lion; Dante, Leonardo, St. Thomas Aquinas, Ste. Jeanne d'Arc, Sta. Teresa, Frederick II, Otto the Great, St. Ferdinand of Spain, Chaucer and Shakespeare, Strafford and Montrose and Mary of Scotland, Washington, Adams and Lee. These are but a few key names; fill out the splendid list for yourselves. By them we unconsciously establish our standard of human beings.

Now to class with them and the unrecorded multitude of their compeers, the savage and ignorant mob beneath, or its leaders and mouthpieces, is both unjust and unscientific. What kinship is there between St. Francis and John Calvin; the Earl of Strafford and Thomas Crumwell; Robert E. Lee and Trotsky; Edison and Capone? None except their human form. They of the great list behave like our ideal of the human being; they of the ignominious sub-stratum do not—because they are not. In other words, the just line of demarcation should be drawn, not between Neolithic Man and the anthropoid ape, but between the glorified and triumphant human being and the Neolithic mass which was, is now and ever shall be.

What I mean is this, and I will give you this as a simile. Some years ago I was on the Island of Hawaii and in the great crater of Kilauea on the edge of the flaming pit of Halemaumau. For once the pit was level full of molten lava that at one end of this pit, at the iron edge of old lava, rose swiftly from the lowest depths, then slid silently, a viscous field of lambent cherry colour, along the length of the great pit, to plunge and disappear as silently, only to return and rise again, when all was to happen once more. Indeterminate, homogeneous, it was an undifferentiated flood, except for one thing. As it slid silkily onward it "fountained" incessantly. That is to say, from all over its surface leaped high in the air slim jets of golden lava that caught the sun and opened into delicate fireworks of falling jewels, beautiful beyond imagination.

Such I conceive to be the pattern of human life. Millennium after millennium this endless flood of basic raw material sweeps on. It is the everlasting Neolithic Man, the same that it was five or ten thousand years B.C. It is the matrix of the human being, the stuff of which he is made. It arises from the unknown and it disappears in the unknown, to return again and again on itself. And always it "fountains" in fine personalities, eminent and of historic record, or obscure yet of equal nobility, and these are the "human beings" on whose personality, character and achievements we establish our standard.

The basic mass, the raw material out of which great and fine personalities are made, is the same today as it was before King Zoser of Egypt and the first architect, Imhotep, set the first pyramid stones that marked the beginning of our era of human culture. Neolithic it was and is, and there has been no essential change in ten thousand years, for it is no finished product, but raw material and because of its potential, of absolute value. We do not realize this, for it is not obvious to the eye since all that greatness has achieved in that period is as free for the use of contemporary Neolithic Man as it is for those who have emerged into the full stature of humanity. Free and compulsory education, democratic government and universal suffrage, and the unlimited opportunities of industrial civilization have clothed him with the deceptive garments of equality, but underneath he is forever the same. It is not until we are confronted in our own time with a thing like the original Bolshevik reign of terror, the futility of popular government, not only national but as we see it close at home in the sort of men that we choose to govern us in our cities, our state legislatures, the national Congress; in the bluntness of intellect and lack of vision in big business and finance, or when we read Mr. Mencken's "Americana" or consider the monkey-shines of popular evangelists, "comic strips," dance- and bicycle- and Bible-reading marathons, that we are awakened to a realization of the fact that there is something wrong with our categories.

Those that live in these things that they have made are *not* behaving like the human beings we have chosen for ourselves out of history as determinants of that entity, and this for the reason that they still are the veritable men of the Neolithic age that no camouflage of civilization can change.

Perhaps we have set our standard too high. Perhaps we should, in accordance with the alleged principles of Mr. Jefferson, count the mob-man as the standard human being; but since the gulf that separates him from the ideal we have made for ourselves is too vast to be bridged by any social, political or biological formula, this would force us back on the Nietzschean doctrine of the Superman which, personally, I reject. It seems to me much more fitting to accept our proved ideal as the true type of human being, counting all else as the potent material of creation.

I cannot blind myself to the fact that if what I have said is taken seriously it will probably seem revolting, if not grotesque and even impious. I do not mean it to be any of these things, nor does it seem so to me. Put into few words, and as inoffensively as possible, all I mean is that the process of creation is continuous. That as the "first man" was said to have been created out of the dust of the earth, so this creation goes on today as it ever has. As this same "dust of the earth" may have been Neolithic or more probably Paleolithic sub-man, so today the formative material is of identical nature and potency— but it is still, as then, the unformed, unquickened, primitive or Neolithic matter. Within its own particular sphere it is invaluable, indispensable, but we treat it unfairly when, through our vaporous theorizing we are led to pitchfork it into an alien sphere where it cannot function properly, and where it is untrue to itself, and by its sheer weight of numbers and deficiency or certain salutary inhibitions, is bound to negative the constructive power of the men of light and leading, while reducing the normal average to the point of ultimate disaster.

If there is any modicum of truth in what I have said I must leave to you the noting of those implications that must follow in respect to the doctrine and workings of democracy as these are manifested today in society, politics and religion.

And now, in these last days we stand aghast at the portent of our own *Götterdämmerung*. The high gods we had revered and before whom we had made sacrifice of so much of the best we had, show thin and impotent, or vanish in the flame of disaster. Political and social democracy, with their plausible devices and panaceas; popular sovereignty, the Protestant religion of the masses; the technological triumphs that were to emancipate labour and redeem the world; all the multiple manifestations of a free and democratic society fail of their predicted issue, and we find ourselves lapped in confusion and numb with disappointment and chagrin.

I suggest that the cause of comprehensive failure and the bar to recovery is the persistence of the everlasting Neolithic Man and his assumption of universal control.

III. The Chosen Heroes & the Chosen Past

BECAUSE THE *liberal, materialistic, and democratic present was often so unsatisfactory, the conservatives frequently felt the need for solace elsewhere. Nock and Santayana traveled frequently to Europe. Davidson and his students lived in the South and worked to create myths that would comfort them, place them in history, and in some way compensate them for the misfortune of having been born in the wrong time and place. T. S. Eliot emigrated to England and changed his citizenship.*

This desire to opt out of American culture was hardly confined to conservatives—as any study of American writers in Paris during the 1920s quickly shows. But the conservatives were often fearsomely articulate about what they disliked in America and preferred in Europe: Belgium and France for Nock, Italy for Santayana, England for Eliot. They were also adept at examining American culture and finding heroes who stood out from the vulgar crowd and submerged traditions that demanded more attention than they usually received. At times they created a whole imaginative world out of past times in order to convey their frustration with life in modern America.

The limitations of space make it impossible to explore many of these efforts, like Cram's evocation of the Gothic world or Paul More's affectionate portrayal of ancient Greece. I have instead selected three simply to indicate the basic point of this section: that conservatives could opt out of liberal culture and choose their heroes and country where they pleased, then feel reinvigorated and better able to live in the present.

Every editor should be allowed one act of self-indulgence, and Nock's little talk on Pantagruelism is my confessed favorite. The Faculty of Medicine at the Johns Hopkins University invited him to speak on October 28, 1932, on the four hundredth anniversary of the publication of Rabelais' Pantagruel, *and in delivering his talk Nock produced one of the undiscovered classics of modern American conservatism. The educational, social, political, and medical values he found in Rabelais became a recipe for living in a world hostile to civilization. The chosen past thus illuminates the present, the tone is relaxed and witty, the result worthy of far more attention than it has received.*

The original typescript is in the Nock Papers, Library of Congress. The obscure libertarian newspaper, Analysis, *printed a somewhat condensed text in its Nock Memorial Edition of August 1946. That is the basis of the text that follows. The policy of the newspaper forbade copyright protection, and so this version is in the public domain.*

10. Pantagruelism

By Albert Jay Nock

When you kindly asked me here, I was a little afraid to come, because I felt that an audience like this would more or less expect me to get at Rabelais by his profes- sional side, and I am not able to do that. I know nothing about the practice of medicine today, let alone how it was practiced four hundred years ago. I have always been pretty healthy, or I might know more, but I am contented. Probably you have noticed how con- tented ignorant people are. I am not sure that Aristotle is right in that fine sentence of his about all mankind naturally desiring knowledge. Most of them would rather get along without knowing anything, if they could, because knowing things is hard work. I often wish I knew less than I do about a great many things, like politics, for instance, or history. When you know a great deal about something, you have hard work to keep your knowledge from going sour—that is, unless you are a Pantagruelist, and if you are a professor of politics, like me, nothing but Pantagruelism will ever save you. Your learning goes so sour that before you know it the Board of Health comes sniffing around, asking the neighbours whether they have been noticing any- thing lately. Maybe something of that sort is true of medicine too, but as I said, I do not know about that. Pantagruelism is a natural sort of preservative, like refrigeration, it keeps the temperature right. Some people put too much bad antiseptic stuff into their learning—too much embalming-fluid.

There seems to be no doubt that Rabelais's professional standing was high. According to all testimony, he must have been one of the most eminent and successful practitioners in Europe. For two years he was at the head of the great hospital at Lyon, perhaps the fore- most in France, and I think also the oldest in continuous service. It is about a thousand years old. It was moved once, from one quarter of town to another, and it has been dusted up and renovated every now and then, but it still stands where Rabelais found it. Some fragments of structure which belong to his day are said to exist, but I could not identify them. The whole affair looked pretty old to me, but I imagine it is probably all right. I should not care to be a patient there, but I should not care to be a patient anywhere.

Rabelais did some good things at that hospital. In two years he ran the death-rate down three percent. It is not easy to see how he did

Note: From *Analysis* 2, no. 10 (August 1946): 5–6.

that. One might suppose that the death-rate would be pretty constant, no matter what diseases the patients had. Rabelais had an average of about two hundred patients, sleeping two in a bed, sometimes three, in air that was warmed only by an open fire, and with no ventilation worth speaking of. It must have been a little stuffy in there sometimes. Rabelais examined all his patients once a day, prescribed medicines and operations, and superintended a staff of thirty-two people. He managed everything. His salary was about forty dollars a year, which was high. His successor got only thirty. I believe he had his board thrown in. The hospital was rich, but the trustees capitalized its prestige. They thought a physician ought to work for nothing, for the honour of it. Probably you never heard of any trustees like that, so I thought I would mention it.

The thing he did that interests me most was to beat that hospital out of five dollars. He did it in his second year there, nobody knows how, nobody can imagine how. I think that is more extraordinary than reducing the death-rate. Any man who could beat a French hospital corporation out of five dollars need not worry about the death-rate. He could raise the dead. The French auditor of the hospital was frightfully depressed about that five dollars. He left a marginal note on the account, saying that it seemed to be all wrong, but there it was, and for some reason apparently nothing could be done about it. The incident makes me think of Panurge and the money-changers, in the sixteenth chapter of the Second Book, where Rabelais says that whenever Panurge "changed a teston, cardecu or any other piece of money, the changer had been more subtle than a fox if Panurge had not at every time made five or six sols vanish away visibly, openly and manifestly, without making any hurt or lesion, whereof the changer should have felt nothing but the wind."

Rabelais held a more important position, even, than this one at Lyon. For twenty years he was personal physician to two of the ablest and most prominent men in the kingdom, Cardinal Jean du Bellay and his brother Guillaume. Both of them were always ailing, always worn down by heavy labours and responsibilities in the public service. They were in pretty constant need of the best medical skill, and could command it; and Rabelais was their chosen physician and confidential friend.

Then, too, there is his record at the University of Montpellier, which you historians of medicine know better than I do, and know how remarkable it was, so I need not go into it. The University of Montpellier always made a great specialty of medicine. It was like the Johns Hopkins in that. Except for a few years when Toulouse was ahead of it, I believe the Faculty of Medicine there was said to be the best in France. It is interesting to go in and look at the pictures of the sixteenth-century professors. Rabelais is there, and Rondellet, who some think was the original of the physician Rondibilis, in the Third Book. I am none too sure of that, but it does not matter. That sort of question never matters. Rondibilis is the same, no matter who his original was, or whether he had any. What of it? Think of scholars like F. A. Wolf and Lachmann tying themselves up for years over the question whether Homer was one man or eighteen. What difference does it make? You don't read Homer for any such notions as that. You read him to keep going, to keep your head above water, and you read Rabelais for the same reason.

Scurron, Rabelais's preceptor at Montpellier, has his picture there, and so has Saporta, whom Rabelais mentions as a fellow-actor in the comedy of The Man Who Married a Dumb Wife. They had college dramatics in those days, too. Anatole France rewrote this comedy from the synopsis of it that Rabelais gives, and Mr. Granville Barker put it on the stage for us. I wish we could see it oftener, instead of so many plays that are only slices out of our own life, and usually out of the dullest and meanest part of our own life, at that. . . .

Rabelais makes some running comments on physicians and their ways that interest a layman. Some physicians are fussy. They want to regulate everybody and lay down the law about what is good for everybody, and especially about what is *not* good for anybody. They begrudge you any interesting food and anything interesting to drink. Then pretty soon another batch of little rule-of-thumb doctors comes along and tells us the first batch was all wrong, and that we ought to do something different. They were just like that in Rabelais's day, too. A friend of mine has been calling my attention to some dietary rules laid down in that period—why, according to those rules, you would say it was not safe to eat anything. This sort of thing even got under Gargantua's skin, you remember. He told Friar John that it was all wrong to drink before breakfast; the physicians said so. "Oh, rot your physicians!" said Friar John. "A hundred devils leap into my body if there be not more old drunkards than old physicians." Friar John went by what philosophers used to call "the common sense of mankind." He believed that the same thing will not work for everybody, and that seems to have been Rabelais's idea too. Rabelais mentions two or three diets in the course of his story, and they seem very reasonable and sensible. He thought that Nature had some resources of her own, and he was willing to let her have something to say about such matters. The little whimsical doctors of his time would not let Nature have any chance at all, if they could help it. They laid out the course that they thought she ought to follow, and then expected her to follow it. Sometimes she did not do that, and then the patient was out of luck.

Of course, you may lay down some general rules. Rabelais knew that. For instance, he says it was sound practice for Gargantua to eat a light lunch and a big dinner, and that the Arabian physicians, who advised a big meal in the middle of the day, were all wrong. There is sense in that. It is a good general rule. But then, you have to remem-

ber that one man's light lunch is another man's square meal. Also
something depends on what you have for breakfast, and when you get
it, and what you have been doing during the morning. If you have
ever been around a French restaurant at lunchtime, you have probably noticed Frenchmen getting away with a pretty hefty square, and
it is a great sight to see the way they dig into it. As Panurge said, it
is as good as a balsam for sore eyes to see them gulch and raven it.
Well, if you had a French breakfast that morning, it is a fair bet that
you would be doing the same thing. A French breakfast disappears
while you are looking at it. Then again, Gargantua was a huge giant,
and his light lunch would founder an ordinary stomach. It would be
worse than an old-style American Sunday dinner. When he was a
baby, it took the milk of 17,913 cows to feed him. No ordinary baby
could do anything with that much milk. So, you see, you have to allow
for exceptions to your general rule, after all, probably quite a lot of
them.

By the way, did you ever hear that our term Blue Monday came out
of those Sunday dinners? The mayor of one of our mid-Western cities told me that. He said he never had such a frightful time with reformers and the moral element in his town as he did on Monday
morning. They ate their heads off every Sunday noon, and when they
came to on Monday morning, they were full of bile and fermentation
and all sorts of meanness, and that made them want to persecute their
neighbours, so they would run around first thing to the mayor's office
to get him to close up something that people liked, or stop something
that they wanted to do. Every Monday morning he knew he was in for
it. It was Blue Monday for him every week.

I have often wondered how much of this sort of thing is behind our
great reform movements. One of them, you know, was started by a
bilious French lawyer. He was a fearful fellow. Most people have no
idea of the harm he did. He was a contemporary of Rabelais, and they
were probably acquainted. He was down on Rabelais, and did as much
as anybody to give him a bad name. That was because Rabelais would
not join in on his reform. That is always the way with these bilious
reformers. You have to reform things their way, or they say you are
a scoundrel and do not believe in any reform at all. That is the way
the Socialists and Communists feel nowadays, when we do not swallow their ideas whole, and yet maybe we want things reformed as
much as they do. Rabelais wanted to see the Church reformed. He
was hand in glove with Erasmus on that. But he was a Pantagruelist,
so he knew that Calvin's way and Luther's way would not really reform anything, but would only make a botch of it. Well, we see now
that it all turned out just as he knew it would. Swapping the authority of a bishop for the authority of a book was not even a theoretical
reform, and all it did practically was to set up a lot of little Peterkins
all over Christendom, each one sure he was the only one who knew
what the book meant, and down on all the others, fighting and squab-

bling with them and saying all sorts of hateful things about them. Rabelais knew that was sure to happen, and knew that kind of reform was just no reform at all. So he would not go in with Calvin, and Calvin, being a good bilious reformer, abused him like a pickpocket. Calvin was an enormously able man, but his liver was out of commission. It is a strange thought, isn't it, that if somebody had fed Calvin eight or nine grains of calomel at night every week or so, and about a quarter of a pound of Rochelle salts in the morning, the whole tone of Protestant theology might have been different. It almost makes mechanists of us.

Rabelais had much the same sort of notion about reform in medicine. His position on that has puzzled a great many people. That is because they look at him in a little, sectarian, rule-of-thumb way. He was for going back to Galen and Hippocrates, cleaning off the glosses on their texts, and finding out what they really said. Well, then, some say that shows he was a hide-bound old Tory in medicine. On the other hand, he made dissections and lectured from them, which was a great innovation. He went in for experiments. He laughed at some ideas of Democritus and Theophrastus, and in the seventh chapter of the Third Book you find him poking fun at Galen himself. Well, then, others say, he was a great radical, and he has even been put forward as the father of experimentation in medicine. All that is nonsense. To the Pantagruelist, labels like radical and Tory mean just nothing at all. You go back to the classics of a subject for the practical purpose of saving yourself a lot of work. You get an accumulation of observation, method, technique, that subsequent experience has confirmed, and you can take it at second-hand and don't have to work it all out afresh for yourself. Maybe you can improve on it, here and there, and that is all right, but if you don't know the classics of your subject, you often find that you have been wasting a lot of time over something that somebody went all through, clear back in the Middle Ages. What is there radical or Tory about that? It is just good sense.

I think Americans are peculiarly impatient about the classics of any subject. In my own line, I know, I next to never meet anybody who seems to have read anything that was written before about 1890. That is one reason why we get done in so often by other people, especially in business and finance. You take a good thing wherever you find it—that was Rabelais's idea. If somebody worked it out satisfactorily for you forty years ago, or four hundred, or four thousand, why, you are just that much ahead. You have that much more chance to work out something else, some improvement maybe, or something new. Knowing the classics matures and seasons the mind as nothing else will, but aside from that, in a practical way, it is a great labour-saver. When I was at Ems a couple of years ago, one of their experimenters had just discovered that the Ems salts helped out a little in cases of pyorrhea. That was known four hundred years ago. It is men-

tioned in a report on the springs, written in the sixteenth century.
Then it was forgotten, and discovered again only the other day.

But I must stop this sort of thing, and speak about Pantagruelism.
I hear you have a good many Pantagruelists here in Baltimore, and
that does not surprise me, because there used to be such a marvelous
lot of germ-carriers in this university. If you caught Pantagruelism
from Gildersleeve or Minton Warren or William Osler, there was no
help for you. You had it for life. There was a big quarantine against
Baltimore on account of those people. That was the most expensive
quarantine ever established in the world. It cost the American people
all their culture, all their intelligence, all their essential integrities,
their insight, their dignity, their self-respect, their command of the
future, to keep Pantagruelism from spreading. We did it, though. The
country is practically free of Pantagruelism now. There is less of it
here than in any other country I know. Hardly anyone ever heard of
it. Probably you know how the great exponent of Pantagruelism is
regarded. Why, only the other day when I was talking to a few people informally about Rabelais, a man came up to me afterward and
said he was sorry his wife was not there. He had left her at home because he thought she might have to hear some improper language.
That was his idea of Rabelais, and he was a professor in one of our
colleges, too. Just think of a miserable little coot like that. When you
look the situation over and see the general part that this country is
playing in the world's affairs, and see what sort of thing she has to
play it with, you begin to think that quarantine cost too much.

Pantagruelism is not a cult or a creed or a frame of mind, but a
quality of spirit. In one place Rabelais says it is "a certain jollity of
mind, pickled in the scorn of fortune," and this is one of its aspects:
an easy, objective, genial, but unyielding superiority to everything external, to every conceivable circumstance of one's life. It is a quality
like that of the ether, which the physicists of my day used to say was
imponderable, impalpable, harder than steel, yet so pervasive that it
permeates everything, underlies everything. This is the quality that
Rabelais communicates in every line. Read the Prologue to the Second
Book, for instance—better read it aloud to yourself—well, there you
have it, you can't miss it, and if it does not communicate itself to your
own spirit, you may as well give up the idea that you were cut out
for a Pantagruelist.

And at what a time in the world's life was that Prologue written.
It was a period more nearly like ours than any other in history. The
difficulties and temptations that the human spirit faced were like
ours. It was a period of unexampled expansion, like ours; of discovery
and invention, like ours; of revolution in industry and commerce; of
the inflation of avarice into a mania; of ruinous political centralization; of dominant bourgeois ideals—not the ideals of the working

bourgeois, but those of the new bourgeois of bankers, speculators, shavers, lawyers, jobholders; and it was a period of great general complacency towards corruption. This is one thing that makes Rabelais particularly a man of our own time. The quality of spirit that he exhibits was brought out under circumstances almost exactly like ours, and contact with it helps us to meet our own circumstances in the way that he met his.

Pantagruelism means keeping the integrity of one's own personality absolutely intact. Rabelais says that Pantagruel "never vexed nor disquieted himself with the least pretence of dislike to anything, because he knew that he must have most grossly abandoned the divine mansion of reason if he had permitted his mind to be never so little grieved, afflicted or altered on any occasion whatsoever. For all the goods that the heaven covereth and that the earth containeth, in all their dimensions of height, depth, breadth and length, are not of so much worth as that we should for them disturb or disorder our affections, trouble or perplex our senses or spirits."

You see, the Pantagruelist never admits that there is anything in the world that is bigger than he is. Not business, not profession, not position. The case of the American business man is much discussed now, as you know. What has the typical American business man come to? He thought his business was bigger than he was, and he went into slavery to it and let it own him, and he was proud to do that, he thought that meant progress, thought it meant civilization, and he thought because his business was so great that he must be a great man; and he kept letting us know he thought so. He was like the misguided girl who had lived with so many gentlemen that she thought she was a lady. Well, then a pinch comes, and now we are all saying the business man is only a stuffed shirt, that there is nothing inside his shirt but wind and fungus. We see that the big men of business have had to have a tariff wall around them, or get rebates from the railways on their freight, or get some other kind of special privilege, and that they were not great men at all, for almost anybody with the same privilege could have done as well.

Then think of the people in politics, the jobholders and jobhunters. There are a lot of them around just now, telling us what ought to be done and what they are going to do if they are elected. The trouble with them is that they think the job is bigger than they are, and so they destroy the integrity of their personality in order to get it or hold it. Why, by the time a man has connived and lied and shuffled his miserable way up to the point where he can be an acceptable candidate, there isn't enough of him left to be a good jobholder, even if he wants to. The Athenians blamed Socrates, you know, because he wouldn't have anything to do with politics; he would not vote or go into any campaigns or indorse any candidates—he let it all alone. He was a great Pantagruelist, one of the greatest, so he told the Athenians that what they were blaming him for was the very reason why he

and his followers were the best politicians in Athens. That closed
them out. He was such a good Pantagruelist that finally the boys had
to get together and poison him.

Pantagruelism is utterly unselfconscious; it works like a kind of
secondary instinct. Have you ever noticed how Rabelais's wonderful
art comes out in the relations between Pantagruel and Panurge? Pantagruel liked Panurge, was interested in him, amused by him, tolerant
of all his ingenious deviltry, but never once compromised his own
character. On the other hand, he was never priggish, never patroniz-
ing or moralistic with Panurge, not even in their discussion on bor-
rowing and lending. His superiority was always unselfconscious, ef-
fortless. I think the delicate consistency that Rabelais shows on this
point is perhaps his greatest literary achievement; and the climax of
it is that Panurge, who was never loyal to anything or anybody, was
always loyal to Pantagruel.

But Pantagruelism is not easy. In the Prologue to the Third Book we
come on another characteristic which is the crowning glory of Pantagruelism. Rabelais has been talking about the blunders of an honest-
minded Egyptian ruler, and some other matters of the kind, how well-
intended things are sometimes misapprehended, and so on, and then
he says that by virtue of Pantagruelism we are always ready to "bear
with anything that floweth from a good, free and loyal heart." Maybe
that is easier for you than it is for me. I don't mind saying frankly
and very sadly that my Pantagruelism breaks down oftener on that
than on anything. On this point Pantagruelism is like Christianity. I
have often thought I might have made a pretty consistent Christian
if it had not been for just that one thing that the blessed Apostle said
about suffering fools gladly. How easily the great Pantagruelists seem
to do that, but it only seems easy, it really is very hard to do. How
easily, how exquisitely Rabelais did it. I wish I might have him in
New York so he could hear some of my friends talk about the great
transformations that are going to take place when Mr. Roosevelt is
elected or Mr. Hoover is reelected. I always walk out on them, but Rabelais would not. He would play with them a while, and probably get
some results, for they are really first-rate people, but all that sort of
thing seems beyond me.

The quarantine I spoke of a moment ago appears to be pretty well
lifted. We are not quarantining against much of anything, these days.
Now, in conclusion, may I ask if it ever occurred to you to think what
a thundering joke on the country it would be if this university should
quietly, without saying anything about it, go back to its old contra-
band business of disseminating Pantagruelism? For that was its business. You got good chemistry with Remsen, and mathematics with
Sylvester, and semitics with Paul Haupt, and a degree at the end of it,
and all that sort of thing, but mark my words, before time gets
through with you it will show that the real distinction of this univer-

sity was that it exposed you to Pantagruelism day and night. Let us dream about it for a moment. Suppose we say you sold your campus and your plant—they may be an asset to you, but they look to me like a liability; suppose you threw out all your undergraduate students— and this time I am very sure they are a liability; suppose you went back to the little brick houses where Huxley found you, and suppose you got together a dozen or so good sound Pantagruelists from some- where and shut them up there with your graduate students, your bachelors and masters. What a colossal joke it would be. The country has virtually ruined itself in the effort to stamp out Pantagruelism. All its institutional voices have been raised in behalf of ignoble, mean, squalid ideals, and telling us that those mean progress, those mean civilization, those mean hundred-percent Americanism. Now that the country has got itself in such distraction from following this doctrine that none of the accepted prophets have a sensible word to say, I re- peat, what a joke it would be if the old original sinner should go back and begin corrupting the youth again.

Then suppose you should use a little selective pressure on your stu- dent body. You know, some people—excellent people, admirable peo- ple—are immune to Pantagruelism. You had some of them here in the old days, like President Wilson and Mr. Newton Baker. They were fine folks, good as gold, most of them, but no good at all for your pur- poses. Well, suppose when these immune people come around, you tell them after a while that they would probably do better up at Har- vard, or maybe Yale. Yes, Yale is the place for them. There is an In- stitute of Human Relations up there, and these immune people are usually strong on human relations. Did you ever notice that? When Mr. Wilson and Mr. Baker got going on human relations, there was no stopping them. So you might off-load your immune people on Yale, and they could go to the Institute. They would probably find a director there—I mean, a Dean—and plenty of card-indexes and ste- nographers, and one thing or another like that that are just what you need to study human relations with; and meanwhile you could be get- ting on with Pantagruelism.

THE ESSENTIAL *quality which Nock found in Rabelais—"a certain jollity of mind, pickled in the scorn of fortune"—was in generally short supply in America. Mencken certainly had it, however, and he knew of at least one friend of his who possessed it as well. In the critic of all the arts, James Gibbons Huneker (1860–1921), Mencken could choose his own past much the way his friend Nock could with Rabelais. In tracing Huneker's life from his depressing origin in Philadelphia through Europe to New York, Mencken emphasizes his friend's contagious gusto and joy in his work. Huneker was a man without cant; he was cosmopolitan and had "the discreet and complete knowledge of a man of culture." His world was "the whole universe of beauty." He scarcely belonged in America at all: "There is something about him as exotic as a samovar, as essentially un-American as a bashi-bazouk, a nose-ring or a fugue. He is filled to the throttle with strange and unnational heresies." He thus becomes a way of finding an American past that is salvageable and that is not a part of the depressing Victorian conformity that was distressing to many conservatives.*

11. James Huneker

By Henry Louis Mencken

James Gibbons Huneker [is] the only critic among us whose vision sweeps the whole field of beauty, and whose reports of what he sees there show any genuine gusto. That gusto of his, I fancy, is two-thirds of his story. It is unquenchable, contagious, inflammatory; he is the only performer in the commissioned troupe who knows how to arouse his audience to anything approaching enthusiasm. The rest, even including Howells, are pedants lecturing to the pure in heart, but Huneker makes a joyous story of it; his exposition, transcending the merely expository, takes on the quality of an adventure hospitably shared. One feels, reading him, that he is charmed by the men and women he writes about, and that their ideas, even when he rejects them, give him an agreeable stimulation. And to the charm that he thus finds and exhibits in others, he adds the very positive charm of his own personality. He seems a man who has found the world fascinating, if perhaps not perfect; a friendly and good-humoured fellow; no frigid scholiast, but something of an epicure; in brief, the reverse of the customary maker of books about books. Compare his two essays on Ibsen, in "Egoists" and "Iconoclasts," to the general body of American writing upon the great Norwegian. The difference is that between a portrait and a Bertillon photograph, Richard Strauss and Czerny, a wedding and an autopsy. Huneker displays Ibsen, not as a petty mystifier of the women's clubs, but as a literary artist of large skill and exalted passion, and withal a quite human and understandable man. These essays were written at the height of the symbolism madness; in their own way, they even show some reflection of it; but taking them in their entirety, how clearly they stand above the ignorant obscurantism of the prevailing criticism of the time—how immeasurably superior they are, for example, to that favourite hymn-book of the Ibsenites, "The Ibsen Secret" by Jennette Lee! For the causes of this difference one need not seek far. They are to be found in the difference between the bombastic half-knowledge of a school teacher and the discreet and complete knowledge of a man of culture. Huneker is that man of culture. He has reported more of interest and value than any other American critic, living or dead, but the essence of his criticism does not lie so much in what he specifically reports as in the civilized point of view from which he reports

Note: Originally published in *A Book of Prefaces* (New York, 1917), pp. 159–194.

it. He is a true cosmopolitan, not only in the actual range of his ad-
venturings, but also and more especially in his attitude of mind. His
world is not America, nor Europe, nor Christendom, but the whole
universe of beauty. As Jules Simon said of Taine: *"Aucun écrivain de
nos jours n'a . . . découvert plus d'horizons variés et immenses."*

Need anything else be said in praise of a critic? And does an ex-
travagance or an error here and there lie validly against the saying of
it? I think not. I could be a professor if I would and show you slips
enough—certain ponderous nothings in the Ibsen essays, already
mentioned; a too easy bemusement at the hands of Shaw; a vacillat-
ing over Wagner; a habit of yielding to the hocus-pocus of the mys-
tics, particularly Maeterlinck. On the side of painting, I am told, there
are even worse aberrations; I know too little about painting to judge
for myself. But the list, made complete, would still not be over-long,
and few of its items would be important. Huneker, like the rest of us,
has sinned his sins, but his judgments, in the overwhelming main,
hold water. He has resisted the lure of all the wild movements of the
generation; the tornadoes of doctrine have never knocked him over.
Nine times out of ten, in estimating a new man in music or letters,
he has come curiously close to the truth at the first attempt. And he
has always announced it in good time; his solo has always preceded
the chorus.

.   .   .   .

It would be difficult, indeed, to overestimate the practical value to all
the arts in America of his intellectual alertness, his catholic hospitality to ideas, his artistic courage, and above all, his powers of persuasion. It was not alone that he saw clearly what was sound and significant; it was that he managed, by the sheer charm of his writings, to
make a few others see and understand it. If the United States is in
any sort of contact today, however remotely, with what is aesthetically
going on in the more civilized countries—if the Puritan tradition, for
all its firm entrenchment, has eager and resourceful enemies beset-
ting it—if the pall of Harvard quasi-culture, by the Oxford manner out
of Calvinism, has been lifted ever so little—there is surely no man
who can claim a larger share of credit for preparing the way. . . .

Huneker comes out of Philadelphia, that depressing intellectual
slum, and his first writing was for the Philadelphia *Evening Bulletin.*
He is purely Irish in blood, and is of very respectable ancestry, his
maternal grandfather and godfather having been James Gibbons, the
Irish poet and patriot, and president of the Fenian Brotherhood in
America. Once, in a review of "The Pathos of Distance," I ventured
the guess that there was a German strain in him somewhere, and
based it upon the beery melancholy visible in parts of that book. Who
but a German sheds tears over the empty bottles of day before yesterday, the Adelaide Neilson of 1877? Who but a German goes into wool-

len undershirts at 45, and makes his will, and begins to call his wife
"Mamma"? The green-sickness of youth is endemic from pole to pole,
as much so as measles; but what race save the wicked one is floored
by a blue distemper in middle age, with sentimental burblings *a cap-
pella*, hallucinations of lost loves, and an unquenchable lacrymor-
rhea? . . . I made out a good case, but I was wrong, and the penalty
came swiftly and doubly, for on the one hand the Boston *Transcript*
sounded an alarm against both Huneker and me as German spies, and
on the other hand Huneker himself proclaimed that, even spiritually,
he was less German than Magyar, less "Hun" than Hun. "I am," he
said, "a Celto-Magyar: Pilsner at Donnybrook Fair. Even the German
beer and cuisine are not in it with the Austro-Hungarian." Here, I suspect, he meant to say Czech instead of Magyar, for isn't Pilsen in Bo-
hemia? Moreover, turn to the chapter on Prague in "New Cosmopolis,"
and you will find out in what highland his heart really is. In this book,
indeed, is a vast hymn to all things Czechic—the Pilsen *Urquell*, the
muffins stuffed with poppyseed jam, the spiced chicken liver *en cas-
serole*, the pretty Bohemian girls, the rose and golden glory of Hradschin Hill. . . . One thinks of other strange infatuations: the Polish
Conrad's for England, the Scotch Mackay's for Germany, the Low
German Brahms' for Italy. Huneker, I daresay, is the first Celto-Czech
—or Celto-Magyar, as you choose. (Maybe the name suggests something. It is not to be debased to *Hoon*-eker, remember, but kept at
Hun-eker, rhyming initially with *nun* and *gun*.) An unearthly marriage of elements, by all the gods! but there are pretty children of
it. . . .

Philadelphia humanely disgorged Huneker in 1878. His father designed him for the law, and he studied the institutes at the Philadelphia Law Academy, but like Schumann, he was spoiled for briefs by
the stronger pull of music and the *cacoëthes scribendi*. (Grandpa
John Huneker had been a composer of church music, and organist at
St. Mary's.) In the year mentioned he set out for Paris to see Liszt;
his aim was to make himself a piano virtuoso. His name does not appear on his own exhaustive list of Liszt pupils, but he managed to
quaff of the Pierian spring at second-hand, for he had lessons from
Theodore Ritter (*né* Bennet), a genuine pupil of the old walrus, and
he was also taught by the venerable Georges Mathias, a pupil of Chopin. These days laid the foundations for two subsequent books, the
"Chopin: the Man and His Music" of 1900, and the "Franz Liszt" of
1911. More, they prepared the excavations for all of the others, for
Huneker began sending home letters to the Philadelphia *Bulletin* on
the pictures that he saw, the books that he read and the music that
he heard in Paris, and out of them gradually grew a body of doctrine
that was to be developed into full-length criticism on his return to the
United States. He stayed in Paris until the middle 80's, and then settled in New York.

All the while his piano studies continued, and in New York he be-

came a pupil of Rafael Joseffy. He even became a teacher himself
and was for ten years on the staff of the National Conservatory, and
showed himself at all the annual meetings of the Music Teachers'
Association. But bit by bit criticism elbowed out music-making, as
music-making had elbowed out criticism with Schumann and Berlioz.
In 1886 or thereabout he joined the *Musical Courier*; then he went,
in succession, to the old *Recorder*, to the *Morning Advertiser*, to the
Sun, to the *Times*, and finally to the Philadelphia *Press* and the New
York *World*. Various weeklies and monthlies have also enlisted him:
Mlle. New York, the *Atlantic Monthly*, the *Smart Set*, the *North American Review* and *Scribner's*. He has even stooped to *Puck*, vainly trying to make an American *Simplicissimus* of that dull offspring of
synagogue and barbershop. He has been, in brief, an extremely busy
and not too fastidious journalist, writing first about one of the arts,
and then about another, and then about all seven together. But music has been the steadiest of all his loves; his first three books dealt
almost wholly with it; of his complete canon more than half have to
do with it.

.   .   .   .

This capacity for making the thing described seem important and
delightful, this quality of infectious gusto, this father-talent of all the
talents that a critic needs, sets off his literary criticism no less than
his discourse on music and musicians. Such a book as "Iconoclasts"
or "Egoists" is full of useful information, but it is even more full of
agreeable adventure. The style is the book, as it is the man. It is arch,
staccato, ironical, witty, galloping, playful, polyglot, allusive—sometimes, alas, so allusive as to reduce the Drama Leaguer and women's
clubber to wonderment and ire. In writing of plays or of books, as in
writing of cities, tone-poems or philosophies, Huneker always assumes
that the elements are already well-grounded, that he is dealing with
the initiated, that a pause to explain would be an affront. Sad work
for the Philistines—but a joy to the elect! All this polyphonic allusive-
ness, this intricate fuguing of ideas, is not to be confused, remember,
with the hollow showiness of the academic soothsayer. It is as natural
to the man, as much a part of him as the clanging Latin of Johnson,
or, to leap from art to art Huneker-wise, the damnable cross-rhythms
of Brahms. He could no more write without his stock company of
heretic sages than he could write without his ration of malt. And, on
examination, all of them turned out to be real. They are far up dark
alleys, but they are there! . . . And one finds them, at last, to be as
pleasant company as the multilingual puns of Nietzsche or Debussy's
chords of the second.
    As for the origin of that style, it seems to have a complex ancestry.
Huneker's first love was Poe, and even today he still casts affectionate
glances in that direction, but there is surely nothing of Poe's elephan-
tine labouring in his skipping, *pizzicato* sentences. Then came Carlyle

—the Carlyle of "Sartor Resartus"—a god long forgotten. Huneker's mother was a woman of taste; on reading his first scribblings, she gave him Cardinal Newman, and bade him consider the Queen's English. Newman achieved a useful purging; the style that remained was ready for Flaubert. From the author of "L'Education Sentimentale," I daresay, came the deciding influence, with Nietzsche's staggering brilliance offering suggestions later on. Thus Huneker, as stylist, owes nearly all to France, for Nietzsche, too, learned how to write there, and to the end of his days he always wrote more like a Frenchman than a German. His greatest service to his own country, indeed, was not as anarch, but as teacher of writing. He taught the Germans that their language had a snap in it as well as sighs and gargles—that it was possible to write German and yet not wander in a wood. There are whole pages of Nietzsche that suggest such things, say, as the essay on Maurice Barrès in "Egoists," with its bold tropes, its rapid gait, its sharp *sforzandos*. And you will find old Friedrich at his tricks from end to end of "Old Fogy."

Of the actual contents of such books as "Egoists" and "Iconoclasts" it is unnecessary to say anything. One no longer reads them for their matter, but for their manner. Every flapper now knows all that is worth knowing about Ibsen, Strindberg, Maeterlinck and Shaw, and a great deal that is not worth knowing. We have disentangled Hauptmann from Sudermann, and thanks to Dr. Lewisohn, may read all his plays in English. Even Henry Becque has got into the vulgate and is familiar to the Drama League. As for Anatole France, his "Revolt of the Angels" is on the shelves of the Carnegie Libraries, and the Comstocks have let it pass. New gods whoop and rage in Valhalla: Verhaeren, Artzibashef, Przybyszewski. Huneker, alas, seems to drop behind the procession. He writes nothing about these second-hand third-raters. He has come to Wedekind, Schnitzler, Schoenberg, Korngold and Moussorgsky, and he has discharged a few rounds of shrapnel at the Gallo-Asiatic petticoat philosopher, Henri Bergson, but here he has stopped, as he has stopped at Matisse, Picasso, Epstein and Augustus John in painting. As he says himself, "one must get off somewhere." . . .

Of all the eminent and noble cities between the Alleghenies and the Balkans, Prague seems to be Huneker's favourite. He calls it poetic, precious, delectable, original, dramatic—a long string of adjectives, each argued for with eloquence that is unmistakably sincere. He stands fascinated before the towers and pinnacles of the Hradschin, "a miracle of tender rose and marble white with golden spots of sunshine that would have made Claude Monet envious." He pays his devotions to the chapels of St. Wenceslaus, "crammed with the bones of buried kings," or, at any rate, to the shrine of St. John Nepomucane, "composed of nearly two tons of silver." He is charmed by the beauty of the stout, black-haired, red-cheeked Bohemian girls, and hopes that enough of them will emigrate to the United States to improve the fading pulchritude of our own houris. But most of all, he has praises for the Bohemian cuisine, with its incomparable apple tarts, and its dumplings of cream cheese, and for the magnificent, the overpowering, the ineffable Pilsner of Prague. This Pilsner motive runs through the book from cover to cover. In the midst of Dutch tulip-beds, Dublin cobblestones, Madrid sunlight and Atlantic City leg-shows, one hears it insistently, deep down in the orchestra. The cellos weave it into the polyphony, sometimes clearly, sometimes in scarcely recognizable augmentation. It is heard again in the wood-wind; the bassoons grunt it thirstily; it slides around in the violas; it rises to a stately choral in the brass. And chiefly it is in the minor. Chiefly it is sounded by one who longs for the Pilsen *Urquell* in a far land, and among a barbarous and teetotaling people, and in an atmosphere as hostile to the recreations of the palate as it is to the recreations of the intellect.

As I say, this Huneker is a foreigner and hence accursed. There is something about him as exotic as a samovar, as essentially un-American as a bashi-bazouk, a nose-ring or a fugue. He is filled to the throttle with strange and unnational heresies. He ranks Beethoven miles above the native gods, and not only Beethoven, but also Bach and Brahms, and not only Bach and Brahms, but also Berlioz, Bizet, Bruch and Bülow and perhaps even Balakirew, Bellini, Balfe, Borodin and Boïeldieu. He regards Budapest as a more civilized city than his native Philadelphia, Stendhal as a greater literary artist than Washington Irving, "Künstler Leben" as better music than "There is Sunlight in my Soul." Irish? I still doubt it, despite the *Stammbaum*. Who ever heard of an Irish epicure, an Irish *flâneur*, or, for that matter, an Irish contrapuntist? The arts of the voluptuous category are unknown west of Cherbourg; one leaves them behind with the French pilot. Even the Czech-Irish hypothesis (or is it Magyar-Irish?) has a smell of the lamp. Perhaps it should be Irish-Czech. . . .

There remain the books of stories, "Visionaries" and "Melomaniacs." It is not surprising to hear that both are better liked in France and Germany than in England and the United States. ("Visionaries" has even appeared in Bohemian.) Both are made up of what the Germans call *Kultur-Novellen*—that is, stories dealing, not with the emotions common to all men, but with the clash of ideas among the civilized and godless minority. In some of them, *e.g.*, "Rebels of the Moon," what one finds is really not a story at all, but a static discussion, half aesthetic and half lunatic. In others, *e.g.*, "Isolde's Mother," the whole action revolves around an assumption incomprehensible to the general. One can scarcely imagine most of these tales in the magazines. They would puzzle and outrage the readers of Gouverneur Morris and Gertrude Atherton, and the readers of Howells and Mrs. Wharton no less. Their point of view is essentially the aesthetic one; the overwhelming importance of beauty is never in any doubt. And the beauty thus vivisected and fashioned into new designs is never the simple Wordsworthian article, of fleecy clouds and primroses all compact; on the contrary, it is the highly artificial beauty of pigments and tone-colours, of Cézanne landscapes and the second act of "Tristan und Isolde," of Dunsanyan dragons and Paracelsian mysteries. Here, indeed, Huneker riots in the aesthetic occultism that he loves. Music slides over into diabolism; the Pobloff symphony rends the firmament of Heaven; the ghost of Chopin drives Mychowski to drink; a single drum-beat finishes the estimable consort of the composer of the Tympani symphony. In "The Eighth Deadly Sin" we have a paean to perfume—the only one, so far as I know, in English. In "The Hall of the Missing Footsteps" we behold the reaction of hasheesh upon Chopin's ballade in F major. . . . Strangely-flavoured, unearthly, perhaps unhealthy stuff. I doubt that it will ever be studied for its style in our new Schools of Literature; a devilish cunning is often there, but it leaves a smack of the pharmacopoeia. However, as George Gissing used to say, "the artist should be free from everything like moral prepossession." This lets in the Antichrist. . . .

Huneker himself seems to esteem these fantastic tales above all his other work. Story-writing, indeed, was his first love, and his Opus 1, a bad imitation of Poe, by name "The Comet," was done in Philadelphia so long ago as July 4, 1876. (Temperature, 105 degrees Fahrenheit.) One rather marvels that he has never attempted a novel. It would have been as bad, perhaps, as "Love Among the Artists," but certainly no bore. He might have given George Moore useful help with "Evelyn Innes" and "Sister Teresa": they are about music, but not by a musician. As for me, I see no great talent for fiction *qua* fiction in these two volumes of exotic tales. They are interesting simply because Huneker the story teller so often yields place to Huneker the playboy of the arts. Such things as "Antichrist" and "The Woman Who Loved Chopin" are no more, at bottom, than second-rate anecdotes; it is the filling, the sauce, the embroidery that counts. But what filling! What sauce! What embroidery! . . . One never sees more of Huneker. . . .

He must stand or fall, however, as critic. It is what he has written about other men, not what he has concocted himself, that makes a figure of him, and gives him his unique place in the sterile literature of the republic's second century. He stands for a *Weltanschauung* that is not only un-national, but anti-national; he is the chief of all the curbers and correctors of the American Philistine; in praising the arts he has also criticized a civilization. In the large sense, of course, he has had but small influence. After twenty years of earnest labour, he finds himself almost as alone as a Methodist in Bavaria. The body of native criticism remains as I have described it; an endless piling up of platitudes, an homeric mass of false assumptions and jejune conclusions, an insane madness to reduce beauty to terms of a petty and pornographic morality. One might throw a thousand bricks in any American city without striking a single man who could give an intelligible account of either Hauptmann or Cézanne, or of the reasons for holding Schumann to have been a better composer than Mendelssohn. The boys in our colleges are still taught that Whittier was a great poet and Fenimore Cooper a great novelist. Nine-tenths of our people—perhaps ninety-nine hundredths of our native-born—have yet to see their first good picture, or to hear their first symphony. Our Chamberses and Richard Harding Davises are national figures; our Norrises and Dreisers are scarcely tolerated. Of the two undoubted world figures that we have contributed to letters, one was allowed to die like a stray cat up an alley and the other was mistaken for a cheap buffoon. Criticism, as the average American "intellectual" understands it, is what a Frenchman, a German or a Russian would call donkeyism. In all the arts we still cling to the ideals of the dissenting pulpit, the public cemetery, the electric sign, the bordello parlour.

But for all that, I hang to a somewhat battered optimism, and one of the chief causes of that optimism is the fact that Huneker, after all these years, yet remains unhanged. A picturesque and rakish fellow, a believer in joy and beauty, a disdainer of petty bombast and moralizing, a sworn friend of all honest purpose and earnest striving, he has given his life to a work that must needs bear fruit hereafter. While the college pedagogues of the Brander Matthews type still worshipped the dead bones of Scribe and Sardou, Robertson and Bulwer-Lytton, he preached the new and revolutionary gospel of Ibsen. In the golden age of Rosa Bonheur's "The Horse Fair," he was expounding the principles of the post-impressionists. In the midst of the Sousa marches he whooped for Richard Strauss. Before the rev. professors had come to Schopenhauer, or even to Spencer, he was hauling ashore the devil-fish, Nietzsche. No stranger poisons have ever passed through the customs than those he has brought in his baggage. No man among us has ever urged more ardently, or with sounder knowledge or greater persuasiveness, that catholicity of taste and sympathy which stands in such direct opposition to the booming certainty and snarling narrowness of Little Bethel.

If he bears a simple label, indeed, it is that of anti-Philistine. And the Philistine he attacks is not so much the vacant and harmless fellow who belongs to the Odd Fellows and recreates himself with *Life* and *Leslie's Weekly* in the barber shop, as that more belligerent and pretentious donkey who presumes to do battle for "honest" thought and a "sound" ethic—the "forward looking" man, the university ignoramus, the conservator of orthodoxy, the rattler of ancient phrases—what Nietzsche called "the Philistine of culture." It is against this fat milch cow of wisdom that Huneker has brandished a spear since first there was a Huneker. He is a sworn foe to "the traps that snare the attention from poor or mediocre workmanship—the traps of sentimentalism, of false feeling, of cheap pathos, of the cheap moral." He is on the trail of those pious mountebanks who "clutter the marketplaces with their booths, mischievous half-art and tubs of tripe and soft soap." Superficially, as I say, he seems to have made little progress in this benign *pogrom*. But under the surface, concealed from a first glance, he has undoubtedly left a mark—faint, perhaps, but still a mark. To be a civilized man in America is measurably less difficult despite the war, than it used to be, say, in 1890. One may at least speak of "Die Walküre" without being laughed at as a half-wit, and read Stirner without being confused with Castro and Raisuli, and argue that Huxley got the better of Gladstone without being challenged at the polls. I know of no man who pushed in that direction harder than James Huneker.

FRANK L. OWSLEY (1890–1956) was one of the most eminent professional historians to be both a conservative and an articulate reconstructor of the American past. It should go without saying that the views in the essay that follows do not represent a consensus of historians even of his own time, let alone of subsequent generations. But Owsley was a clear and gifted writer whose expertise on his subject is simply not open to question, however much one might legitimately disagree with his bias and conclusions.

Basic to his essay is the concept of fraud in the course of American history, as well as the use of fraud by plutocratic elements intent on controlling the nation through "legal" but improper means. The great symbols of this rule by money are Alexander Hamilton and the Supreme Court as dominated by John Marshall and his Federalist-Republican successors. The Court has consistently interpreted the Constitution to help consolidate wealth and to prevent average citizens from enjoying their proper liberties.

The hero of the essay is of course Thomas Jefferson, with his key principle of "the absolute denial of the totalitarian State." Within the Jeffersonian cosmos there are five natural rights: to life, liberty, the pursuit of happiness, self-government, and the ownership of property. These rights in the 1930s were in grave danger from a fascism of the right or a communism of the left, which would grant security but deny these liberties, and Owsley wants to return as much private property as possible to the average citizen and thus in a very Jeffersonian way guarantee the health of the nation through genuine democracy. If Jefferson were alive, Owsley feels, he would be a regionalist rather than a narrow states' rightist, because the region has become the logical unit for a viable democracy. As for the government, some remains necessary. America needs "enough government to prevent men from injuring one another." In so writing, Owsley has chosen his own southern, Jeffersonian past to provide a counterhistory to Hamiltonian Federalist-Republican history, with definite implications about how one should think about the everyday problems of governing.

12. The Foundations of Democracy

By Frank L. Owsley

I

Neither Congress, President, nor Supreme Court knows at this moment what is the Constitution of the United States; and it can hardly be proved that the remaining one hundred and thirty million inhabitants of the United States possess any greater certainty about their Constitution than the three departments of the Federal Government which are sworn to uphold, maintain, and defend it. We are, indeed, in a constitutional fog which has constantly grown thicker since the original document was presented to the country for ratification in 1787.

Let me point out a few of the leading factors which have caused the people and their organs of government to become thus enveloped. It will be recalled that the convention which drew up the Federal Constitution in 1787 was in essence a revolutionary, secessionist body. Its actions were in violation of State instructions and of the Articles of Confederation which, at the time, were the Constitution of the United States. It performed its work in secret, and the document which it presented to the country in 1787, while it contained many fine principles of government, was essentially reactionary and undemocratic. The President was to be chosen by uninstructed electors, who in turn were to be chosen either by a suffrage based upon property qualifications or by State legislatures based upon a similar suffrage. The Federal Senate was to be elected by these same legislatures which usually held office—as today in many States—by the approbation of the county court or some other local political hierarchy which was in practice self-perpetuating. The Federal Judiciary was to be chosen by the President with the consent of the Senate. The social philosophy of the Constitution was in keeping with its undemocratic mechanism. In short, the original Constitution was so contrived as to remove the Federal Government as far as possible from the sound of *vox populi* and to place it in the hands of the few men of wealth.

The vote upon this document could scarcely be called a plebiscite: out of a population of four million or more, only about one hundred and sixty-five thousand voted on the State ratification conventions.

Note: Originally published in *Who Owns America?*, edited by Herbert Agar and Allen Tate (Boston: Houghton Mifflin, 1936), pp. 52–67. Reprinted by permission of Mrs. Harriet C. Owsley.

Cajolery, trickery, and bribery were used to obtain ratification, and even so the margin in favor of ratification was only a few thousand. A Constitution obtained by such methods and one which repudiated many of the fundamental principles for which the American Revolution had been fought only a few years before could not be regarded by its contemporaries or by a well-informed, intelligent person, today, as sacrosanct or as falling within the same category as the Ten Commandments.

The impending dissolution of the American State and reconquest by England brought many liberal leaders like James Madison to support such a Constitution. But even so—and despite the doubtful methods used to obtain ratification—the friends of the Constitution would have failed had they not pledged the immediate incorporation into the Constitution of the first ten amendments, which contain, to a great extent, the Bill of Rights or the rights of man for which the intellectual leaders of the American Revolution had contended, and for which the common man had thought the war was fought. But the incorporation of the rights of man within a document reactionary in its philosophy of human society as well as in its mechanism could only thicken the fog which had already been raised. On the face of it, it appears to be an attempt to fuse in one short charter the philosophy of plutocracy and that of democracy, which was the impossible proverbial mixture of oil and water. In reality it was the hopes of the old revolutionary leaders, soon to be called Jeffersonians, that the Bill of Rights would, by mere force of principle, correct the undemocratic features of the main body of the Constitution. Tacked on at the end and forming no organic part of the whole, the Bill of Rights was a liberal postscript added to an illiberal document.

Fortunately for the plutocratic philosophy, that government is in essence the executive committee of great wealth, the Federalists under the leadership of Alexander Hamilton secured control of the executive branch of the Government for twelve years and the legislative during most of this time. But most fortunate of all, the Federalists for forty years held possession of the Judiciary, which arrogated to itself the power to declare laws of Congress unconstitutional and in general to declare the law and the Constitution. For a brief period, under Chief Justice Taney, the Jeffersonians gained control of the Court. With the Civil War the Court came again under the control of jurists who professed the Hamiltonian philosophy.

After the Civil War, during so-called reconstruction, the Federalists, now bearing the Jeffersonian name 'Republican,' obtained two amendments, the Fourteenth and the Fifteenth, which were intended to change, and did change to a certain extent, the fundamental nature of the original Constitution. Now, all the historians of reconstruction except three Negro writers and one carpetbag ex-governor agree that these two amendments were incorporated into the Federal Constitution by open fraud and violence supported by Federal troops in the

South, and congressional legislation which even the Federalist Supreme Court would have thrown out had they not been intimidated
by the Radical leaders. Regardless of what may be thought of the desirability of such amendments—and that irrelevant question is not to
be raised here—no self-respecting, well-informed American can look
with reverence upon this portion of the Federal document. But I wish
to call attention, in passing, to the fact that it is the Fourteenth
Amendment which corporate wealth holds, next to the Jeffersonian
Fifth Amendment, most sacred and most dear. Among other things,
the Fourteenth Amendment guarantees that the States can deprive no
person of life, liberty, and property without due process of law, while
the Fifth Amendment prohibits the Federal Government from depriv-
ing any person of life, liberty, and property without due process of
law. By giving a corporation the status of a person, the Federalist
Judiciary has caused these colossal bodies of organized wealth to become the undefeated champions of personal liberty! The irony of
these two amendments is withering. One was honorably secured by
the Jeffersonians as safeguards for the liberty of the white man; the
other, violently and corruptly secured by the Republicans, ostensibly
in behalf of the liberty of the black man: both—like other Jeffersonian amendments in behalf of human liberty—have been erected
by the Supreme Court, not into bulwarks of human freedom, but into
impregnable fortresses of corporate wealth.

I have pointed out, thus far, various factors which have obscured
the meaning of the original Federal Constitution and the Jeffersonian
amendments, and which deprive that document of any claim to
sacredness: the unconstitutional procedure of the Convention of
1787; the secrecy of its operations; the trickery and fraud used in the
adoption of the Constitution in 1787–89 and in the adoption of the
reconstruction amendments; the packing of the Judiciary with Federalists when Jefferson was elected; the doubtful assumption of power
by the Supreme Court to declare a Federal law unconstitutional; and
above all the interpretation rendered the Fifth and Fourteenth
Amendments. Another factor of paramount importance in darkening
the glass through which we view the Constitution is, or was, the sectional interpretation of the original document. One has only to remember New England's threats of secession during the Jeffersonian Embargo, or the War of 1812, or even at the annexation of Texas; or the
Southern threat of secession in the Virginia and Kentucky Resolutions, the Nullification movement, and the final secession in 1860—
all centering in the meaning of the Constitution—in order to see that
sectional interpretation was a major factor up until 1865, in creating
doubt as to the meaning of the Constitution.

I wish to comment further upon the rôle of the Supreme Court in
befogging the meaning of the original Constitution and the amendments. Under the Hamiltonian philosophy that government is run for
and by the rich, the Supreme Judiciary has stretched the Constitution

of 1787 and the amendments in many different directions; meanings have been read between the lines, into the lines, and beyond the lines; lines have been added, subtracted, divided, and multiplied to fit the exigencies of the occasion and to benefit great wealth (and destroy small wealth). One reads many of these decisions and looks about himself in vain for a familiar constitutional landmark. The Constitution, he feels, has been made to serve God and Mammon, human liberty and human bondage. The Supreme Court has rendered hundreds of decisions which have defined the Constitution in all its aspects; yet, despite the fact that this High Court has usually been in the hands of jurists who are disciples of Hamilton, the hundreds of decisions which it has rendered are consistent chiefly in this one principle: excessive amiability toward those who possess great wealth and great indifference toward those who own nothing or small private properties. Outside of this excessive amiability to great wealth, the decisions of the Supreme Court, which cover about twenty thousand pages and over two hundred and ninety volumes, are confusion and contradiction piled upon confusion and contradiction: here we behold a constitutional Tower of Babel. Yet these twenty thousand pages of decisions, rather than the document printed in the backs of our textbooks, are the working Constitution of the United States. It is out of this welter of decisions which the executive, legislative, and judicial branches of the Federal Government select the precedents on which they estimate the constitutionality of a bill or law. It is possible, of course, to go back to the original Constitution itself and ignore the principle of *stare decisis*; but it is too much to expect of our jurists. The Supreme Court have determined and will determine the constitutionality of a measure in accordance with their social and political philosophy, for they will have little difficulty in finding precedents to support their positions. The personnel of the Great Judiciary determines everything. In view of this, I am strongly tempted to assert that the Constitution of the United States is not the original document adopted in 1789 or the twenty thousand pages of decisions, but the Supreme Court itself. Such an assertion would be equivalent to saying that we are living under a judicial despotism.

This perennial uncertainty as to what is our Constitution has been one of the most dangerous and disruptive forces in our history; and now that the economic, social, and political systems of the world are in chaos, such uncertainty adds to the uneasiness among all classes. While the Hamiltonians have the Court today and are rejoicing that the Constitution has been saved, people are asking, 'What Constitution?' Tomorrow, the Jeffersonians may control the Court and save still another Constitution. But eventually the fascists or communists may gain control of the Court and what Constitution will they save?

It seems impossible to escape the conclusion that we need a new Constitution which will reconstruct the Federal Government from center to circumference. Such a reconstruction must take into consideration the realities of American life, past and present; and one of the greatest realities is sectionalism or regionalism; and above all, it must be based upon the eternal verity that while man must eat, he does not live by bread alone.

II

While I wish to put myself on record here as being an advocate of the reconstruction of the American State, and most particularly the Federal Judiciary in all its branches, it is not my purpose in this essay to propose a plan of reconstruction. Rather do I wish to urge this: it is high time that we—and this applies most pertinently to our judiciary —re-examine the principles upon which the American State was founded in 1776. Lincoln and Seward as spokesmen for those interests which found the Constitution as interpreted under the Jeffersonian Chief Justice Taney too narrow for their full expansion, called upon a 'higher law' and it was upon this 'higher law' that the Republican Party came into power. The interests which Seward consciously, and Lincoln, perhaps innocently, represented were industrial and corporate wealth, located chiefly in the East. These great industrial and financial groups had set good but ill-informed men upon a crusade against slavery in the South, where it was already destined through economic causes to disappear rapidly. The ends of Abolition could not be obtained within the Constitution, so the 'higher law' was invoked. It was only after Lincoln's death that it became apparent that the 'higher law' had been invoked, not to bring freedom and happiness to the slave, but rather to the great bankers, railroad magnates, and industrialists—freedom to gambol between the great protecting walls of the Fourteenth and Fifth Amendments! In short, it was in reality the industrialists and corporations who invoked the 'higher law' to gain control of the National Government and make it over according to their desire. The Abolitionists were futile, ill-informed idealists who were ruthlessly brushed aside when their services were no longer useful. Today, because we do not know what is the Constitution—unless it is the Supreme Court—and because if it were the simple document of 1787 it is absolutely inadequate and has always been so, even during the 'horse-and-buggy' stage, we invoke the 'higher law' against these same interests who falsely invoked it to destroy the South and reduce both South and West to the status of proconsular provinces of the old Roman Empire. The 'higher law' is the fundamental principles upon which the American State was founded, the early American principles which became known, as I have said, as Jeffersonian principles. It is time that we re-examine and reassess these principles. Such principles thus disinterred should control the constitutional reconstruction of the United States which must ultimately come; and in the meanwhile they must be made to guide our political action and our conduct of government. Otherwise we cannot escape the communist or fascist totalitarian State.

The whole body of founding fathers subscribed to these principles, to this 'higher law,' some with mental reservations, others with deathless devotion. Among the greatest of these were: James Otis and Samuel Adams, of Massachusetts; George Mason, Patrick Henry, James Madison, and Thomas Jefferson, of Virginia; John Dickinson, of Pennsylvania, and Christopher Gadsden, of South Carolina. The leadership of Thomas Jefferson, which lasted over half a century, attached his name to these principles. He embodies and symbolizes them. *These principles upon which the American State was founded fall into one great category which in turn contains at least five cardinal principles; from these five cardinal principles numerous other principles stem like the branches of a tree. This great category was and is the absolute denial of the totalitarian State: neither kings nor parliaments, foreign or domestic, had complete sovereignty over the individual.* 'Thus far shalt thou go and no further,' was said to Government. The founding fathers drew their principles from the experience of the English race; from the Anglo-Saxon days when God was supposed to have made the laws and the king and his council only declared what they were; from the charter of Henry I, who acknowledged the supremacy of immemorial customs and laws; from King John, who signed the Magna Charta, and all the kings who came after him, who, in a similar fashion, admitted that their sovereignty over their subjects was limited. The jurists Coke, Littleton, and Blackstone confirmed the limitation of sovereignty, and Brown, Hobbes, Milton, and Locke, the philosophers, stated in broad abstract terms the theories of limited sovereignty. The philosophers of the American Revolution stated these principles more clearly, and, as I have said, they made these principles the foundation of the American State. They were called 'natural rights.' There were five great rights which no government could legitimately destroy: the right to life; the right to liberty; the right to property; the right to the pursuits of happiness (so long as the exercise of this right did not encroach upon the rights of others); and the right of self-government— that is, government was made to serve man, man was not made to serve government, and when government failed to serve man it should be changed, peaceably if possible, forcibly if need be.

These principles, as I have said, were partly repudiated by Alexander Hamilton and many of his followers; but on the other hand Jefferson and many of his colleagues clung to the original American doctrines and founded a party upon them. There can be no doubt that liberty in all its magnificent meaning was to Jefferson the greatest of the five principles; liberty was indeed the flowering, and end of being, of the other cardinal principles: freedom of thought, freedom of conscience, freedom of speech, all the things, indeed, which we call personal liberty, were parts of that freedom which Jefferson and his colleagues visualized. The other four principles were both ends in themselves and instruments by which liberty could be secured. What seem to be three additional principles which have been attached to Jeffersonianism almost to the exclusion of the others are State rights, strict construction, and *laissez-faire.* Any student of Jefferson and his likeminded colleagues is aware that State rights was only another form for the cardinal principle of self-government. The knowledge gained from experience as English colonists demonstrated irrefutably to these men that government from a great distance, by legislators not equally affected by their laws with the people for whom they were legislating, was ignorant government because it had no understanding of the local situation; and it was despotic government because the opinion and wishes of the people for whom the laws were passed were not considered or even known. Any believer, then, in the right of a people to govern themselves would naturally adhere in the early days of our history to the doctrine of State rights. This doctrine was also an instrument by which the other Jeffersonian principles could be obtained or protected; particularly so when the Hamiltonian philosophy dominated the Government. The Virginia and Kentucky Resolutions and the Nullification movement are good illustrations of the use of State rights and State sovereignty as defense weapons, for sectional protection as well as for protecting the five cardinal principles, already enumerated as the basic Jeffersonian principles.

The strict construction doctrine was primarily an instrument of defense against the Hamiltonian philosophy. Like State rights it was meant to preserve local and, therefore, self-government; and uphold the other great principles of human rights. It was not an end or a virtue in itself, for when Jefferson and his successors were in power they violated the doctrine of strict construction and added to the territory of the United States until it reached the Pacific, and they undertook many other measures which only a loose construction of the Constitution could justify. *What I wish to make clear is that State rights and strict construction were either aspects of the great principles of the right of self-government or that they were defense weapons against what the Jeffersonians believed to be enemies of the basic principles of the American State.* If Jefferson and Samuel Adams were here today they would hardly be State rights advocates. They would, probably, according to their own logic, advocate *regional governments*; and realists as they were, they would hardly be able to look at the two hundred and ninety-odd volumes of Supreme Court decisions and remain strict constructionists. Without doubt they would demand a new Constitution which guaranteed unequivocally the basic principles of democracy.

Jefferson's doctrine of *laissez-faire*, that the best government was the one which governed least, has been most ironically appropriated by the Hamiltonians just as has the Fifth Amendment and the Fourteenth, as another sanctuary for great wealth. To hear the United States Chamber of Commerce or the House of Morgan or the Liberty

League quote Jefferson, whom they hate, to prove that government should not interfere with business, is the perfect example of the Devil's well-known facility in quoting Scriptures. There is one part of Jefferson's statement concerning the so-called *laissez-faire* doctrine which the corporations and their political representatives fail to quote: *he specified that there should be enough government to prevent men from injuring one another.* It may be supposed that in a simple agricultural society, where land and natural resources were plentiful and every factory hand could quit his job and move West, little national or State government would be necessary. Such has often been the assumption of historians who have not studied closely the career of Jefferson and that of his aides. It is thus that Jefferson's so-called *laissez-faire* doctrine has so often been explained. But a careful study of Jefferson will disclose that he found a tremendous amount of government intervention necessary, even in an agricultural society, to prevent men from injuring one another. Jefferson's career as a legislator in Virginia during the American Revolution and as President of the United States should be contemplated by those who quote the great democrat in support of the non-intervention of government. Jefferson, Pendleton, and Wythe drew up a new code, which was calculated eventually under the leadership of Jefferson, Mason, and Madison, to revolutionize the social and economic fabric of Virginia. The laws of primogeniture and entail were abolished, with the result that a redistribution of landed property took place not unlike that which resulted from the French Revolution. Jefferson was thoroughly familiar with the destruction of the yeomanry in England by the entail, primogeniture, and the Enclosure Acts. Tidewater Virginia was in his day rapidly developing into a country not unlike England which Goldsmith was describing as a land 'where wealth accumulates and men decay.' Under the influence of Jefferson the Episcopalian Church was disestablished, its property appropriated; he introduced bills to establish a system of public schools the like of which had not been dreamed of since the days of Plato. He lived to see the University and part of the lower system established. The Embargo of 1808–09 upon all commerce, laid down at the behest of Jefferson as President, was the strongest intervention of government in business known in America till 1917. These are fundamental illustrations of the Jeffersonian conception of the rôle of government in the affairs of man. He was unafraid of government except when in the hands of the enemies of free government.

I have said that the cardinal principles of the Jeffersonian or early American doctrine of government were the rights to life, liberty, pursuits of happiness, self-government, and property, and that these rights were great ends in themselves and that in turn each was an instrument to secure the other. The greatest of these instruments, indeed, the *sine qua non* for making possible the other rights, was the right to own property. If they had thought of the great political principles enumerated as stones in the arch which upholds the State, then the Jeffersonians would have considered private property as the keystone of the arch, without which the whole thing must fall. But what was the Jeffersonian conception of private property? Not great corporations, trusts, monopolies, banks, or princely estates, in brief, not great wealth concentrated in the hands of the few, but land and other property held or obtainable by all self-respecting men. Such property thus widely held must, of course, in the very nature of things, be *personally controlled,* or it would cease to have much value as the basic instrumentation of the right to life, liberty, the pursuits of happiness, and self-government. The *ownership* and *control* of productive property sufficient for a livelihood gave a man and his family a sense of economic security; it made him independent; he was a real citizen, for he could cast his franchise without fear and could protect the basic principles of his government. Jefferson regarded stocks and bonds as an insecure economic basis for a free State, for even in the eighteenth century directors and presidents of corporations understood, perfectly, the art of avoiding the payment of dividends to small stockholders who had no voice in directing the management of the business. The insecurity of citizens who depended upon such property over which they no longer had control was doubtless a strong factor in the Jeffersonian advocacy of the agrarian State. Perhaps the Jeffersonians believed that city life was not a good life, but the loss of economic independence and security which accompanied this life was what made the great Virginian and his colleagues fear urbanization and look upon land as the best form of private property and the only safe basis of a free State.

The Hamiltonian conception of property was great wealth concentrated in a few hands, and he and his disciple Marshall, and their disciples, proposed and propose that government and society be run in the interest of the rich and the well-born. Under the Hamiltonian philosophy, Dives might throw crumbs to Lazarus and permit his dogs to lick the sores of Lazarus; but that is the end of his obligation.

If one combines the economic and social unbalance created by technological development with the friendliness of government to great wealth, which I have just sketched, he has in his hands the principal factors which have produced conditions from whose worst consequences we may not be able to escape. Primarily as a result of government by and for great wealth, private property has almost been destroyed. Forty or fifty million American citizens are living on an economic level hardly more comfortable and less secure than that of the cave man of twenty thousand years ago. Another fifty million are desperately, and with a constant sense of insecurity, struggling to meet the daily needs of existence. Perhaps the other twenty or thirty million are living well, but I challenge that. As for the two hundred corporations and the few thousand men who own the bulk of the resources of the United States, at least it can be said that they are able to meet their desires; but they are living in great insecurity because they fear that they will be heavily taxed, and that there may be danger of communism. From top to bottom, from rich to poor, there is a feeling of insecurity. No one but a fool feels safe.

In simple words, let me repeat that private property, widely distributed, which formed the basis of the early American State, has all but disappeared. The keystone of the arch which supported the free State, the property State, which was able to challenge the theory of the totalitarian State, whether the absolutism of a monarch by divine rights, an absolutist British Parliament, or a modern fascist or communist State, is crumbling. With the disappearance of private property has disappeared much of the popular reverence for property. The average man does not truly know what property is. To him—in a vague way—it is something he can touch or see or comprehend with his senses; but he is dispossessed of such. Stocks and bonds and banks and securities are meaningless. He owns none and his friends own none. In any case he has no control over his property.

The propertyless folk of Italy, Russia, Germany, and even Japan have given up claims to freedom, or any of the human rights which the Jeffersonians thought of as the natural rights of man, in exchange for economic and social security or promise of such security. In America, where the tradition of freedom still persists, such an exchange would not be made readily and openly; yet millions—I dare not contemplate how many millions—of Americans are this day ready to trade in (as they would trade in the battered remains of an old car which will not run and which they doubt can be made to run) any residue of abstract liberty which they still may lay claim to, in exchange for bread and circuses; and millions more are half-decided; while the great mass of American people must, within no distant time, come to the conclusion that it is better to be well-fed slaves with their families secure than to cling to a freedom which leaves them upon the streets and their children to die of exposure or grow up as beggars, and their franchise to be bought for a cup of coffee. The right to life, the right to liberty, to the pursuit of happiness, the right to govern oneself, the right to own property, all natural rights must give way to the fascist or communist totalitarian State which guarantees security and denies freedom—unless private property is put back into the hands of the disinherited American people.

IV. Humanism & the Originality of the Artist

DURING THE *late 1920s and early 1930s, conservatives received far more attention than was customary. A group of critics calling themselves the New Humanists created something of a stir with their denunciations of naturalism, romanticism, and much that went under the rubric of modernism. The leaders were Irving Babbitt (1865– 1933) and Paul Elmer More (1864–1937), while the followers had been chiefly students or friends of these men. Their opponents had little in common except a rejection of the humanist position. The controversy lasted only a few years as a public phenomenon, but it did serve to cause conservatives to state positions, define terms, and receive pointed criticisms in a way unusual for their normally secluded lives.*

The New Humanist position is best examined within a much larger critical movement back to classicism in criticism, religion, and politics —a movement that actually helped foster modernism in poetry and music and that dominated many centers of creativity during the second and third decades of the twentieth century. One of the key statements of the position came in 1919 from Thomas Stearns Eliot (1888– 1965), then a leading modernist poet and about to enter a major phase of his creative life as a literary critic. A former student of Babbitt, Eliot left America for England and immediately adopted British tastes and positions in religion, poetry, and politics, some of them distinctly unattractive to Babbitt.

The key Eliot essay is called "Tradition and the Individual Talent" and may be found in both The Sacred Wood *(New York, 1920) and* Selected Essays of T. S. Eliot *(New York, 1950). It is too well known and readily available to warrant reprinting in this volume, but a brief précis of it serves admirably to introduce other important documents of this phase of American cultural conservatism. Eliot begins by defending the idea of "tradition" in the face of criticism by innovative personalities who disliked anything that smacked of the old and the dead. Critics too often examined new art in terms of what it seemed to have that was new, instead of asking how the new work participated in the traditions of the past. Tradition, he insists, is something that cannot be inherited and that must be obtained by great labor. Artists must perceive not only the pastness of their past but the presentness of it, and they must tie the timeless and the temporal in their work. No artists of any kind, Eliot insisted firmly, had their complete meaning alone. They had to develop their consciousness of the past, keep it steadily in mind when they created, and realize that to progress as artists they had to experience a continual sacrifice of self. Good art demanded not the expansiveness of the self but its extinction as it increasingly participated in the development of tradition. Genuinely mature artists combine the elements of the past in a new way; they do not suddenly create something original. Ultimately all lasting art allows artists an escape from emotion; it enables artists to escape from their personality rather than to express their personality.*

This position astonished and dismayed many readers who regarded Eliot as a major force in modernism. Often unaware of the learning and discipline that went into his art, they had misread him and supposed that his critical values were as radical as his poetic forms and that he was rebellious against tradition instead of happy to embrace it. He was, instead, typical of a substantial group of creative artists who seemed rebellious but who were in fact neoclassical in their general attitudes. Igor Stravinsky used the material supplied to him by Pergolesi; Aaron Copland advocated a return to the hard and the classical even when using jazz themes; E. E. Cummings resuscitated forgotten Greek forms: the tendency was quite widespread and productive of innovations within traditions in just the way Eliot specified. Whether they knew it or not, the modernists and rebels of the 1920s were often radicals within very old and very usable traditions.

This new emphasis on classicism and tradition began at the turn of the twentieth century. Irving Babbitt very early in his life began defending such a position in his essays on education and literature, and Eliot may well have first encountered his later views while a student in Babbitt's classes at Harvard. At roughly the time that Eliot was there, Babbitt published a small book that dealt chiefly with the teaching of literature. In it he discussed concepts like humanism and humanitarianism and established his own position in favor of the aristocracy, a disciplined and selective sympathy, and the perfecting of the individual according to some classical ideal of what a human being should be. In Eliot's essay, the focus of attention was clearly critical; in Babbitt's the political and social implications are somewhat more clear even though the basic focus remains literary.

13. What Is Humanism?

By Irving Babbitt

A good example of the confusion arising from general terms is the term that is more important than any other, perhaps, for our present argument. To make a plea for humanism without explaining the word would give rise to endless misunderstanding. It is equally on the lips of the socialistic dreamer and the exponent of the latest philosophical fad. In an age of happy liberty like the present, when any one can employ almost any general term very much as he pleases, it is perhaps inevitable that the term humanism, which still has certain gracious associations lingering about it, should be appropriated by various theorists, in the hope, apparently, that the benefit of the associations may accrue to an entirely different order of ideas. Thus the Oxford philosopher, Mr. F. C. S. Schiller, claims to be a humanist, and in the name of humanism threatens to "do strange deeds upon the clouds." Renan says that the religion of the future will be a "true humanism." The utopists who have described their vision of the future as "humanism" or the "new humanism" are too numerous to mention. Gladstone speaks of the humanism of Auguste Comte, Professor Herford of the humanism of Rousseau, and the Germans in general of the humanism of Herder; whereas Comte, Rousseau, and Herder were all three not humanists, but humanitarian enthusiasts. A prominent periodical, on the other hand, laments the decay of the "humanitarian spirit" at Harvard, meaning no doubt humanistic. We evidently need a working definition not only of humanism, but of the words with which it is related or confused,—humane, humanistic, humanitarian, humanitarianism. And these words, if successfully defined, will help us to a further necessary definition,—that of the college. For any discussion of the place of literature in the college is conditioned by a previous question: whether there will be any college for literature to have a place in. The college has been brought to this predicament not so much perhaps by its avowed enemies as by those who profess to be its friends. Under these circumstances our prayer, like that of Ajax, should be to fight in the light.

The first step in our quest would seem to go back to the Latin words from which all the words of our group are derived. Most of the material we need will be found in a recent and excellent study by M.

Note: Originally published in *Literature and the American College* (Boston: Houghton Mifflin, 1908), pp. 2–5.

Gaston Boissier of the ancient meanings of *humanitas*. From M. Boissier's paper it would appear that *humanitas* was from the start a fairly
elastic virtue with the Romans, and that the word came to be used
rather looosely, so that in a late Latin writer, Aulus Gellius, we find a
complaint that it had been turned aside from its true meaning. *Humanitas*, says Gellius, is incorrectly used to denote a "promiscuous
benevolence, what the Greeks call philanthropy," whereas the word
really implies doctrine and discipline, and is applicable not to men in
general but only to a select few,—it is, in short, aristocratic and not
democratic in its implication.

The confusion that Gellius complains of is not only interesting in
itself, but closely akin to one that we need to be on guard against
to-day. If we are to believe Gellius, the Roman decadence was like our
own age in that it tended to make love for one's fellow man, or altru-
ism, as we call it, do duty for most of the other virtues. It confused
humanism with philanthropy. Only our philanthropy has been profoundly modified, as we shall see more fully later, by becoming associated with an idea of which only the barest beginnings can be found
in antiquity—the idea of progress.

It was some inkling of the difference between a universal philanthropy and the indoctrinating and disciplining of the individual that
led Aulus Gellius to make his protest. Two words were probably needed in his time; they are certainly needed to-day. A person who has
sympathy for mankind in the lump, faith in its future progress, and
desire to serve the great cause of this progress, should be called not a
humanist, but a humanitarian, and his creed may be designated as
humanitarianism. From the present tendency to regard humanism as
an abbreviated and convenient form for humanitarianism there must
arise every manner of confusion. The humanitarian lays stress almost
solely upon breadth of knowledge and sympathy. The poet Schiller, for
instance, speaks as a humanitarian and not as a humanist when he
would "clasp the millions to his bosom," and bestow "a kiss upon the
whole world." The humanist is more selective in his caresses. Aulus
Gellius, who was a man of somewhat crabbed and pedantic temper,
would apparently exclude sympathy almost entirely from his conception of *humanitas* and confine the meaning to what he calls *cura et
disciplina*; and he cites the authority of Cicero. Cicero, however,
seems to have avoided any such one-sided view. Like the admirable
humanist that he was, he no doubt knew that what is wanted is not
sympathy alone, nor again discipline and selection alone, but a disciplined and selective sympathy. Sympathy without selection becomes
flabby, and a selection which is unsympathetic tends to grow disdain-
ful.

The humanist, then, as opposed to the humanitarian, is interested
in the perfecting of the individual rather than in schemes for the elevation of mankind as a whole; and although he allows largely for
sympathy, he insists that it be disciplined and tempered by judgment.

IRVING BABBITT *and Paul Elmer More first met at Harvard University graduate school, where they were among the few serious students of Oriental literature. They became lifelong friends, conservative spokesmen, and at the end of their lives the most conspicuous leaders of the New Humanist movement.*

Most of Babbitt's career was spent at Harvard, where he taught, and frequently attacked, French literature. A brilliant if erratic teacher, he soon attracted a significant college audience, and he was a pioneer in studies of romanticism and its place in comparative literature. His conservative views, based largely on his studies of the classical ideals of the Orient, Greece, and Rome, permeated not only his scholarly work on French criticism and Rousseau but also his frequent forays into education, art, and politics. He became probably the most influential polemicist of his day, willing to defend notions of measure, restraint, and self-control.

More, in contrast, was quiet and shy and not nearly as outspoken as his friend. He never equaled his colleague's academic performance, preferring to remain an independent literary critic and journalist for publications like the Nation. *Although devoted to Babbitt, More could never bring himself to accept Babbitt's skepticism about religion, and for much of his life he was something of a heretic, seeking an acceptable orthodoxy and religious peace of mind—a successful quest, as a later selection will demonstrate. He also had the sense to devote himself to the classical literature and thought that he loved, and his contributions are thus probably more enduring than Babbitt's often relentlessly hostile discussions of romanticism.*

These differences of emphasis come out clearly in More's affectionate sketch: he the seeker, shifting and developing; Babbitt the man who knows, rigid and argumentative from his graduate school days, who changed his examples but never his basic ideas. The sketch also conveys clearly and briefly the essential message of the humanism which the two men shared: "Humanism has to do primarily with that plane of practical ethics where the natural and the supernatural meet together, producing a world of harmony and order and mediation."

14. Irving Babbitt

By Paul Elmer More

It is not an easy thing, with the cold page of print in mind, to write of a friend, a very close friend, and it is only with reluctance that I have acceded to the request to undertake such a task. And there was a special reason for hesitating in this case. Babbitt was an author and a teacher, and in these capacities is known to a larger and a smaller circle; others may estimate—indeed Professor Mercier has already estimated—the value of his books as well as I could do, or better; and of his astonishing manner and power in the lecture room, his pupils, many of them now holding prominent places in the academic world, can speak from a knowledge which I do not possess. But he was a talker too, greater in that vein, I believe, than as a teacher, greater, I know, than as an author. And it is just of his genius in the give and take of conversation that I am qualified, by long association and by a fundamental sympathy of mind not incompatible with clashing differences, to write as probably no one else can do. Yet a record of the spoken word without its intonation and the accompanying gesture leaves it but a dead thing, and a reported argument is likely to lose its point unless the second party to the discussion brings himself into the scene to a degree that may seem egotistic.

My acquaintance with Babbitt began in the autumn of 1892, when I came to Cambridge from the West to prosecute my study of Sanskrit and Pâli. Babbitt was then twenty-six or -seven years old. He had graduated from Harvard, had taught for a time in Montana, and had then spent a year in Paris, working in the same languages with Sylvain Lévi. We two formed the whole of the advanced class under Professor Lanman, and naturally were thrown much together. I can well remember our first meeting in Lanman's marvellously equipped library. Babbitt was rather above the average height, powerfully built, with the complexion of radiant health. But it was his eyes that caught and held one's attention. They were of a dark, not pure blue, and even then, though of a lustre that dimmed somewhat in later years, had in repose the withdrawn look of one much given to meditation. He had a way of gazing downwards or forwards or anywhere rather than into the face of his interlocutor, in a manner which could never be described as timid or shifty, but which gave often the impression of remoteness, as if he had lost the individual before him in some general

Note: Originally published in the *University of Toronto Quarterly* 3 (1933–34): 25–42, by permission of the University of Toronto Press.

view of life or some question of fundamental principles which might be occupying his mind. But if the unlucky individual thought to escape into that remoteness from the consequences of a rash statement or a logical fallacy, he was likely to be caught up by a swift direct glance that seemed to shoot out tentacles, as it were, into his very soul. At such moments that restless energy of Babbitt's, which was wont to work itself off in walking or by pacing back and forth as he talked, would appear to be gathered together, holding his body in an attitude of tense rigidity. The effect—I am speaking of his early years of combat—was startling, sometimes almost terrific, as if in an evening ramble under the shadow of familiar trees one were brought up sharply by the gleam of watching eyes from a form crouching ready to spring. One such instance I may recall. We were strolling up what was then known as North Avenue, engaged in debate over I cannot remember what matter, when suddenly he stopped short, faced about upon me, and, with both hands rigidly clenched, ejaculated: "Good God, man, are you a Jesuit in disguise?" The words may sound flat enough in the repeating; but as they were hurled out, with the accompanying gesture and glance of indignation, they made an impression not to be forgotten. I have never been able to answer the question satisfactorily.

The old North Avenue and Brattle Street, both thoroughfares at that time leading out into the open country, are particularly associated in my memory with these talks. Babbitt was always delicately sensitive to the charms of New England scenery, and in such places as Squam Lake and Dublin, N.H., where later I visited him in the long vacations, he would manifest a romantic love of nature which might surprise those who know only the classical and rather austere side of his intellect. But again, in those Cambridge days, owing to the weather or the hour we would meet indoors, sometimes in his room, oftener in my own narrow quarters. And I can see, almost hear, him now as he used to pace back and forth the few steps from wall to wall, arguing vehemently on whatever question might be broached, or recounting the adventures of his youth (a strange and mixed experience), pausing at every fourth or fifth turn to take huge draughts from the water jug on my washstand, and pretty well emptying it in the course of an evening. I cannot recall the range of topics discussed—no doubt in part they were those which young men have been worrying over since the beginning of human speech—nor can I recapture the excitement of hearing the world and the destinies of man tossed about in thesis and counter-thesis after a fashion quite new to me. Literature was one of the fields in which he exercised his dialectic, naturally; and what remains with me now is chiefly the fact that his views were already formed and fixed. My taste, on the contrary, was in a state of transition. I had brought with me to Cambridge a mind steeped in Heine and Novalis and the Schlegels, and though my enthusiasm for these German dreamers had cooled before I met him and I was feeling my way towards more classical standards, there was enough of the old virus left in me to call out all the vigour of his critical powers. I am afraid that I held for him then the place afterwards occupied by Rousseau, who in those days, so far as I can remember, was never mentioned, but first comes to the front in the comparison with Bacon in *Literature and the American College*, one of Babbitt's best and most finished pieces of writing and an epitome of all he was to fight for in later years. Of the classics Horace, I think, was at that time the poet most frequently referred to or quoted by him. And at the frosty touch of that Lord of Common Sense the exquisites of romanticism would shrivel up and drift away in the winds. How he came to his love and mastery of the Roman and Greek poets, I do not know. According to his own account the taste was born in him. The astonishing fact, as I look back over the years, is that he seems to have sprung up, like Minerva, fully grown and fully armed. No doubt he made vast additions to his knowledge and acquired by practice a deadly dexterity in wielding it, but there is something almost inhuman in the immobility of his central ideas. He has been criticized for this and ridiculed for harping everlastingly on the same thoughts, as if he lacked the faculty of assimilation and growth. On the contrary, I am inclined to believe that the weight of his influence can be attributed in large measure to just this tenacity of mind. In a world visibly shifting from opinion to opinion and, as it were, rocking on its foundation, here was one who never changed or faltered in his grasp of principles, whose latest word can be set beside his earliest with no apology for inconsistency, who could always be depended on. It will be remembered that Socrates was charged with the same monotony of ideas, and his retort to the sophist might have been uttered by Babbitt: "Why, my dear young man, not only am I always talking in the same manner, but I am forever talking about the same things." It comes down to one's conception of truth: is truth something fixed which can be discovered, and when discovered is it of a nature to demand a man's unwavering allegiance; or is truth too, like opinion, only a glimpse of some momentary aspect of the flux, no sooner beheld than lost in the flowing stream of impressions?

And not only had Babbitt at an early age—how early I do not know —reached these settled convictions, but at least from the beginning of our acquaintance they were knit together into a system by logical bonds which were perfectly clear to his mind, so clear, indeed, that he tended to take them for granted as equally obvious to others. The consequence to his writing was not wholly fortunate. For one thing, it gave a kind of rotary movement instead of a regular progression to his books. A rhetorician would say that he did not know how to manage his paragraphs. Instead of finishing one link of his argument and then proceeding to the next and so on from premise to conclusion, he is somewhat inclined to crowd his whole thesis, at least implicitly, into each single paragraph, so that the book, despite the inexhaustible variety of his illustrations, gives the impression of endless repetition. That is undoubtedly a fault of construction, and has stood in the way of his full recognition as a thinker. But it is a rhetorical fault only, owing to a failure to put himself as a writer into the mind of his reader; the constructive faculty was really there; he had reasoned out his position step by step, but, having done this for himself, he would forget that his reader had not been present at the process, and he would pitch into his exposition at any point—beginning, middle, or ending.

And this is one reason why he seemed to me more effective as a talker than as a writer. Here again the uninstructed or uninterested listener might criticize his conversation as displaying the same lack of method as his books. And I can remember the complaint of a distinguished but rather commonplace historian of Harvard that my friend's conversation had no sense at all, being a jumble of terms with no definite meaning for him or for anyone else, and of dogmatic assertions which severally had no logical basis and collectively no sequence. But for the sympathetic listener there needed to be no such difficulty. By a question interposed here and there, or by an occasional sharp contradiction, it was easy to bring him back to the order of his thoughts and to lay bare the whole hidden working of his mind from axiomatic principles to inevitable conclusions.

I am trying to describe Babbitt's talk at its highest, when the subject brought out all his resources, and to show how, in the give and take of argument and by the need of defending his position against an antagonism not incompatible with large agreement, certain qualities came to the light which many readers fail to detect in his published works. But I would not leave the impression that he was addicted to preaching in season or out of season; there might be something of the prophet in his tone when grave moral issues were raised, never of the prig; he might reduce his antagonist physically to a rag by the pertinacity of his attack, he was never a bore. His ordinary intercourse, as a matter of fact, was notable for flashes of wit and strokes of keen repartee that could set the table on a roar, and in his earlier days might be seasoned by touches of almost Rabelaisian humour which would never be guessed from the reticences of his later manner.

Literature and the problems of education were much in his thought; but the staple of his more serious talk, owing chiefly to his own inclination but partly, no doubt, to provocation, from my side, was ethical and religious. This remained true to the end; in those days, however, the discussions were coloured by his, or I may say our, special studies. From the beginning, Babbitt was drawn to the Buddhistic side of Hinduism rather than to the Brahmanic, and to the Pâli language, in which the most authentic record of Buddha's teaching is preserved, rather than to the Sanskrit. There was something in this corresponding to his classical taste in works of the imagination and

to his rejection of romanticism. Primarily what attracted him to the
Pâli texts may have been the clarity and concreteness of the style
(which the uninitiated may best feel in De Lorenzo's Italian version
of *I Discorsi di Buddho*), as compared with the elusive mistiness of
the Sanskrit, particularly of the *Upanishads*. With this clarity, almost
hardness, of expression went the ethical doctrine of Buddha. Here I
am unable to say whether Babbitt favoured the doctrine, the *dhamma*,
because it fell in with conclusions at which he had already arrived
by independent reflection, or whether his ethical ideas were largely
the result of reading in the Pâli. Of the two alternatives I surmise
that the former is the truer, though in either case the important point
is the native affinity of his mind with that of the Oriental sage. This
comes out in a footnote to his criticism of the Arcadian dream of
Rousseau in his first publication:

> The greatest of vices according to Buddha is the lazy yield-
> ing to the impulses of temperament (*pamâda*); the greatest
> virtue (*appamâda*) is the opposite of this, the awakening from
> the sloth and lethargy of the senses, the constant exercise of
> the active will. The last words of the dying Buddha to his dis-
> ciples were an exhortation to practise this virtue unremitting-
> ly.

That was the lesson Babbitt had for the world when I first knew
him; it is the heart and essence of what he inculcated in book after
book, to the discomfiture and disgust of his hostile critics; it is what
he was hoping to confirm by a translation and exposition of the
Dhammapada which he was preparing when his health failed.

On the other hand, I had started my Oriental studies with a predilection for the Sanskrit literature of the *Upanishads*, the *Bhagavad
Gîta*, and the Vedantic theosophy. To this I was brought in part, I suppose, by the romantic virus not yet expelled from my system, though
a deeper attraction was in the mythological elements of the Vedânta,
which, in fact, range from an absolute pantheism to a grotesque
polytheism, but which might lead, as I think I even then felt instinctively, to a more concrete monotheism. However that may be, it is
easy to see that here was a situation to call out all Babbitt's fighting
powers in debate; and nobly did he respond to the summons. I would
never acknowledge defeat, but I was often left prostrate on the field
of battle.

This Harvard period extended over three years, the first when we
were students together, the second when he returned as instructor in
French after an interval of a year at Williams, and the third in 1899–
1900 when I was there again doing some special work for Lanman.
It is a digression but a fact worthy of note that, though Babbitt began—and ended—his teaching career at Harvard in the modern field,
his heart at first was set on working in the classics. I often wonder

what might have been the consequences if the Classical Department
had not rejected him at the beginning and continued systematically
more suo to ignore him. What might have happened if he had spent
his energies on expounding a literature to which he could have given
his positive allegiance instead of one which he studied chiefly to
annihilate? His diagnosis of our modern ailments would have lost
something of its fervour and scientific completeness; but the exemplary wisdom of Greece might have been brought back to us alive,
and the teaching of the classics might have been made once more a
discipline in the humanities. I may be pardoned for adding here my
complaint that a very great teacher, perhaps even the greatest this
country has ever produced, was overlooked by one department and,
where accepted, had to force his way up against resistance and
through protracted depreciation. There was a moment in his mid-
career when it was even touch and go whether he would not be
dropped altogether. It was the response to his genius by a large and
growing number of the better students in the University that ultimately brought full recognition from the Faculty. But this is a digression.

A long period elapsed before the discussions of that early association were renewed in all their intimacy and intensity. During this
interval I had visited him more than once in his summer homes and
he had passed a number of months in Princeton, but the real fun began again in the second term of the academic year 1925–1926 (if my
dates are correct), when I was a substitute at Harvard for an absent
member of the Classical Department. Fortunately I was able to rent
the home of Professor Ropes, who also was enjoying a "sabbatical."
There was a large and comfortably furnished library attached to the
house, and here night after night, two or three times a week, Babbitt
used to come, and, sitting on one side of the great fireplace, with me
—shall I say, his glad victim?—on the other side, poured out such a
stream of argument, invective, and persuasion as had not, I am sure,
been heard in Cambridge before and probably will never be heard
again. It was *magnifique, et c'était la guerre*! The battle-ground was
the same as in the old Harvard days, but with a difference. Babbitt's
fundamental ideas had not changed by a jot, though they were now
reinforced by an appalling mass of erudition at the service of an un-
hesitating, unfailing, unerring memory. Meanwhile, I had quite definitely moved away from my absorption in the theosophical speculations of India; my heart was now all in a Platonism supplemented by
Christian theology of the Greek type. Against the Platonic philosophy
of Ideas, Babbitt brought up Aristotle's positive and scientific humanism, and with the claims of theology contrasted the merits of Buddha's
non-theological religion which offered the same ethical and spiritual
results as Christianity without demanding credence in a dogma and
a mythology impossible, he insisted, for the modern mind to accept.
Of course my cue was to contend that Aristotle himself, seeing that

his positive humanism could not stand on its own feet, was driven at
the last to brace it with a metaphysic of the Absolute beside which
Plato's Idealism is as easy to swallow as a breath of spring air, and
that in religion Buddha had won his army of adherents by the example of his own supposed ascent through countless aeons to absolute
knowledge, a myth as difficult to credit as the Incarnation. Naturally
I thought at the time I was right, as I still think; but if victory ever
lodged on my side, it was of a very private sort, known only to myself
when I had crept to bed. But oh the wonder and glitter of those
defeats!

It will be seen how Babbitt's attitude towards the great religions of
the world might be brought out in such debates with a sharpness that
would scarcely be guessed by those who know him only in his books.
And this is particularly true in the case of Christianity, where for a
double reason he exercised a certain reserve, or "economy," in his
public statements. For one thing, he wrote always not for display but
for conviction. His mind was eminently practical in that he aimed at
getting results and thought much of strategy in attack. He held it a
law of sound tactics not to arouse the hostility of those whom he desired to convince, but to make concessions where this could be done
with honour; and he used to scold me laughingly, sometimes almost
pathetically, for going out of my way, as he said, to make enemies
among every party to a controversy. Thus it was that he took pains in
his writing to avoid irritating the sensibility of Christian readers. But
besides the strategic motive, perhaps explaining it, was the fact that
he recognized in what he would call the psychological effects of dogmatic faith a moral and spiritual discipline to be acclaimed and fostered, whatever its source might be. He saw, and admitted whole-
heartedly, that belief in the Grace of God had in times past operated
to awaken the soul "from the sloth and lethargy of the senses," and
to produce a "constant exercise of the active will" profoundly akin to
the *appamâda* of Buddhism. In all this there was not the slightest intention to deceive or to palter about first principles; but it happened,
nevertheless, that many Christians were misled by these concessions.
The dogma of Grace, the notion of help and strength poured into the
soul from a superhuman source, was in itself repugnant to him, and
the Church as an institution he held personally in deep distaste, however he may have seemed to make an exception of the disciplinary
authority of Romanism. There should be no misunderstanding left on
this point. The naked truth will, I believe, redound to his credit; it will
clarify and strengthen his influence with the large body of his pupils
who feel the need of religion but cannot subscribe to a definite creed.
I can remember him in the early days stopping before a church in
North Avenue, and, with a gesture of bitter contempt, exclaiming:
"There is the enemy! there is the thing I hate!" Undoubtedly that sentiment was softened as time went on, and as he grew more charitably
disposed towards those who, for whatever reason, were ranged on the

side of decency and restraint; but it never disappeared. On the other hand, he was much closer to Buddhism than would appear from his public utterances. I wish not to exaggerate. In private as well as in public he refused to be denominated a Buddhist, and with perfect sincerity. But in the denial by Buddha (the real Buddha as seen in the authentic texts) of anything corresponding to Grace, in his insistence on the complete moral responsibility of the individual, in the majesty of his dying command, "Work out your own salvation with diligence," Babbitt perceived the quintessential virtue of religion, purged of ephemeral associations, of outworn superstition, of impossible dogma, of obscurantist faith, and based on a positive law which can be verified by experiment, pragmatically, step by step. It was in this way he sought to bring together a positivism in the religious plane with a positivism in what he distinguished as the purely humanistic plane of life and letters.

So much I can say to elucidate what might be gathered from his books. And it seems to me worth saying for the reason that, however pungent and straightforward his language may be in other matters, his frequent allusions to the supernatural left a good many of his readers puzzled over its exact relation to the natural. The difficulty is that in print, so far as I remember, he never distinguishes between the supernatural and the superhuman, or makes clear why he accepted the one and rejected the other. Now Buddhism holds to the supernatural, holds to it, indeed, in the extreme form of an Absolute utterly different from, and separable from, the flux and distintegration and relativity of the natural. But the supernatural so conceived is, properly speaking, not superhuman; it is within man, a part of man's being, just as the natural is; and the ultimate goal of ethics and religion is a state wherein, entirely by human effort, the dualism in man of the supernatural and the natural is dissolved, and all the passions and insatiate desires and all the unattainable strivings of nature are forever stilled. In Christianity, on the other hand, the supernatural in man is regarded as akin to, but not identical with, a supernatural which is also superhuman. Grace is the medium of cooperation between the supernatural will in man and the divine will which is God.

With this distinction between the supernatural and the superhuman in mind one can understand how Christianity brings a disturbing factor into "humanism" as Babbitt conceived it, whereas Buddhism falls quite easily into the whole scheme. Humanism has to do primarily with that plane of practical ethics where the natural and the supernatural meet together, producing a world of harmony and order and mediation. Religion is an attempt to live in a plane above the humanistic, where the supernatural departs from the natural into its own citadel of imperturbable peace. Humanism is thus not anti-religious, in so far as it depends on the controlling power of the supernatural; but it may be non-religious in so far as its business is with the world and does not seek to escape the world. The humanist is not hostile to religion, but he should be careful not to confuse the plane of the non-religious with that of the religious. At the same time, his passage from the non-religious to the religious plane, when he wishes to make it, is simplified by the fact that the higher sphere is still human in the sense that no demand is made upon him to go outside of himself (his higher self), nor to introduce any element of the superhuman as contrasted with the supernatural which was already present and operative in the humanistic sphere.

All this I could understand from our conversations at Harvard. But there was still something in Babbitt's personal attitude towards religion not clear to me, and I had even ventured in an essay published in *The Bookman* to challenge him on this point. In response he said more than once that the time had come when he ought to define his position in such terms as to leave no room for misunderstanding; and this, in fact, he undertook to do in the Introduction to his essays *On Being Creative*, published in 1932. But even there his definition is so complicated with his whole theory of humanism that I doubt if it has cleared up all the difficulties which his followers had felt; the weakness of the written word, as Plato long ago complained, is that it can make no reply to the questioner. And that is why I would supplement his published *apologia* with a reference to a last conversation with him not many months before his health was finally broken.

It was at my home in Princeton. We were sitting in a flagged porch looking out over a stretch of lawn to a background of shrubs and trees arrayed in the rich greens of early summer and bathed in the slanting light of late afternoon. Something of the magic charm of nature, to which Babbitt was always warmly responsive, perhaps also a foreboding of the end so near, opened his heart, and he spoke of his religious convictions with a simplicity and gentleness quite different from his ordinary combative manner. It was like a confession of faith, to be held sacred except in so far as it may serve to complete and elucidate his public profession.

There is in man as distinguished from the animal, he said, a something of which he is immediately, though it may be dimly, aware at the centre of his being, a something which exists apart from the desires and affections and ambitions and dejections of that lower self which is ordinarily thought of as our personality. It may be called the "ethical" will, because, though not to be confused with the lower will which is active in the affairs of life, it does yet, in some untraceable manner, make its effects felt ethically in the plane of nature. To express this indefinable relation, while maintaining intact the distinction between the supernatural and the natural, the higher faculty may be spoken of as the will to refrain, the *frein vital* as contrasted with the *élan vital*; but though it can be defined only in negative terms, it is in itself real and positive, the highest reality and the supreme factor in that which we know as our individual character. At the same time, in this deepest stratum of our consciousness, we are aware of the great paradox that this ethical will is at once both individual and universal, so that he who is most himself is also most human, thinking and acting not as an isolated atom in conflict with other atoms, but as a being at one with the great heart of the world, strong in the strength drawn from that silence of the soul beyond the curtain of perplexing lights and noises, wherein all distractions end in peace.

I should be untrue to myself if I did not say that the refusal to admit responsibility to the superhuman, in the full theistic sense of the word, seems to me to deprive religion of its richest source of inspiration, and to leave it too often a sort of flimsy and unpractical sentiment. But I should be false to my friend if, with that last conversation in mind, I did not assert that, beneath all the fret of controversy, he himself had reached to a fountain of perennial peace and strength. In his books he may have written sometimes vaguely, and not always consistently, of religion; his life was a steady growth, not in Grace, but in obedience to the unrelenting exactions of conscience and in a sense of the littleness of men protesting against the law of their own being. There lay at once his humility and his magnanimity, and therein shines the virtue of his example.

Some time ago I was dining with Frank Mather, whom Babbitt had first met at Williams, and who from that association had come to be united with us in bonds of triple comradeship. He, too, as all readers are aware, is an advocate of humanism, and contends that only the perfect agnostic can lay claim to the Simon-Pure article. Among the guests was a Hindu gentleman of broad culture and keen perceptions, who had been recently in Cambridge and through my introduction had called on Babbitt. In the course of the evening, I asked him how Babbitt had impressed him, and his response was quick and enthusiastic: "Oh, Babbitt, he is a holy man, a great saint!" Now holiness is the last trait that most of us in the West would attribute to one of Babbitt's self-assertive character, but the word came quite naturally from an Oriental to whom the saint is a man notable rather for his will-power than for meek submissiveness. It was, perhaps, because I ventured upon some criticism of this kind that the Hindu visitor put me in my place: "You are not a saint at all, but only a philosopher"; and then, answering a question of our host about himself, added, with a twinkle in his eye: "And you, my dear Frank, are the wickedest man I know."

BETWEEN *Paul More and H. L. Mencken there existed differences of style and temperament so great as to mark the outside boundaries of conservatism in America. Mencken was one of the most flagrant of the voices which distressed the humanists, while More was a tempting target for all the witty young people who scoffed at self-control and classical decorum. Yet the brief book review that follows shows quite clearly Mencken's great if grudging respect for More. Mencken does not go into the many ways the two men resembled each other, as in their suspicions of government, their stress on the need for a genuine aristocracy, and their general hostility to much of the liberalism of their day. The differences in temperament and rhetorical style are quite evident. More's taste tended to run to classical studies and the Christian religion; Mencken preferred romantic modernists like Nietzsche and Conrad and detested much of the Christianity of his day. Mencken's piece thus provides a brief critique of More and the humanist position from within the conservative camp.*

15. Paul Elmer More

By Henry Louis Mencken

Nothing new is to be found in the latest volume of Paul Elmer More's Shelburne Essays. The learned author, undismayed by the winds of anarchic doctrine that blow down his Princeton stovepipe, continues to hold fast to the notions of his earliest devotion. He is still the gallant champion sent against the Romantic Movement by the forces of discipline and decorum. He is still the eloquent fugleman of the Puritan ethic and aesthetic. In so massive a certainty, so resolute an immovability there is something almost magnificent. These are somewhat sad days for the exponents of that ancient correctness. The Goths and the Huns are at the gate, and as they batter wildly they throw dead cats, perfumed lingerie, tracts against predestination, and the bound files of the *Nation*, the *Freeman* and the *New Republic* over the fence. But the din does not flabbergast Dr. More. High above the blood-bathed battlements there is a tower, of ivory within and solid ferro-concrete without, and in its austere upper chamber he sits undaunted, solemnly composing an elegy upon Jonathan Edwards, "the greatest theologian and philosopher yet produced in this country."

Magnificent, indeed—and somehow charming. On days when I have no nobler business I sometimes join the barbarians and help them to launch their abominable bombs against the embattled bluenoses. It is, in the main, fighting that is too easy, too Anglo-Saxon to be amusing. Think of the decayed professors assembled by Dr. Franklin for the *Profiteers' Review*; who could get any genuine thrill out of dropping *them*? They come out on crutches, and are as much afraid of what is behind them as they are of what is in front of them. Facing all the horrible artillery of Nineveh and Tyre, they arm themselves with nothing worse than the pedagogical birch. The janissaries of Adolph Ochs, the Anglo-Saxon supreme archon, are even easier. One has but to blow a *shofar*, and down they go. Even Prof. Dr. Stuart P. Sherman is no antagonist to delight a hard-boiled heretic. Sherman is at least honestly American, of course, but the trouble with him is that he is *too* American. The Iowa hayseed remains in his hair; he can't get rid of the smell of the chautauqua; one inevitably sees in him a sort of *reductio ad absurdum* of his fundamental theory—to wit, the

Note: Originally published in *Prejudices: Third Series*, by H. L. Mencken (New York: Knopf, 1922), pp. 176–179. Copyright © 1922 and renewed 1950 by H. L. Mencken. Reprinted by permission of Alfred A. Knopf, Inc.

theory that the test of an artist is whether he hated the Kaiser in 1917, and plays his honorable part in Christian Endeavor, and prefers Coca-Cola to Scharlachberger 1911, and has taken to heart the great lessons of sex hygiene. Sherman is game, but he doesn't offer sport in the grand manner. Moreover, he has been showing sad signs of late of a despairing heart: he tries to be ingratiating, and begins to hug in the clinches.

The really tempting quarry is More. To rout him out of his armored tower, to get him out upon the glacis for a duel before both armies, to bring him finally to the wager of battle—this would be an enterprise to bemuse the most audacious and give pause to the most talented. More has a solid stock of learning in his lockers; he is armed and outfitted as none of the pollyannas who trail after him is armed and outfitted; he is, perhaps, the nearest approach to a genuine scholar that we have in America, God save us all! But there is simply no truculence in him, no flair for debate, no lust to do execution upon his foes. His method is wholly *ex parte*. Year after year he simply iterates and reiterates his misty protests, seldom changing so much as a word. Between his first volume and his last there is not the difference between Gog and Magog. Steadily, ploddingly, vaguely, he continues to preach the gloomy gospel of tightness and restraint. He was against "the electric thrill of freer feeling" when he began, and he will be against it on that last gray day—I hope it long post-dates my own hanging—when the ultimate embalmer sneaks upon him with velvet tread, and they haul down the flag to half-staff at Princeton, and the readers of the New York *Evening Journal* note that an obscure somebody named Paul E. More is dead.

IN 1930 *two books focused the arguments for and against the New Humanism. Norman Foerster edited* Humanism and America, *stating the essential positions, while C. Hartley Grattan edited* The Critique of Humanism. *Many of the essays in both volumes are diffuse and hard to excerpt briefly and clearly, but I have chosen one which is so organized as to state with reasonable clarity both sides of the argument.*

Allen Tate (1899–) was an active member of the Fugitive poets and the southern agrarians. He was, however, uncharacteristically modernist in his views on literature, and he admired Eliot inordinately, a distinctly minority position in the Nashville of that day. He thus managed to be both conservative in his chief values and yet critical of many of the conservative positions taken by others. He did not contribute to the conservative volume at all but rather placed his critique in Grattan's book, where it had rather odd company. The essence of Tate's position was that humanism as normally phrased was based too often on naturalistic premises and was therefore subject to many valid criticisms much as liberalism and positivism were. For Tate, as for Eliot in related essays mentioned in the bibliographical essay, religious views were essential to make humanism work in any meaningful way. Since Babbitt disliked organized religion intensely and More was essentially heretical in ways unacceptable to Tate, the whole enterprise was flawed at the core. The essay is very long, not always clear, and has been severely condensed.

16. The Fallacy of Humanism

By Allen Tate

If the necessity for virtue could tell us how to practice it, we should be virtuous overnight. For the case of the American Humanists against modern culture is damaging to the last degree. The truth of their indictment, negatively considered, cannot be denied. But this is not enough.

There is widespread belief that the doctrines of Humanism are fundamentally sound. It would be truer to say that they are only partly and superficially so, and that they are being rejected for superficial reasons—the Humanists are dogmatic, they ignore contemporary literature, they lack the "esthetic sense." These limitations unhappily go deeper. Humanism is obscure in its sources; it is even more ambiguous as to the kind of authority to which it appeals. And yet believers in tradition, reason, and authority—among whom this essayist counts himself—will approach the writing of Messrs. Babbitt, More and Foerster with more than an open mind; they will have in advance the conviction that

> the rightful concern of man is his humanity, his world of
> value . . . that marks him off from a merely quantitative order;

but, after a great deal of patient reading, they will come away with that conviction—and with no more than that conviction. They will have got no specific ideas about values—that is to say, they will have gained no medium for acquiring them; and such a medium, they will reflect, is morally identical with the values themselves. Values are not suspended in the air to be plucked. They will reflect, suspiciously, that the vague method of Humanism resembles the vague method of the so-called Romantic in the very respect in which agreement or difference is fundamental: the Humanist pursues Humanism for its own sake—or, say, restraint for restraint's sake, or proportion for proportion's sake—and while this is doubtless better than pursuing disorder for disorder's sake, the authority of the worthier pursuit is no clearer than that of the baser. His doctrine of restraint does not look

Note: Originally published in *The Critique of Humanism,* edited by C. Hartley Grattan (New York: Brewer & Warren, 1930), pp. 131–138, 148–155, 160–166. Later collected in Allen Tate, *Memoirs and Opinions: 1926–1974* (Chicago: The Swallow Press, 1974). Reprinted by permission of The Swallow Press, Inc., Chicago.

to unity, but to abstract and external *control*—not to a solution of the moral problem, but an attempt to get the social results of unity by main force, by a kind of moral Fascism.

The reader will decide, moreover, that this defect of the Humanist is a central one and that, critically examined, it will turn out to be the philosophical malady of the so-called naturalist. Doctrinal differences in themselves may be negligible; the man who supposes himself a naturalist may practice the Humanistic virtues (Montaigne): the Humanist in doctrine may exhibit the method of naturalism (More). But if the appearance of mere doctrine is deceptive, the operation of a technique cannot be. The Humanists have no technique. How, under the special complexities and distractions of the modern world, they intend to make good their values they do not say; they simply urge them. And this discrepancy between doctrine and method their hardier readers will find adequately described in Book II, Chapter IV, of the *Nicomachean Ethics*:

> . . . yet people in general do not perform these actions, but taking refuge in talk they flatter themselves they are philosophizing, and that they will so be good men: acting in truth very like those sick people who listen to the doctor with great attention but do nothing that he tells them: just as these people cannot be well bodily under such a course of treatment, neither can those be mentally by such philosophizing.

The Humanists have listened not only to one doctor but to a great many doctors, and they tell us what they say; but they have not learned, and they cannot teach us, how to take the medicine.

I propose, in the first place, therefore, to analyze the position held by those Humanists in whom the minimum of doctrine appears: I mean by the minimum of doctrine that their thought refuses to exceed the moralistic plane: they steadily repudiate all religious and philosophical support. The Humanists of this type are Babbitt and Foerster. Secondly, I shall try to discover how this Humanism differs, if it differ, from that of Mr. More, who appears to lean heavily upon religious values. Different as the religious and the non-religious brands of Humanism seem to be, they may turn out in the end to founder on the same reef. At the last, if Humanism shall save itself—that is to say, if it shall find a method—what is the position into which it will be logically driven?

The Humanism formulated by Mr. Norman Foerster in the last chapter of his *American Criticism* is actually a summary of the views of Professor Babbitt. The summary is, of course, an over-simplification, and does scant justice to Professor Babbitt's intellectual resourcefulness; yet I think it contains the fundamental scheme of his position. (It omits one of his chief difficulties, which I will bring out in a moment.) The assumptions of Humanism, according to Mr. Foerster, are as follows:

(1) "... that assumptions are necessary." Foerster points out the self-deception of the naturalist, or the anti-authoritarian, who thinks he has got rid of assumptions.

(2) "... that the essential elements of human experience are precisely those which appear to conflict with the reality explored by naturism. It [Humanism] recognizes, indeed, the service of naturism ... in showing the power of the natural man's impulses."

(3) "... the central assumption of humanism is that of a dualism of man and nature ... the rightful concern of man is his humanity, his world of value and quality that marks him off from a merely quantitative natural order."

(4) "Finally, humanism assumes the freedom of the will to conform to a standard of values, as opposed to the deterministic assumption of naturism."

From these assumptions Mr. Foerster proceeds to a doctrine which I reproduce in a greatly abridged form:

(1) An adequate human standard calls for *completeness*. This includes "natural" human nature.

(2) But it also calls for *proportion*: it demands the harmony of the *parts with the whole* (italics mine).

(3) The complete, proportionate standard may be said to consist of the *normally* or *typically human*.

(4) Although such an ethos has never existed, it has been approximated in the great ages of *the past*. Foerster looks mainly to Greece, but he includes the Romans, Vergil and Horace; the Christians, Jesus, Paul, Augustine, others; the Orientals, Buddha and Confucius; the moderns, Shakespeare, Milton, Goethe. (But he has misgivings about Shakespeare.)

(5) Unlike Romanticism, Humanism is true to its Hellenic origin in its faith in *reason*. It seeks to deal positively with the whole of human experience, including those elements of experience that do *not* fall within the scope of what is termed science.

(6) Unlike the conceptions of life that grow out of science, Humanism seeks to press beyond reason by the use of *intuition* or *imagination* ... the human or ethical imagination, as distinguished from the natural or pathetic imagination, which is below the reason.

(7) The ultimate ethical principle is that of restraint or control.

(8) This center to which Humanism refers everything . . . is
the reality that gives rise to religion. But pure Humanism
is content to describe it *in physical terms* . . . it hesitates
to pass beyond its experimental knowledge to the dogmatic affirmations of any of the great religions . . . it
holds that *supernatural revelation must be tested by the
intellect* . . . it should be clear that Humanism, like Greek
philosophy, *begins with science* and *not* with religion.

Now Mr. Foerster says that human values are those which *appear*
to conflict (do they or do they not?) with the reality explored by naturism; and yet Humanism demands the cultivation of all human nature, including "natural" human nature. He says, too, that Humanism
rejects the elements of experience that fall within the "scope of what
is termed science." However this may be, Humanism puts its faith in
reason (because of its Hellenic origin) and it is based upon science,
and yet it is unlike the conceptions of life that grow out of science. It
demands a dualism of man and nature opposed to the monistic assumption of naturism. But how, it may be asked, is this dualism to be
preserved along with that other requirement of a "harmony of the
parts with the *whole*"? Mr. Foerster has just denounced the monistic
whole. And, further, it may be asked, upon which side of the duality
does reason take its stand? If science is naturism, and reason science,
the question answers itself.

Humanism is based upon science, which is naturism and yet it is
unlike the conceptions of life that grow out of science. And here it
may be asked upon which science Mr. Foerster performs his miracle
of accepting rejection? Is it just *science*? Or is it an unconscious attitude whose vision of reality is mechanism, a popular version of genuine science? In this case, it is the quantitative natural order of which
he speaks. But how did it get quantified? Is it *naturally* quantified?
The only plausible answer is that it was quantified by Mr. Foerster's
kind of reason, but that being unaware of this he can, with an effective "chaser" handy, drink "reason" off neat.

The chaser is the "ethical imagination," which presses beyond reason. We have seen that he puts his faith in reason, and it is difficult
to see why he wishes a faith beyond faith, or why he selects this particular super-faith: he refuses to press beyond reason in favor of
religion.

.   .   .   .

If Professor Babbitt's Humanism is eclectic, Mr. More's is equally
so—but the apparent synthesis takes place on the religious plane. Humanists like Babbitt and Foerster have to meet the problem of access
to truth beyond the personality; it is obvious that Babbitt is a sound
man, that his views are sound because he is; but there is no other
guarantee of the soundness of his views. He is a "personality," and

there is nothing to do about personality but to feel that it is sound or unsound. Mr. More, however, compels us to answer the question: Is his religion as a source of moral authority sound or unsound?

The problem is harder than that of personality, but in the end it is the same. What, in the first place, is Mr. More's religion? Is it Christianity? It is possible that it is. He has written time and again about the insight afforded us by Christian writers, and to them he has brought no inconsiderable insight of his own. There is also, according to Mr. More, a profound insight in Plato—perhaps the profoundest. Again, his studies in the Hindu religions and philosophies have stimulated him to some of his best and most sympathetic writing: the Hindus teach a deep religious dualism. Mr. More's *Studies of Religious Dualism* is a kind of breviary of the good he finds in half a dozen or more religious attitudes. The question remains: which of these religions is Mr. More's? The answer to this, I believe, is: Mr. More's religion is Mr. More's.

Now one of Mr. More's apologists has justly called the five volumes of *The Greek Tradition* an "original and profound work"; yet does its originality and profundity bear upon the question of religious authority—the sole question that I am putting to Mr. More's religious writings? However, Mr. More's defender indirectly attempts to answer this very question: he says: "The Christ of the New Testament [contains] an exact and unmistakable explanation of his [More's] acceptance of the historic Christian revelation." I have read this explanation in addition to the rest of Mr. More's religious writings; yet what "acceptance" means is not clear, for Mr. More's Christianity excludes belief in the Miracles and the Virgin Birth. There is a detailed analysis yet to be made of Mr. More's religious books; still I think that my conclusion will be found to be correct: the historic revelation that Mr. More has accepted is largely one of his own contrivance. It is revelation on Mr. More's own terms—revelation as revealed by Mr. More. It is a reconstruction of the historical elements in a pattern satisfactory to the needs of Mr. More's "independent faith," the authority for which is to be found solely in his own books.

He has written a good deal on religion, but it is not easy to put one's finger on his idea of it. Because of the discrepancy between the individualism of his religion and the dogmatism of his judgments his explicit statements on the subject tend to be vague—something like pulpit rhetoric. And yet he does have definite ideas. Their most significant expression is in incidental remarks, when he is off his guard. About twenty years ago he took to task an interpreter of the Forest Philosophers for trying

> to convert into hard intellectualism what was at bottom a religious and thoroughly human experience.

Is intellectualism hard (or soft) incompatible with religion? If the experience was thoroughly human, was it also religious? Mr. More thinks that it was. If intellectualism has no place in religion, where does it belong? Mr. More's reply to this is undoubtedly Mr. Foerster's conception of reason: reason is the exclusive privilege of what the Humanists call naturism. Religion is an indefinite, unutterable belief. Mr. More, as well as Babbitt and Foerster, cannot get out of this notion of reason. Now, if religion is not allowed to reason, what may it do? Shall it be contented with visions? I think that Mr. More would say no; but he could not rationally say it. Mr. More repeats implicitly the dilemma of Babbitt and Foerster—and it is very different from a dualism. You have on the one hand scientific naturalism: on the other, irrational belief—the "illusion of a higher reality" that is only an illusion. It is the familiar doctrine of the *philosophe*, that the religious or ethical imagination is an aberration of the intellect, of naturalism. Mr. More would say that the religious and the human join in opposing the natural. But if the religious and the human combine in the present state of Mr. More's religion, which is individualistic, he is opposing naturalism with opposition, or in other words with itself. You cannot overcome naturalism with an illusion of higher reality or an individualistic faith; the illusion and the individualism are properties of the thing to be overcome. In spite of Mr. More's religious attitude, most of my criticism of Babbitt and Foerster apply to him.

Mr. More's dilemma is implicit through *Christ the Word*, the most recent volume of *The Greek Tradition*, and it becomes explicit in an essay entitled "An Absolute and An Authoritative Church" (*The Criterion*, July, 1929). Harassed by the demon of the absolute, he tries to find religious authority apart from the Protestant claim of infallibility for the biblical texts, on the one hand, and, on the other, from the Roman claim of absolute interpretation of these texts. The solution of the problem seems to lie in the Eastern and the Anglican Churches, which offer "the kind of revelation which neither in book nor in Church is absolute, but in both book and Church possesses a sufficient authority." The merit of any particular church is beside my point, but Mr. More's idea of authority is very much to it, and he fails to make it clear. He admits that his authority may bring "the reproach of uncertainty," and the reader must conclude that the uncertainty is rooted in his persistently independent faith. The new essay is a summary of Mr. More's religious thought, and it is forthright and fearless; but it ends in vague appreciation of tradition tempered by individualism. The dilemma of absolutes remains untouched because Mr. More seems to lack the philosophical impulse to think himself out of it.

He gives us, in the first chapter of *Studies of Religious Dualism*, something of his religious history up to that time (1909). He had repudiated Calvinism. He was drifting, but suddenly he found a book that initiated him into the "mysteries of independent faith"—the kind of faith, one observes, that the romantic, the naturist, the Rousseauist, has supported all along. Calvinism, it seems, was not independent enough or too independent. Now just how much independence was necessary? Mr. More had to make his decision individualistically, and he had, like Professor Babbitt, no way of knowing when he came to more than a personal stop.

His critics have accused him of a defective "esthetic sense"; he has seemed to be preoccupied with the content of literature; he has little to say of style, almost nothing, except what he says impatiently, of the craft of writing from the point of view of the writer. With Professor Babbitt, he never permits us to forget his conviction that the problems of craft are secondary and "esthetic" and that, if the writer is virtuous, the writing will take care of itself. The reply to this is not that such confusion of thought is unworthy of Mr. More—which it is. It is not enough to oppose to it an equal confusion—that his is due to a lack of esthetic perception. His failure to understand the significance of style is a failure to understand most of the literature that he has read. It is his intention to extract from any given book the doctrine that coincides with his own. We have just seen that it is difficult to find out what Mr. More's doctrine is. With what is literature, then, to coincide? Mr. More entertains false hopes of literature; he expects it to be a philosophy and a religion because, in his state of "independent faith," he has neither a definite religion nor a definite philosophy prior to the book he happens to be reading.

In his most recent volume, *The Demon of the Absolute*, he remarks somewhat complacently, that he is not concerned at the moment with artistic means; only with "results." This distinction runs all through Mr. More's writings: he is not concerned with the letter of religion or of literature—the means through which it exists and is preserved, the religion or the literature itself. Religious results, separate from religious means, become—if they become anything—independent faith. Literary results, that is the moral paraphrase of a work of literature, become independent morality. In either case the full content of the literary or religious text is left behind. When Mr. More tells us that a writer has a sound moral attitude, he may be right, but there is no reason to believe that he may not be wrong. His judgments, for us, are thus neither right nor wrong: strictly speaking they are meaningless. He cannot cite his independent faith because he has no text outside himself; it is rationally inarticulate; there is no way to communicate it.

.   .   .   .

How shall we know when we have values?—a more difficult problem than the mere conviction that we need them. There is no such thing as pure value, nor are there values separate from the means of creating and preserving them. There are certain definite ways in which men have had access to value in the past (the Humanists tell us that Dante had values, but not how he got them); but our problem is, Have

we any of those ways now? If we have, how may they be used? Is
there a condition or are there several conditions that must be met before we may use them?

We have seen the assumptions of the Humanists. The assumptions
of this essay are that Humanism is not enough, and that if the values
for which the Humanist pleads are to be made rational, even intelligible, the parallel condition of an objective religion is necessary. There
should be a living center of action and judgment, such as we find in
the great religions, which in turn grew out of this center. The act of
"going into the Church" is not likely to supply the convert with it.
Yet, for philosophical consistency, this is what the Humanists should
do. It is clear that this essay urges the claim of no special church, and
it is in no sense a confession of faith; but the connection between the
Reformation and the rise of Naturalism, and what I conceive the religious imagination to be, define the position that the Humanists must
occupy if they wish to escape intellectual suicide. The religious unity
of intellect and emotion, of reason and instinct, is the sole technique
for the realization of values.

The virtue of religion is its successful representation of the problem
of evil, for no metaphysical system has been able to account for evil
in a unified world. We have seen how Mr. Foerster, wishing at once
to cultivate natural human nature and to reject it, could not decide
how far he wished to go in either direction. This was because his
dualism was verbal; there were no really opposed principles; there was
simply an infinite number of points on the same scale. And thus his
opposition between Quality and Quantity was verbal too; it was Quantity versus Quantity, presided over by rootless Restraint, the referee
who checked nothing but coherent thought. The Humanists tell us
that somehow we have to do with Quality, yet since, for them, nature
is the quantified nature of scientism and the mind is a quantified machine of moral ideas, it is difficult to see where Quality comes from.
The Humanists seem to use the word to mean something "better"
than something else—the philosophical level at which the fashionable
tailor uses it. For Quality in itself is neither good nor bad.

There is, then, a preliminary question to be asked: What is the
source of qualitative experience? Both horns of his dualism being reduced to Quantity, the Humanist cannot tell us; and that is why
much of his criticism gives you the feeling that he expects you to
pluck values out of the air. Since the Humanist has not been philo-
sophically hardy enough to work out of the naturalistic version of nature (which he naïvely accepts), since, in fact, he cannot root the concept of nature as Quantity out of his mind, his idea of Quality is irresponsible, foot-loose, highly transcendental in a kind of Concord sense.

The source of Quality is nature itself because it is the source of experience. It is only by holding to an idea that leaves nature an open
realm of Quality that experience is possible at all; and, conversely,
experience alone is the road to Quality. If an American zoölogist sees

a certain Philippine cobra he doubtless says, *"Naja samaransis"*; the snake is merely an instance of the quantification of nature. The head-hunter, however, has a more vivid feeling for the unique possibilities of the particular cobra; it may bite him; it may give him the evil eye —both richly qualitative experiences. For the Humanist, *opposing* Quality to nature, has got it on the wrong side of his duality. Pure Quality would be pure evil, and it is only through the means of our re-covery from a lasting immersion in it, it is only by maintaining the precarious balance upon the point of collapse into Quality, that any man survives his present hour; pure quality is pure disintegration. The scientist says, *"Naja samaransis"*; Mr. More, a cadence of the same theme—"Immoral"; Quality is quantified before we ever see it as Quality; and nature becomes a closed system of abstraction in which man is deprived of all experience whatever and, by being so deprived, reduced to an abstraction himself.

The religious attitude is the very sense (as the religious dogma is the definition) of the precarious balance of man upon the brink of pure Quality. But if you never have Quality, never have the challenge of evil, you have no religion—which is to say, you have no experience either. It is experience, immediate and traditional fused—Quality and Quantity—which is the means of validating values. Experience gives the focus to style, and style is the way anything is done. Rhetorical de-vice is our abstract term for properties of style after style is achieved; they have never of themselves made one poem better than another.

Religion's respect for the power of nature lies in her contempt for knowledge of it; to quantify nature is ultimately to quantify ourselves. Religion is satisfied with the dogma that nature is evil, and that our recovery from it is mysterious ("grace"). For the abstraction of nature ends, as we have seen, with the destruction of the reality of time, and immediate experience being impossible, so do all ideas of tradition and inherited order become timeless and incoherent. It is the indis-pensable office of the religious imagination that it checks the abstract-ing tendency of the intellect in the presence of nature. Nature ab-stract becomes man abstract, and he is at last condemned to a perma-nent immersion in pure and evil Quality; he is forever condemned to it because he can no longer see it for what it is. The protection of re-ligion is the abstraction, not of nature, which so conceived would be the abstraction of abstraction, but of experience. It proposes a system of Quantity *against* nature; it is a quantitative version of the encoun-ter between the head-hunter and the cobra; but it says nothing about the cobra-in-itself. The organized meaning of the encounters of man and nature, which are temporal and concrete, is religious tradition, and religious tradition is not exclusively the Church, but necessarily implies a way of life historically protected by the Church. The dogma acts for the recoil of the native from the snake: it is his technique for finding out the value of the encounter. Every such encounter is rich and unique in Quality: it is the temporal, never recurring focus, the new triumph, the re-affirmation of the preserved experience of man. The modern Humanist, because of habitual reactions, recoils, but he has no reason for doing so, and his recoil is without value. He and the snake are one: Quantity versus Quantity; nature against nature; snake against snake; or, for that matter, man against man.

It is the failure of the Humanist to get out of this dilemma which makes his literary criticism feeble and incomplete. Mr. Foerster says: "It is best to face the issue in all candor"—the issue being Shakespeare. This poet merely "presents" life; he does not "interpret" it. If I had never read Shakespeare and had not read the rest of Mr. Foerster's book, his distinction would sound plausible; but having read his book, I know what he means, which is something very different from what he thinks he means. He means that the mind of Shakespeare was not a mechanism of moral ideas. The Humanists quarrel with literature because it cannot give them a philosophy and a church; but they keep turning to literature because they cannot find these things elsewhere. You cannot have the sense of literature without the prior, specific, and self-sufficient sense of something else. Without this you expect too much of literature; you expect of it a religion and a philosophy; and by expecting of it the wrong thing, you violate it, and in the end you get from it less than it is meant to yield; you get neither literature nor religion, nor anything that is intelligible. You destroy literature without constructing a religion.

For, as M. Ramon Fernandez has recently said, with Aristotelian tact, Humanism should not pretend to be a "body of Doctrine"; it is "a resultant situation."

The American Humanists have tried to make the resultant situation its own background, because they lack the resultant situation itself. Humanism is too ambitious, with insufficient preparation. (I do not mean erudition.) It tries to take a short-cut to the resultant situation, and ignores the social difficulty of making or reconstructing an appropriate background. It ignores the philosophical difficulty of imagining what the background should be; it is an effort to imitate by rote the natural product of culture; it is a mechanical formula for the recovery of civilization. It is the cart before the horse, and because it gets the "philosophy" in the wrong place, it invites philosophical attack. Humanism should be culture, but it may be a little untamed in the Humanists until, as the digging of graves in the grave-diggers, "custom hath made it in them a property of easiness."

V. Agrarianism & the South

AT ROUGHLY *the same time that the New Humanists were developing their position, the followers of Donald Davidson and John Crowe Ransom at Vanderbilt were also refining a position about the place of themselves and their region in the modern world. In their first incarnation, Davidson, Ransom, Tate, and Robert Penn Warren called themselves the "Fugitives," wrote poetry for each other's criticisms, and attacked both the romantic myths of the Old South and the business ethic of the New South. Originally, these poets had no cult of the South themselves, but the famous "monkey trial" of John Scopes in nearby Dayton, for attempting to teach Darwinian ideas in the public schools, put them and their region on the defensive. They began to formulate reasons for their preference of the South over the North. In time, their position, generally called southern agrarianism or simply agrarianism, became a defense of values which seemed to them to have set the Old South apart from the industrialized North: its aristocracy, its hierarchical social structure, its uniform religion and code of conduct, its pervasive sense of ritual and mystery. Much of this remained in the more recent South, and with effort more could be recovered. The North was hopelessly gone and could never be redeemed.*

By the late twenties, the agrarian position had become refined enough and the opposition irritating enough for the leaders of the group to plan a book. The result, after numerous difficulties, was published as I'll Take My Stand. *As a whole the book itself was not distinguished: its arguments were often sprawling and its sense of history highly erratic. Most of the contributors did their best work elsewhere. Nevertheless, the introductory statement of principles remains a valuable position paper.*

The twelve contributors were Allen Tate, John Crowe Ransom, John Donald Wade, Frank L. Owsley, Herman C. Nixon, Robert Penn Warren, Andrew N. Lytle, Lyle H. Lanier, Henry B. Kline, Donald Davidson, Stark Young, and John Gould Fletcher.

17. Introduction: A Statement of Principles

By Twelve Southerners

The authors contributing to this book are Southerners, well acquainted with one another and of similar tastes, though not necessarily living in the same physical community, and perhaps only at this moment aware of themselves as a single group of men. By conversation and exchange of letters over a number of years it had developed that they entertained many convictions in common, and it was decided to make a volume in which each one should furnish his views upon a chosen topic. This was the general background. But background and consultation as to the various topics were enough; there was to be no further collaboration. And so no single author is responsible for any view outside his own article. It was through the good fortune of some deeper agreement that the book was expected to achieve its unity. All the articles bear in the same sense upon the book's title-subject: all tend to support a Southern way of life against what may be called the American or prevailing way; and all as much as agree that the best terms in which to represent the distinction are contained in the phrase, Agrarian *versus* Industrial.

But after the book was under way it seemed a pity if the contributors, limited as they were within their special subjects, should stop short of showing how close their agreements really were. On the contrary, it seemed that they ought to go on and make themselves known as a group already consolidated by a set of principles which could be stated with a good deal of particularity. This might prove useful for the sake of future reference, if they should undertake any further joint publication. It was then decided to prepare a general introduction for the book which would state briefly the common convictions of the group. This is the statement. To it every one of the contributors in this book has subscribed.

Nobody now proposes for the South, or for any other community in this country, an independent political destiny. That idea is thought to have been finished in 1865. But how far shall the South surrender its moral, social, and economic autonomy to the victorious principle

of Union? That question remains open. The South is a minority section that has hitherto been jealous of its minority right to live its own
kind of life. The South scarcely hopes to determine the other sections,
but it does propose to determine itself, within the utmost limits of
legal action. Of late, however, there is the melancholy fact that the
South itself has wavered a little and shown signs of wanting to join
up behind the common or American industrial ideal. It is against that
tendency that this book is written. The younger Southerners, who are
being converted frequently to the industrial gospel, must come back
to the support of the Southern tradition. They must be persuaded to
look very critically at the advantages of becoming a "new South" which
will be only an undistinguished replica of the usual industrial
community.

But there are many other minority communities opposed to industrialism, and wanting a much simpler economy to live by. The communities and private persons sharing the agrarian tastes are to be
found widely within the Union. Proper living is a matter of the intelligence and the will, does not depend on the local climate or geography, and is capable of a definition which is general and not Southern
at all. Southerners have a filial duty to discharge to their own section.
But their cause is precarious and they must seek alliances with sympathetic communities everywhere. The members of the present group
would be happy to be counted as members of a national agrarian
movement.

Industrialism is the economic organization of the collective American society. It means the decision of society to invest its economic
resources in the applied sciences. But the word science has acquired
a certain sanctitude. It is out of order to quarrel with science in the
abstract, or even with the applied sciences when their applications
are made subject to criticism and intelligence. The capitalization of
the applied sciences has now become extravagant and uncritical; it
has enslaved our human energies to a degree now clearly felt to be
burdensome. The apologists of industrialism do not like to meet this
charge directly; so they often take refuge in saying that they are devoted simply to science! They are really devoted to the applied sciences and to practical production. Therefore it is necessary to employ
a certain skepticism even at the expense of the Cult of Science, and
to say, It is an Americanism, which looks innocent and disinterested,
but really is not either.

The contribution that science can make to a labor is to render it
easier by the help of a tool or a process, and to assure the laborer of
his perfect economic security while he is engaged upon it. Then it
can be performed with leisure and enjoyment. But the modern laborer has not exactly received this benefit under the industrial re-

gime. His labor is hard, its tempo is fierce, and his employment is insecure. The first principle of a good labor is that it must be effective, but the second principle is that it must be enjoyed. Labor is one of the largest items in the human career; it is a modest demand to ask that it may partake of happiness.

The regular act of applied science is to introduce into labor a labor-saving device or a machine. Whether this is a benefit depends on how far it is advisable to save the labor. The philosophy of applied science is generally quite sure that the saving of labor is a pure gain, and that the more of it the better. This is to assume that labor is an evil, that only the end of labor or the material product is good. On this assumption labor becomes mercenary and servile, and it is no wonder if many forms of modern labor are accepted without resentment though they are evidently brutalizing. The act of labor as one of the happy functions of human life has been in effect abandoned, and is practiced solely for its rewards.

Even the apologists of industrialism have been obliged to admit that some economic evils follow in the wake of the machines. These are such as overproduction, unemployment, and a growing inequality in the distribution of wealth. But the remedies proposed by the apologists are always homeopathic. They expect the evils to disappear when we have bigger and better machines, and more of them. Their remedial programs, therefore, look forward to more industrialism. Sometimes they see the system righting itself spontaneously and without direction: they are Optimists. Sometimes they rely on the benevolence of capital, or the militancy of labor, to bring about a fairer division of the spoils: they are Coöperationists or Socialists. And sometimes they expect to find super-engineers, in the shape of Boards of Control, who will adapt production to consumption and regulate prices and guarantee business against fluctuations: they are Sovietists. With respect to these last it must be insisted that the true Sovietists or Communists—if the term may be used here in the European sense—are the Industrialists themselves. They would have the government set up an economic super-organization, which in turn would become the government. We therefore look upon the Communist menace as a menace indeed, but not as a Red one; because it is simply according to the blind drift of our industrial development to expect in America at last much the same economic system as that imposed by violence upon Russia in 1917.

Turning to consumption, as the grand end which justifies the evil of modern labor, we find that we have been deceived. We have more time in which to consume, and many more products to be consumed. But the tempo of our labors communicates itself to our satisfactions, and these also become brutal and hurried. The constitution of the natural man probably does not permit him to shorten his labor-time and enlarge his consuming-time indefinitely. He has to pay the penalty in satiety and aimlessness. The modern man has lost his sense of vocation.

Religion can hardly expect to flourish in an industrial society. Religion is our submission to the general intention of a nature that is fairly inscrutable; it is the sense of our rôle as creatures within it. But nature industrialized, transformed into cities and artificial habitations, manufactured into commodities, is no longer nature but a highly simplified picture of nature. We receive the illusion of having power over nature, and lose the sense of nature as something mysterious and contingent. The God of nature under these conditions is merely an amiable expression, a superfluity, and the philosophical understanding ordinarily carried in the religious experience is not there for us to have.

Nor do the arts have a proper life under industrialism, with the general decay of sensibility which attends it. Art depends, in general, like religion, on a right attitude to nature; and in particular on a free and disinterested observation of nature that occurs only in leisure. Neither the creation nor the understanding of works of art is possible in an industrial age except by some local and unlikely suspension of the industrial drive.

The amenities of life also suffer under the curse of a strictly-business or industrial civilization. They consist in such practices as manners, conversation, hospitality, sympathy, family life, romantic love—in the social exchanges which reveal and develop sensibility in human affairs. If religion and the arts are founded on right relations of man-to-nature, these are founded on right relations of man-to-man.

Apologists of industrialism are even inclined to admit that its actual processes may have upon its victims the spiritual effects just described. But they think that all can be made right by extraordinary educational efforts, by all sorts of cultural institutions and endowments. They would cure the poverty of the contemporary spirit by hiring experts to instruct it in spite of itself in the historic culture. But salvation is hardly to be encountered on that road. The trouble with the life-pattern is to be located at its economic base, and we cannot rebuild it by pouring in soft materials from the top. The young men and women in colleges, for example, if they are already placed in a false way of life, cannot make more than an inconsequential acquaintance with the arts and humanities transmitted to them. Or else the understanding of these arts and humanities will but make them the more wretched in their own destitution.

The "Humanists" are too abstract. Humanism, properly speaking, is not an abstract system, but a culture, the whole way in which we live, act, think, and feel. It is a kind of imaginatively balanced life lived out in a definite social tradition. And, in the concrete, we believe that this, the genuine humanism, was rooted in the agrarian life of the older South and of other parts of the country that shared in such a tradition. It was not an abstract moral "check" derived from the classics—it was not soft material poured in from the top. It was deeply founded in the way of life itself—in its tables, chairs, portraits, festivals, laws, marriage customs. We cannot recover our native humanism by adopting some standard of taste that is critical enough to question the contemporary arts but not critical enough to question the social and economic life which is their ground.

The tempo of the industrial life is fast, but that is not the worst of it; it is accelerating. The ideal is not merely some set form of industrialism, with so many stable industries, but industrial progress, or an incessant extension of industrialization. It never proposes a specific goal; it initiates the infinite series. We have not merely capitalized certain industries; we have capitalized the laboratories and inventors, and undertaken to employ all the labor-saving devices that come out of them. But a fresh labor-saving device introduced into an industry does not emancipate the laborers in that industry so much as it evicts them. Applied at the expense of agriculture, for example, the new processes have reduced the part of the population supporting itself upon the soil to a smaller and smaller fraction. Of course no single labor-saving process is fatal; it brings on a period of unemployed labor and unemployed capital, but soon a new industry is devised which will put them both to work again, and a new commodity is thrown upon the market. The laborers were sufficiently embarrassed in the meantime, but, according to the theory, they will eventually be taken care of. It is now the public which is embarrassed; it feels obligated to purchase a commodity for which it had expressed no desire, but it is invited to make its budget equal to the strain. All might yet be well, and stability and comfort might again obtain, but for this: partly because of industrial ambitions and partly because the repressed creative impulse must break out somewhere, there will be a stream of further labor-saving devices in all industries, and the cycle will have to be repeated over and over. The result is an increasing disadjustment and instability.

It is an inevitable consequence of industrial progress that production greatly outruns the rate of natural consumption. To overcome the disparity, the producers, disguised as the pure idealists of progress, must coerce and wheedle the public into being loyal and steady consumers, in order to keep the machines running. So the rise of modern advertising—along with its twin, personal salesmanship—is the most significant development of our industrialism. Advertising means to persuade the consumers to want exactly what the applied sciences are able to furnish them. It consults the happiness of the consumer no more than it consulted the happiness of the laborer. It is the great effort of a false economy of life to approve itself. But its task grows more difficult every day.

It is strange, of course, that a majority of men anywhere could ever as with one mind become enamored of industrialism: a system that has so little regard for individual wants. There is evidently a kind of thinking that rejoices in setting up a social objective which has no relation to the individual. Men are prepared to sacrifice their private dignity and happiness to an abstract social ideal, and without asking whether the social ideal produces the welfare of any individual man whatsoever. But this is absurd. The responsibility of men is for their own welfare and that of their neighbors; not for the hypothetical welfare of some fabulous creature called society.

Opposed to the industrial society is the agrarian, which does not stand in particular need of definition. An agrarian society is hardly one that has no use at all for industries, for professional vocations, for scholars and artists, and for the life of cities. Technically, perhaps, an agrarian society is one in which agriculture is the leading vocation, whether for wealth, for pleasure, or for prestige—a form of labor that is pursued with intelligence and leisure, and that becomes the model to which the other forms approach as well as they may. But an agrarian regime will be secured readily enough where the superfluous industries are not allowed to rise against it. The theory of agrarianism is that the culture of the soil is the best and most sensitive of vocations, and that therefore it should have the economic preference and enlist the maximum number of workers.

These principles do not intend to be very specific in proposing any practical measures. How may the little agrarian community resist the Chamber of Commerce of its county seat, which is always trying to import some foreign industry that cannot be assimilated to the life-pattern of the community? Just what must the Southern leaders do to defend the traditional Southern life? How may the Southern and the Western agrarians unite for effective action? Should the agrarian forces try to capture the Democratic party, which historically is so closely affiliated with the defense of individualism, the small community, the state, the South? Or must the agrarians—even the Southern ones—abandon the Democratic party to its fate and try a new one? What legislation could most profitably be championed by the powerful agrarians in the Senate of the United States? What anti-industrial measures might promise to stop the advances of industrialism, or even undo some of them, with the least harm to those concerned? What policy should be pursued by the educators who have a tradition at heart? These and many other questions are of the greatest importance, but they cannot be answered here.

For, in conclusion, this much is clear: If a community, or a section, or a race, or an age, is groaning under industrialism, and well aware that it is an evil dispensation, it must find the way to throw it off. To think that this cannot be done is pusillanimous. And if the whole community, section, race, or age thinks it cannot be done, then it has simply lost its political genius and doomed itself to impotence.

THE CONTRIBUTORS *to* I'll Take My Stand *worked out their ideas in a number of preliminary essays and continued to elaborate on their ideas after the publication of the anthology. In one of the best of these essays, John Crowe Ransom (1888–1974) summed up the case for the South as a uniquely European culture with particular resemblances to the experiences of England and Scotland. The culture of these regions, he insisted, should never be too practical, as in the North, but rather should exercise the mind. In the North, this was hardly possible, for there industrialism was rampant and people could never fully develop. In a quote which he repeated later in the anthology he stated:* "For it is the character of a seasoned provincial life that it is realistic, or successfully adapted to its natural environment, and that as a consequence it is stable, or hereditable. But it is the character of our urbanized, anti-provincial American life that it is in a condition of eternal flux." *The South simply could never agree that* "the whole duty of man was to increase material production" *or that one's culture was in any way related. Concerns of religion, hierarchy, stability, and order came first.*

18. The South Defends Its Heritage

By John Crowe Ransom

It is out of fashion in these days to look backward rather than forward; and about the only American given commonly to this disgraceful conduct is some unreconstructed Southerner, who persists in his regard for a certain terrain, a certain history, and a certain inherited way of living. He is punished as his crime deserves. He feels himself in the American scene as an anachronism, and knows he is felt by his neighbors as a reproach.

Fortunately, he is a tolerably harmless reproach. He is like some quaint local character of eccentric but fixed principles who is thoroughly and almost pridefully accepted by the village as a rare exhibit of the antique kind. His position is secure from the interference of the police, but it is of a rather ambiguous dignity.

I could wish that he were not so entirely taken for granted, and that as a reproach he might bear a barb and inflict a sting.

His fierce devotion is to a lost cause, but I am grieved that his contemporaries are so sure it is lost. They are so far from fearing him and his example that they even in the excess of confidence offer him a little honor, a little petting. As a Southerner, I have observed this indulgence, and I try to be grateful. Obviously, it does not constitute a danger to the Republic; distinctly, it is not treasonable. They are good enough to attribute a sort of glamour to Southern life as it is defined for them in the popular tradition. They like to use the South as the nearest available locus for the scenes of their sentimental songs, and sometimes they send their daughters to the Southern seminaries. Not too much is to be made, of course, of this last graceful gesture. For they do not expose to this hazard their sons, who in our still very masculine order will have to discharge the functions of citizenship, and who must accordingly be sternly educated in the principles of progress at progressive institutions of learning. But it does not seem to make so much difference what principles of a general character the young women acquire, since they are not likely to be impaired by principles in their peculiar functions, such as virtue and the domestic duties. And so, at suitable seasons, and on the mainline trains, one may see them in some numbers, flying south or flying north like migratory birds; and one may wonder to what extent their

Note: Originally published in *Harper's* 159 (June 1929): 108–118. Copyright © 1956 by *Harper's* magazine. Reprinted by permission of Helen Ransom Forman, executrix of John Crowe Ransom's estate.

philosophy of life will be affected by two or three years in the South. One must remember that probably their parents have already made this calculation and are prepared to answer, Not much.

The Southerner must know and, in fact, he does very well know, that his antique conservatism does not exert a large influence against the American progressivist doctrine. The Southern idea to-day is down, and the progressive or American idea is up. Nevertheless, the historian and the philosopher, who take views that are thought to be respectively longer and deeper than most, may very well reverse this order and find that the Southern idea rather than the American has in its favor the authority of example and the approval of theory. And some prophet may even find it possible to expect that it may yet rise again.

I will propose a thesis which seems to have about as much cogency as generalizations usually have: The South is unique on this continent for having founded and defended a culture which was according to the European principles of culture; and the European principles had better look to the South if they are to be perpetuated in this country.

The nearest of the European cultures which we could examine is that of England; and this is of course the right one in the case, quite aside from our convenience. England was actually the model employed by the South, in so far as Southern culture was not quite indigenous. And there is in the South even to-day an Anglophile sentiment quite anomalous in the American scene.

England differs from America doubtless in several respects, but most notably in the fact that England did her pioneering an indefinite number of centuries ago, did it well enough, and has been living pretty tranquilly on her establishment ever since, with infrequent upheavals and replacements. The customs and institutions of England seem to the American observer very fixed and ancient. There is no doubt that the English tradition expresses itself in many more or less intangible ways, but it expresses itself most importantly in a material establishment; and by this I mean the stable economic system by which Englishmen are content to take their livelihood from the physical environment. The chief concern of England's half-mythical pioneers, as with pioneers anywhere, was with finding the way to make a living. Evidently they found it. But fortunately the methods they worked out proved transmissible, proved, in fact, the main reliance of the succeeding generations. The pioneers explored the soil, determined what concessions it might reasonably be expected to make them, housed themselves, developed all their necessary trades, and arrived by painful experiment at a thousand satisfactory recipes by which they might secure their material necessities. Their descendants have had the good sense to consider that this establishment was good enough for them. They have elected to live their comparatively easy and routine lives in accordance with the tradition which they inherited, and they have consequently enjoyed a leisure, a security, and an intellectual freedom that were never the portion of pioneers.

The pioneering life is not the normal life, whatever some Americans may suppose. It is not, if we look for the meaning of European history. The lesson of each of the European cultures now extant is in this—that European opinion does not make too much of the intense practical enterprises, but is at pains to define rather narrowly the practical effort which is prerequisite to the reflective and aesthetic life. Boys are very well pleased to employ their muscles almost exclusively, but men prefer to exercise their minds. It is the European intention to live materially along the inherited line of least resistance, in order to put the surplus of energy into the free life of the mind. Thus is engendered that famous, or infamous, European conservatism, which will appear stupid, necessarily, to men still fascinated by materialistic projects, men in a state of arrested adolescence; for instance, to some very large if indefinite fraction of the population of these United States.

Perhaps England is being "quickened" or Americanized; then, *tant pis!* I have in mind here the core of unadulterated Europeanism, with its self-sufficient, backward-looking, intensely provincial communities. The human life of English provinces long ago came to terms with nature, fixed its roots somewhere in the spaces between the rocks and in the shade of the trees, founded its comfortable institutions, secured its modest prosperity—and then willed the whole in perpetuity to the generations which should come after, in the ingenuous confidence that it would afford them all the essential human satisfactions. For it is the character of a seasoned provincial life that it is realistic, or successfully adapted to its natural environment, and that as a consequence it is stable, or hereditable. But it is the character of our urbanized, anti-provincial, progressive, and mobile American life that it is in a condition of eternal flux. Affections, and long memories, attach to the ancient bowers of life in the provinces; but they cannot attach to what is always changing. Americans, however, are somewhat averse to such affections for natural objects and to such memories.

.   .   .   .

The Southern states were settled of course by miscellaneous strains. But evidently the one which determined the peculiar tradition of the South was the one which came out of Europe most convinced of the virtues of establishment, contrasting with those strains which seem for the most part to have dominated the other sections, and which came out of Europe feeling rebellious towards all establishments. There are a good many faults to be found with the old South, but hardly the fault of being intemperately addicted to work and to gross material prosperity. The South never conceded that the whole duty of man was to increase material production, or that the index to the degree of his culture was the volume of his material production. His business seemed to be rather to envelop both his work and his play with a leisure which permitted the activity of intelligence. On this assumption the South pioneered her way to a sufficiently comfortable and rural sort of establishment, considered that an establishment was something stable, and proceeded to enjoy the fruits thereof. The arts of the section, such as they were, were not immensely passionate, creative, and romantic; they were the Eighteenth Century social arts of dress, conversation, manners, the table, the hunt, politics, oratory, the pulpit. These were arts of living and not arts of escape; they were also community arts, in which every class of society could participate after its kind. The South took life easy, which is itself a tolerably comprehensive art.

But so did other communities in 1850, I believe. And doubtless some others do so yet; in parts of New England, for example. If there are such communities, this is their token, that they are settled. Their citizens are comparatively satisfied with the life they have inherited, and are careful to look backward quite as much as they look forward. Before the Civil War there must have been many such communities this side of the frontier. The difference between the North and the South was that the South was constituted by such communities and made solid. But solid is only a comparative term here. The South as a culture had more solidity than another section, but there were plenty of gaps in it. The most we can say is that the Southern establishment was completed in a good many of the Southern communities, and that this establishment was an active formative influence on the spaces between, and on the frontier spaces outlying, which had not yet perfected their organization of the economic life.

The old Southern life was of course not nearly so fine as some of the traditionalists like to believe. It did not offer serious competition among the world-types against the glory that was Greece, or the grandeur that was Rome. It hardly began to match the finish of the English, or any other important European civilization. It is quite enough to say that it was a way of life which had been considered and authorized. The establishment had a sufficient economic base, it was meant to be stable rather than provisional, it had got beyond the pioneering stage, it provided leisure, and its benefits were already being enjoyed. It may as well be admitted that Southern society was not an institution of very showy elegance, for the so-called aristocrats were mostly home-made and countrified. Aristocracy is not a word which defines this social organization so well as squirearchy, which I borrow from a recent article by Mr. William Frierson in the *Sewanee Review*. And even the squires, and the other classes too, did not define themselves very strictly. They were loosely graduated social orders, not so fixed as in Europe. Their relations were personal and friendly. It was a kindly society, yet a realistic one; for it was a failure if it cannot be said that people for the most part were in their right places.

Slavery was a feature monstrous enough in theory but, more often than not, humane in practice; and it is impossible to believe that its abolition alone could have effected any great revolution in society.

The fullness of life as it was lived in the ante-bellum South by the different social orders can be estimated to-day only by the application of some difficult sociological technic. It is my thesis that all were committed to a form of leisure, and that their labor itself was leisurely. The only Southerners who went abroad to Washington, and elsewhere, and put themselves into the record, were those from the top of the pyramid. They held their own with their American contemporaries. They were not intellectually as seasoned as good Europeans, but then the Southern culture had had no very long time to grow, as time is reckoned in these matters; it would have borne a better fruit eventually. They had a certain amount of learning, which was not as formidable as it might have been; but at least it was classical and humanistic learning, not highly scientific, and not wildly scattered about over a variety of special studies.

It seems important to reflect that the South as a going society would not have countenanced the innovation of an elective college curriculum. The first aim of such a society is to protect its social concept, and this means the ascendancy in education of that group of studies which has social significance; they used to be called the humanities, before they were forbidden the use of so proud a term. The admission that one study is as important as another is a plea in spiritual bankruptcy, and it invites and produces just that ceaseless dissipation of human energies which now defines our intellectual Americanism—it pictures man as a creature without a center, without a substantial core of interests, and unable to give to his destiny any direction. In a true society there are historical and philosophical principles which compose the staple of an educational requirement, leaving the physical sciences to shift somewhat for themselves. And beyond the learning prescribed for its lay leaders, it is logical for this society to give an educational preference to certain professions which are peculiarly committed to its defense. Such professions are the Church, the bar, and the higher teaching profession; when they lose caste society is in danger. But this is somewhat of a digression; for in 1860 there was not much difference between Northern and Southern ideals of education. Certainly there was less difference between Northern and Southern colleges than there was between North and South. The colleges tended to be conservative social instruments everywhere.

Then the North and the South fought, and the consequences were disastrous to both. The Northern temper was one of jubilation and expansiveness, and now it was no longer shackled by the weight of the conservative Southern tradition. Industrialism, the latest form of pioneering and the worst, presently overtook the North, and in due time has now produced our present American civilization. Poverty and pride overtook the South; poverty to bring her institutions into disrepute, and to sap continually at her courage; and a false pride to inspire a distaste for the thought of fresh pioneering projects, and to doom her to an increasing physical enfeeblement.

It is only too easy to define the malignant meaning of industrialism. It is the contemporary form of pioneering; yet since it never consents to define its goal, it is a pioneering on principle, and with an accelerating speed. Industrialism is a program under which men, using the latest scientific paraphernalia, sacrifice comfort, leisure, and the enjoyment of life to win Pyrrhic victories from nature on points of no strategic importance. Ruskin and Carlyle feared it nearly a hundred years ago, and now it may be said that their fears have been realized partly in England, and with almost fatal completeness in America. Industrialism is an insidious spirit, full of false promises and generally fatal to establishments since, when it once gets into them for a little renovation, it proposes never again to leave them in peace. Industrialism is rightfully a menial, of almost miraculous cunning but no intelligence; it needs to be strongly governed or it will destroy the economy of the household. Only a community of tough conservative habit can master it.

The South did not become industrialized; she did not repair the damage to her old establishment, either, and it was in part because she did not try hard enough. Hers is the case to cite when we would show how the good life depends on an adequate pioneering, and how the pioneering energy must be kept ready for call when the establishment needs overhauling. The Southern tradition came to look rather pitiable in its persistence when the Twentieth Century had arrived, for the establishment was quite depreciated. Unregenerate Southerners were trying to live the good life on a shabby equipment, and they were grotesque in their effort to make an art out of living when they were not decently making the living. In the country districts great numbers of these broken-down Southerners are still to be seen in patched blue-jeans, sitting on ancestral fences, shotgun across their laps and hound-dog at their feet, surveying their unkempt acres while they comment shrewdly on the ways of God. It is their defect that they have driven a too easy, an unmanly bargain with nature, and that their aestheticism is based on insufficient labor.

. . . .

And now the crisis in the South's decline has been reached.

Industrialism has arrived in the South. Already the local Chambers of Commerce exhibit the formidable data of Southern progress. A considerable party of Southern opinion, which might be called the New South party, is well pleased with the recent industrial accomplishments of the section, and eager for many more. Southerners of another school, who might be said to compose an Old South party, are apprehensive lest the section become completely and uncritically devoted to the industrial ideal precisely as the other and dominant sections of the Union are devoted to it. But reconstruction is actually under way, and it is an industrial reconstruction. Tied politically and economically to the Union, her borders wholly violable, all the South now sees very well that she can restore her prosperity only within the competition of an industrial system.

After the war the Southern plantations were often broken up into small farms. These have yielded less and less of a living, and it is said that they will never yield a good living until once more they are integrated into large units. But these units will be industrial units, controlled by a board of directors or an executive rather than by a squire, worked with machinery, and manned not by farmers living at home but by "labor." Even so they will not, according to Mr. Henry Ford, support the population that wants to live on them; in the off-seasons the laborers will have to work in factories, which henceforth are to be counted on as among the charming features of Southern landscape. The Southern problem is very complicated, but at its center is the farmer's problem, and this problem is simply the most acute version of that general agrarian problem which inspires the despair of many thoughtful Americans to-day.

The agrarian discontent in America is deeply grounded in the love of the tiller for the soil, which is probably, I must confess, not peculiar to the Southern specimen but one of the more ineradicable human attachments, be the tiller as progressive as he may. In proposing to wean men of this foolish attachment, industrialism sets itself against the most ancient and the most humane of all the modes of human livelihood. Do Mr. Hoover and the distinguished thinkers at Washington see how essential is the mutual hatred between the industrialists and the farmers, and how mortal is their conflict? The gentlemen at Washington are mostly preaching and legislating to secure the fabulous "blessings" of industrial progress; they are on the industrial side. But though the industrialists have a doctrine which is monstrous, they themselves are no monsters, but forward-lookers with very nice manners, and no American progressivist is against them. The farmers seem boorish and stubborn by comparison; American progressivism is against them in the fight, though their traditional status is still so strong that they are not too flagrantly antagonized. All the solutions recommended for their difficulty are really enticements held out to them to become a little more co-operative, more mechanical, more mobile—in short, a little more industrialized. But the farmer who is not a mere laborer, even the farmer of the comparatively new places like Iowa and Nebraska, is necessarily among the more stable and less progressive elements of society. He refuses to mobilize himself and become a unit in the industrial army, because he does not approve of army life.

I will use some terms which are hardly in his vernacular. He identifies himself with a spot of ground, and this ground carries a good deal of meaning; it defines itself for him as nature. He would till it not too hurriedly and not too mechanically to observe in it the contingency and the infinitude of nature; and so his life acquires its philosophical and even its cosmical consciousness. A man can contemplate and explore, respect and love an object as substantial as a farm or a native province. But he cannot contemplate nor explore, respect nor love a mere turnover, such as an assemblage of "natural resources," a pile of money, a volume of produce, a market, or a credit system. It is into precisely these intangibles that industrialism would translate the farmer's farm. It means the dehumanization of his life.

However that may be, the South at last, looking defensively about her in all directions upon an industrial world, fingers the weapons of industrialism. There is one powerful voice in the South which, tired of a long status of disrepute, would see the South made at once into a section second to none in wealth, as that is statistically reckoned, and in progressiveness, as that might be estimated by the rapidity of the industrial turnover. This desire offends those who would still like to regard the South as, in the old sense, a home; but its expression is loud and insistent. The urban South, with its heavy importation of regular American ways and regular American citizens, has nearly capitulated to these novelties. It is the village South and the rural South which supply the resistance, and it is lucky for them that they represent a vast quantity of inertia.

Will the Southern establishment, the most substantial exhibit on this continent of a society of the European and historic order, be completely crumbled by the powerful acid of the Great Progressive Principle? Will there be no more looking backward but only looking forward? Is our New World to be dedicated forever to the doctrine of newness?

It is in the interest of America as a whole, as well as in the interest of the South, that these questions press for an answer. I will enter here the most important items of the situation as well as I can; doubtless they will appear a little over-sharpened for the sake of exhibition.

(1) The intention of Americans at large appears now to be what it was always in danger of becoming: an intention of being infinitely progressive. But this intention cannot permit of an established order of human existence, and of that leisure which conditions the life of intelligence and the arts.

(2) The old South, if it must be defined in a word, practiced the contrary and European philosophy of establishment as the foundation of the life of the spirit. The ante-bellum Union possessed, to say the least, a wholesome variety of doctrine.

(3) But the South was defeated by the Union on the battlefield with remarkable decisiveness, and the two consequences have been dire: the Southern tradition was physically impaired, and has ever since been unable to offer an attractive example of its philosophy in action;

and the American progressive principle has developed into a pure industrialism without any check from a Southern minority whose voice
ceased to make itself heard.

(4) The further survival of the Southern tradition as a detached
local remnant is now unlikely. It is agreed that the South must make
contact again with the Union. And in adapting itself to the actual
state of the Union, the Southern tradition will have to consent to a
certain industrialization of its own.

(5) The question at issue is whether the South will permit herself
to be so industrialized as to lose entirely her historic identity, and to
remove the last substantial barrier that has stood in the way of
American progressivism; or will accept industrialization, but with a
very bad grace, and will manage to maintain a good deal of her
traditional philosophy.

The hope which is inherent in this situation is evident from the
terms in which it is stated. The South must be industrialized—but to
a certain extent, and in moderation. The program which now engages
the Southern leaders is to see how the South may handle this fire
without being badly burned. The South at last is to be physically re-
constructed; but it will be fatal if the South should conceive it as her
duty to be regenerated, her spirit re-born with a totally different
orientation towards life.

And fortunately, the Southern program is not perfectly vague, but
is capable of a certain definition. There are at least two lines, along
either of which an intelligent Southern policy may move in the right
general direction; and it may even move back and forth between them
and still advance.

The first course would be for the Southern leaders to arouse the
sectional feeling of the South to its highest pitch of excitement in defense of all the old ways that are threatened. It may seem rather
ungrateful towards the industrialists to accept their generous services
in such a churlish spirit. But if one thing is more certain than another, it is that these gentlemen will not be found standing by while
they wait for human sympathy. They are already on the scene, and
manifesting an inextinguishable enthusiasm for their role. The only
attitude that needs artificial respiration is the resistant attitude of
the natives. The resistance will be the fiercest and most effective if
industrialism is represented to the Southern people as—what it undoubtedly is for the most part—a foreign invasion of Southern soil,
which is capable of much more devastation than was wrought when
Sherman marched to the sea. From this point of view, it will be a
great gain if the present peaceful invasion will now and then forget
itself by some indiscretion and be less peaceful. The native and the
invader will be sure to come to an occasional clash, and that may
offer the chance to revive ancient and almost forgotten animosities. It
will be in order to proclaim to Southerners that the carpetbaggers are

again in their midst. And it will be well to seize upon and advertise certain Northern industrial communities as horrible examples of a way of life which Southerners traditionally detest; not failing to point out the human catastrophe which occurs when a Southern village or rural community becomes the cheap labor of a miserable factory system. It will be doubtless a little bit harder to impress the people with the fact that the new so-called industrial "slavery" not only fastens upon the poor, but blights the middle and better classes of society too; and to make this point it may be necessary even to revive such a stale antiquity as the old Southern gentleman, and his scorn for the dollar-chasers and the technical specialists.

Such a policy as this would show decidedly a sense of what the Germans call Realpolitik. It could be nasty and unscrupulous, but it could accomplish results.

Its net result might be to give to the South eventually a position in the Union analogous more or less to the position of Scotland under the British crown—a section with a very local and peculiar culture that would, nevertheless, be secure and respected. And Southern traditionalists may take courage from the fact that it was Scottish stubbornness which obtained this position for Scotland; it did not come gratuitously; it was the consequence of an intense sectionalism that fought for a good many centuries before its fight was won.

That is one policy; and though it is not the only one, it may be necessary to employ it, with discretion, and to bear in mind its Scottish analogue. But it is hardly handsome enough for the best Southerners. Its methods are too easily abused; it offers too much room for the professional demagogue; and one would only as a last resort like to have the South stake upon it her whole chance of survival. After all, the reconstruction may be undertaken with some imagination, and not necessarily under the formula of a literal restoration. It does not greatly matter to what extent the identical features of the old Southern establishment are restored; the important consideration is that there be an establishment for the sake of stability.

The other course may not be so easily practicable, but it is certainly more idealistic and statesmanlike. That course is for the South to re-enter the American political field with a determination and an address quite beyond anything she has exhibited during her half-hearted national life of the last half a century. And this means specifically that she may pool her own stakes with the stakes of other minority groups in the Union which are circumstanced similarly. There is in active American politics already, to start with, a very belligerent if somewhat uninformed Western agrarian party. Between this party and the South there is much community of interest; both desire to defend home, stability of life, the practice of leisure, and the natural enemy of both is the insidious industrial system. There are also, scattered here and there, numerous elements with the same general attitude which would have some power if united; the persons and even communities who are thoroughly tired of progressivism and its spurious benefits, and those who have recently acquired, or miraculously through the generations preserved, a European point of view—sociologists, educators, artists, religionists, and ancient New England townships. The combination of these elements with the Western farmers and the old-fashioned South would make a formidable bloc. The South is numerically much the most substantial of these three groups, but has done next to nothing to make the cause prevail by working inside the American political system.

The unifying effective bond between these geographically diverse elements of public opinion will be the clean-cut policy that the rural life of America must be defended, and the world made safe for the farmers.

THE MANY *sharp attacks on agrarianism that followed the publication of* I'll Take My Stand *soon moved several of the contributors to reply. Frank L. Owsley was one of these. In the essay that follows he defends agrarian notions about the economy, with its "small units owned and controlled by real people." After the pattern set by Thomas Jefferson so long ago, he wanted more widespread public ownership of property and a more decentralized governmental system.*

Somewhat condensed, Owsley's five pillars of agrarianism were his desire to rehabilitate current farmers, reinvigorate the soil they worked, encourage more sensible production of both subsistence and money crops, institute a just political economy where agriculture was as important as industry, and instigate a new regional conception of the Constitution which would protect the rights of farmers and Southerners.

19. The Pillars of Agrarianism

By Frank L. Owsley

Since the appearance of *I'll Take My Stand* in 1930, the Agrarians have been subjected to a fusillade of criticism. I suspect that our philosophy as set forth in that book and in later essays, published in certain periodicals, especially in the Distributist-Agrarian AMERICAN REVIEW, has irked the devotees of our technological civilization. Venturing an even stronger word, it begins to appear that the doctrines announced in *I'll Take My Stand* have actually *infuriated* these people. Just recently, on an important examination for a certain scholarship, it seems that the Committee inquired of each candidate what he thought of agrarianism. It was noteworthy that the successful candidate summed up his opinion by saying that the advocates of such a system were "cockeyed." One of the candidates who was not only rejected, but was urged not to apply again on the grounds of age (he has just celebrated his twenty-second birthday, and the age limit of the scholarship is several years above this age) answered that as far as he understood it he heartily approved of agrarianism. The most recent and, perhaps, the most violent attack upon the advocates of an agrarian state is that of H. L. Mencken. While Mencken's attack is so violent and lacking in restraint that it does not fall far short of libel, I have no desire to single him out as a critic worthy of an answer. However, I must confess that Mencken's attack, because it is typical—outside of the billingsgate—of those coming from the pillars of Industrialism, has prompted, to a certain extent, this essay. Such essays as his, appearing with amazing regularity, have without doubt troubled the mind of the neophyte, and, in many cases, have utterly confused him and made him lose sight of the principles and specific objectives of agrarianism.

Few if any of the Agrarians have expended any effort in answering the criticism of those who attack our principles. From the beginning we have pursued the attack rather than the defence; nor have we—if I may continue the military figure of speech—seen fit to consolidate our positions. However, it seems to me very proper, at the present time, for the sake of those who have been confused, or those whom we hope to draw into our way of thinking, to restate and elaborate the fundamental economic and political principles on which an

Note: Originally published in the *American Review* 4 (March 1935): 529–547. Reprinted by permission of Mrs. Harriet C. Owsley.

agrarian society will probably have to rest in the United States, and most particularly in the South.

I shall not attempt to restate and discuss all the principles and programmes of our hoped-for agrarian society, for this, as John Crowe Ransom has said in another connection, would indeed institute an infinite series. My purpose is to confine my discussion to the five great pillars upon which this society will have to rest. Before going into an exposition of the foundation of a restored agrarianism in the South (or other regions), it will be well to restate our definition of an agrarian state as set forth in the introduction of *I'll Take My Stand*:

> Opposed to the industrial society is the agrarian, which does not stand in particular need of definition. An agrarian society is hardly one that has no use at all for industries, professional vocations, for scholars and artists and for the life of the cities. Technically, perhaps, an agrarian society is one in which agriculture is the leading vocation, whether for wealth, for pleasure, or prestige—a form of labour that is pursued with intelligence and leisure, and that becomes the model to which the other forms approach as well as they may.

I shall edit this definition. We had in mind a society in which, indeed, agriculture was the leading vocation; but the implication was more than this. We meant that the agrarian population and the people of the agricultural market towns must dominate the social, cultural, economic, and political life of the state and give tone to it. Today, the Scandinavian countries are fair examples of such a state. France before the World War was a most beautiful example, where 30,000,000 people lived on the land and 10,000,000 lived in the towns and cities engaging in commerce and industry. Even today, after the disastrous War and its effects upon mechanization of industry, France presents the best balanced economic system of any first-class nation in the world. The ownership of property is more widely distributed there than in any nation comparable in wealth and population. Governments may rise and fall, but the French peasant and farmer seems eternal when compared to those of the United States. Today there are about 350,000 persons unemployed in France as against hardly less than 12,000,000 in the United States. Yet the United States has less than three times as large a population as France.

Before entering into the details of our fundamental programme, let me say that we are not exotics, nor a peculiar sect living in a vacuum, untouched by public affairs, merely irked by the noise of factory wheels and machinery. We fully realize that our programme cannot be put into operation until matters affecting the nation as a whole are set aright. Everything which affects the agrarian interests also touches industry, finance, and commerce. Our programme, there-

fore, intimately involves national problems. We are on the side of
those who know that the common enemy of the people, of their government, their liberty, and their property, must be abated. This enemy
is a system which allows a relatively few men to control most of the
nation's wealth and to regiment virtually the whole population under
their anonymous holding companies and corporations, and to control
government by bribery or intimidation. Just how these giant organizations should be brought under the control of law and ethics we are not
agreed. We are, however, agreed with the English Distributists that
the most desirable objective is to break them down into small units
owned and controlled by real people. We want to see property restored
and the proletariat thus abolished and communism made impossible.
The more widespread is the ownership of property, the more happy
and secure will be the people and the nation. But is such a decentralization in physical property as well as in ownership possible? We are
confident that it is, however much we may differ among ourselves as
to the degree of decentralization that will prove desirable in any given
industry. We are all convinced, though we hold no doctrinaire principles as to method, that these robber barons of the twentieth century
will have to be reduced and civilized in some form or other before any
programme can be realized by our state and Federal governments.

While we are deeply interested in the whole nation, yet, as Agrarians and Southerners, we are not desirous of launching a crusade to
convert or coerce the other sections of the country into our way of
thinking. We therefore, while inviting all who wish, to go with us,
have a fundamental programme for the south to which I have referred as the five pillars of agrarianism.

II

The first item in our agrarian programme is to rehabilitate the population actually living on the soil. This farming population falls into
several categories: large and small planters; large and small farmers,
both black and white; black and white tenants who own their stock
and tools, and rent land; black and white tenants who own no stock
or tools, but are furnished everything and get a share of the crop for
their labour. Finally, there is the wage-hand either coloured or white
who is furnished a house, and perhaps food and a certain cash wage.

Today the farm population in the South whether wage-hand or
large planter is in a precarious and often miserable state. The exploi-
tations by the industrial interests through high tariffs and other
special favours from the Federal government, which force the farmer
to buy in a protected market and sell in a world market, and the
periodic industrial depressions following in close order since the Civil
War, have greatly oppressed the Southern agricultural population.
The majority of the planters do not really own their lands; the real

owners are the life insurance companies or the banks. The payment
of the interest on his mortgage leaves the almost mythical landowner
little on which to subsist. Repayment of the principal is out of the
question. Actually, most of the planters are without credit, and are
no better off than the tenant or share-cropper. In fact the renter and
share-cropper frequently come out of debt with some cash, their corn,
sorghum, potatoes, pigs, cows, and other live stock above the board.
The fate of the small or large farmer is much better. As a rule he is
thrifty, owes less than the other classes, and lives to a great extent
off his farm. Sometimes he sends his children to college, especially
the agricultural college. His house is usually comfortable and sometimes painted. For the farmer as a class, there is less need of state
intervention in his affairs than in the affairs of the tenant and planter
classes. Yet a new political economy is necessary for him as well as
the planters and tenants, or he will eventually lose his land and
status. This new political economy will be discussed later. As for the
planter class, there are many whom even the new political economy
cannot save. Their equity in the once broad acres which they held in
fee simple is too small. It will be best for them to liquidate and begin
over as small farmers under the plan which I shall presently offer in
connection with the tenant farmers.

The most serious problem, however, is not the bankrupt planters
but the tenant-farmers, black or white, because of their great number.
I do not know the exact ratio between the tenant-farmer class and
the landholding class; but I have heard it said that 75% of the population living on the land in the South are tenants. If this estimate is
too high, it will not long remain so unless strong measures are taken,
for the tenant class has been increasing so rapidly in recent years
that it threatens to engulf the entire agricultural population of the
South. Most of the white tenants were once landowners, but have
been thrust near to the bottom of the economic and social order by
the loss of their lands through industrial exploitation, depression,
and, frequently, through high pressure salesmanship of radio, automobile, and farm machinery agents. Industrialism has persuaded, or
created a public opinion which has virtually driven, the farmer to
accept industrial tastes and standards of living and forced him to
mortgage and then to lose his farm. Battered old cars, dangling radio
aerials, rust-eaten tractors, and abandoned threshing machines and
hay balers scattered forlornly about are mute witnesses to the tragedy
of Industrialism's attempt to industrialize the farmer and planter.

A portion of the lower class of white tenants, especially the adults,
are beyond redemption. Through diseased tonsils, adenoids, unbal-
anced rations, tuberculosis, hook worm, malaria, and the social
diseases, many have been made into irresponsible, sometimes—but
not often—vicious people who are lacking in mental alertness and the
constancy of will to enable them to till the soil without close supervision. Such people would not be able to make a living on land which

might be granted or sold to them on easy terms by the government. However, the county and state public health departments should be enabled to take the steps necessary to salvage the children of such families in order that they may become owners of small farms and good citizens when of proper age. It is this class of whites in particular, who own no stock, plant no gardens, raise no chickens, who are frequently and perhaps accurately described as the "po' white trash."

The higher class white tenants, those who own their stock and cattle and have their gardens and truck patches, are ready to become the proprietors of farms. Frequently they are good farmers and send their children through the high schools. They are probably in the majority in most of the Southern states and, as I have suggested, their families have been landowners: they were, in short, once a part of the Southern yeomanry; and for a nation or section to allow these people to sink lower and lower in the social and economic scale is to destroy itself.

As for the Negro tenant class, the majority of the Agrarians agree that the really responsible farmers among them who know how to take care of the soil and who own their own stock and cattle, should be made proprietors of small farms.

The planters and large farmers who are left after liquidating their debts will still have an abundance of tenants who work well under supervision, but who are irresponsible and incapable of taking care of themselves without supervision. In the South, the wage-hand is usually the son of a tenant. He is frequently young and more intelligent than the lower tenant class. He should, where his intelligence and sense of responsibility permit, be homesteaded like the better-class tenant. Otherwise, he should be kept where he is, under the supervision of one who has good judgment and a sense of responsibility.

Now, instead of the Federal or state government spending $2500 in building a house for the homesteaders, with whom they are very gingerly experimenting, and several hundred dollars on small tracts of land, let the national and state governments buy up all the lands owned by insurance companies and absentee landlords—which are being destroyed rapidly by erosion—and part of the land owned by the large planters who are struggling to save a portion of their lands, and give every landless tenant who can qualify, 80 acres of land, build him a substantial hewn log house and barn, fence him off twenty acres for a pasture, give him two mules and two milk cows and advance him $300 for his living expenses for one year. By this means 500,000 persons can be rehabilitated in one year at $1,500 a family or $300 per person. An outright gift of the land is advocated to the homesteader with one condition attached: the land must never be sold or mortgaged, and when abandoned it should automatically escheat to the state which should be under immediate obligation to rehabilitate another worthy family.

The next step would be to bring the technologically unemployed, intelligent city people back to the country. First, those who have had experience as farmers should be rehabilitated; next, but relatively few at a time, those without experience should be permitted to become tenants on plantations, whereupon, if such tenants and their families should feel that they would like to go on, the government should grant them a homestead with sufficient stock and cattle and enough cash to subsist them one year. It seems quite clear to the Agrarians that technological unemployment is destined to increase with rapid acceleration until the majority of the population once employed in industry will be thrown out of the system. The government will be faced with perhaps three alternatives: it could put these permanently unemployed on a dole—until the government becomes bankrupt or an orderly slave state is established; it could refuse the dole and have a revolution; or it could rehabilitate the unemployed by giving them small farms. We, as interested citizens of the United States, urge this last policy upon the government as the only permanent relief from permanent technological unemployment. As Agrarians we urge it as an opportunity to restore the healthy balance of population between city and country, which will aid in the restoration of agrarianism and in the restoration and preservation of civilization.

Next in order of importance but simultaneous with the first step should be the rehabilitation of the soil. We, in common with the agricultural colleges of the country, urge that small and large farmer, small and large planter, regard the enrichment and preservation of the soil as a first duty. Those who own the soil must be held accountable in some way for their stewardship. Undrained, unterraced, single-cropped land, and lack of reforestation, should be *prima facie* evidence that the homesteader is not a responsible person and his land should, after fair warning and action in Chancery Court, escheat to the state. As for those farmers and planters who acquire their land by purchase or inheritance, a heavy suspended fine should be imposed upon them; and unless the planter or farmer remedies the abuses within a reasonable time or gives good reason why he has not been able to do so, the fine should be collected. The county agent and three men appointed by the state department of agriculture, should serve in each county as a kind of court to pass on such matters, and appeal from their decision should be allowed to go to Chancery Court. In short, land must be conserved for future generations and not exploited, as has too often been the practice, by the present owners. Another drastic proposal, which would aid in conserving the land as well as preventing its being alienated or becoming encumbered with debt, is that by state constitutional amendment, no land could be mortgaged, except by consent of a court of equity; nor should any kind of speculative sale be permitted. It must become impossible for land to be sold to real estate and insurance companies or banks. In thus making alienation of the soil difficult and its proper management necessary, I am suggesting a modified form of feudal tenure where, in theory, the King or state has a paramount interest in the land.

When the rehabilitation and conservation of the soil and stability of tenure have been provided for, the next consideration must be the products of the soil.

Subsistence farming must be the first objective of every man who controls a farm or plantation. The land must first support the people who till it; then it must support their stock. In the olden days when there were no money taxes or mortgages to meet, nor automobiles and fine carriages to buy, nor life and fire insurance to keep up, and when the priest and the teacher were paid in kind, this type of farming, if carried on with the scientific knowledge available today, would have supported the grandest of establishments. But today, a minimum outlay of cash is necessary even for those fortunate souls who are without debts: taxes, insurance, clothing, certain articles of luxury, and medical attention require cash.

After subsistence come the money crops. In the South these crops, too often planted at the expense of the subsistence crops, are peanuts, rice, sugar cane, tobacco, and cotton. Cotton and tobacco, the two leading staples, can be raised in the South in almost limitless quantities and must always depend, to a large extent, upon the foreign or world market. Considerable talk has been going its rounds concerning the danger of losing the foreign market because of crop limitation. Crop limitation, however, has no bearing at the present time, at least, upon the problem of cotton and tobacco. There are between nine and twelve million surplus bales of cotton and large quantities of tobacco above current crops, stored in the United States; and there can hardly be any question about loss of world markets because of crop limitation when we are unable to dispose of this terrific surplus. Further, considerable alarm has been expressed concerning the inability of American cotton growers to compete with Russia, Egypt, Brazil, Turkey, China, and India. This is a groundless fear, for even in the days when the South produced the scrub variety of cotton, the world depended largely upon American cotton, because, with the exception of limited areas in Egypt, the Sudan, and South Africa, no part of the world could raise as much cotton per acre or as good a fibre as the American South. Now that Coker of South Carolina and other plant breeders have produced an upland staple with a fibre about two inches in length, which will grow on any soil in the South, and which is being rapidly introduced everywhere, there can hardly be any serious competition with the South, as far as cheapness of production, quality, and quantity are concerned.

Everything being equal in the world markets, the South could soon drive its competitors out, as it did until past the turn of the century when other factors entered. These factors will have to be dealt with intelligently by the government of the United States or by the regional governments to be discussed later, else the South will be wiped out economically. One factor is that within the last twenty years America has ceased to be a debtor nation and become a creditor. As a debtor we shipped cotton to England, France, or Germany which created foreign exchange with which to pay the principal and interest on our debts and purchase foreign goods. The South could raise large cotton and tobacco crops and be sure that the world markets would take all. As soon as we became a creditor we could no longer ship our cotton and tobacco with the assurances of a sale. England and Germany and France and even Japan, wherever possible, have bought cotton from those countries which owed them money. This loss of a foreign market was seemingly made permanent by the rising tariff scale in America, which effectually cut off foreign goods from our markets, and thereby destroyed the chief sources of foreign exchange in this country with which Southern staples could be bought. The tariff, which was a guarantee of the home markets for the industrial interests of the country, principally located in the East and a belt following the Great Lakes, has been the greatest permanent factor in destroying the foreign market on which the South chiefly depended.

It must be said, at this point, that such a situation was envisaged in 1833 when South Carolina nullified the tariff law of 1832, and again when the Southern states seceded from the Union in 1861. The belief that industrialism, as soon as it got control of the Federal government, would not only exploit agriculture but would destroy the South was behind the whole secession movement. Today, we Agrarians witness the fulfillment of the jeremiads of Robert Barnwell Rhett and John C. Calhoun. We, however, are not hoping for or advocating another break-up of the Union; but we are demanding a fair hearing for the fundamental cause of the South—now that slavery can no longer befog the real issue. If the industrial interests continue the monopoly of the home market and thereby cause the agricultural South (and West) to pay a much higher price for goods than the world price level, we must have a *quid pro quo*: a subsidy on every bale of cotton and pound of tobacco or other important agricultural products shipped abroad, based on the difference between world and domestic prices. In order that foreign countries shall have sufficient American exchange with which to purchase our staple farm exports we further insist that all farm products and raw material shipped into the United States be used in creating foreign exchange with which cotton and tobacco may be purchased and exported. (James Waller in *A New Deal for the South* suggests this technique of establishing parity between agriculture and industry.) In short, the South—and, if I may be so bold as to speak for the agrarian interests of another section, the West—must have agriculture put upon the same basis as industry.

III

With such political economy the South would soon become one of the most important parts of the world, and it would add much to the prosperity of the other sections of the country. It is doubtful, however, whether such intelligent legislation is possible under a government so dominated by particular sectional interests.

For that reason—which is founded upon the history of the last one hundred and forty-six years—we are striving for a new constitutional deal which will help put the several sections on equal footing and prevent the exploitation of one by the other. We are in the front ranks of those who insist that the United States is less a nation than an Empire made up of a congeries of regions marked off by geographic, climatic, and racial characteristics. It has been suggested that New England would form a distinct region, the Middle States another, the Middle West another, the Rocky Mountain and Pacific States another, perhaps, and the South another. Of course the region to which a state wished to affiliate would be determined by a plebiscite. W. Y. Elliott of Harvard suggests that the regional governments be granted the present powers of the states, and that the states themselves be deprived of anything save administrative functions. He further suggests that one set of courts should serve both as Federal and state courts, thus eliminating the maze of courts by which justice is delayed and defeated and encouragement thereby given to lynch law.

Mr. Elliott suggests that in the new set-up the Federal government retain its present powers much more clearly defined. He further urges that all concurrent powers be eliminated. As far as I know, Mr. Elliott is not an agrarian; but his plan is essentially what the Agrarians have urged constantly, except in the matter of division of power between Federal and regional governments. His plan seems very reasonable and conservative. Something like it will have to be adopted if the United States is to endure. The Agrarians, I believe, advocate that, in the redivision of powers in a new constitutional convention, the regional governments should have much more autonomy than the states have ever had. The Federal government should have supreme control over war and peace, the army and navy, interregional or even interstate commerce, banking, currency, and foreign affairs. On the other hand, the sections should have equal representation in the Federal legislative body and in the election of the president and in the cabinet. The legislative body should be composed of a senate only and should be elected by the regional congresses. Finally, the regions should have control of the tariff: that is, the several regions should have an equal share in making the tariff, which would be in the form of a treaty or agreement between all the sections, somewhat in the fashion of the late Austro-Hungarian tariff treaties. In case one region, say the South, failed to agree to the tariff treaty, then the South should be exempted from the operation of the law until an agreement could be reached. Such an agreement does not mean that there would be interregional tariffs; it does mean that, if the South should have a lower tariff than the other regions, goods imported through the South from abroad would have to pay an extra duty on entering the other regions operating under the treaty. There would be some smuggling across the Potomac and Ohio, but not any more than through Mexico and Canada.

The Supreme Court, like the proposed Senate, should have equal representation from all the sections, regardless of political parties, and the members of the Supreme Court should not be the creatures of the Senate or the President, but, like the Senate, should be appointed by the regional governors subject to the ratification of the regional legislature, which also should be only a senate. The courts— that is, courts of appeal and circuit courts—should be constituted regionally, but should be considered both Federal and regional, sitting one time as Federal and one time as regional.

In our Agrarian programme, not only does it seem necessary to grant more local autonomy because of differences of economic interest, but because of differences on social and racial interests as well. Under such a government, the Civil War would not have been possible, nor would Reconstruction and the ensuing difficulties and hatreds have arisen. And what is more to the point at the present time, Communist interference in the Southern courts, and even conservative interference from other sections, would hardly take place. In other words, the Agrarians—who come nearer representing the opinion of Southern people than do newspapers largely subsidized by Northern-owned power companies and Wall-Street-owned banks, or the Southern liberals fawning for the favour of these corporations or of other powerful Northern groups—believe that under regional government each section will find it less difficult to attend to its own social and economic problems, and thereby will be encouraged to restore the old friendships which were crippled or destroyed under our present system.

Let me sum up. The five pillars on which it would appear that an agrarian society must rest are: (1) The restoration of the people to the land and the land to the people by the government purchasing lands held by loan companies, insurance companies, banks, absentee landlords, and planters whose estates are hopelessly incumbered with debt, and granting to the landless tenants, who are sufficiently able and responsible to own and conserve the land, a homestead of 80 acres with sufficient stock to cultivate the farm, and cash enough to feed and clothe the family one year; (2) The preservation and restoration of the soil by the use of fines and escheat, and by making land practically inalienable and non-mortgageable—that is by restoring a modified feudal tenure where the state had a paramount interest in the land and could exact certain services and duties from those who possessed the land; (3) The establishment of a balanced agriculture where subsistence crops are the first consideration and the money crops are of secondary importance; (4) The establishment of a just political economy, where agriculture is placed upon an equal basis with industry, finance, and commerce; (5) The creation of regional governments possessed of more autonomy than the states, which will sustain the political economy fitted for each region, and which will prevent much sectional friction and sectional exploitation.

Once this foundation is securely built, the agrarian society will grow upon it spontaneously and with no further state intervention beyond that to which an agricultural population is accustomed. The old communities, the old churches, the old songs would arise from their moribund slumbers. Art, music, and literature could emerge into the sunlight from the dark cramped holes where industrial insecurity and industrial insensitiveness have often driven them. There would be a sound basis for statesmanship to take the place of demagoguery and corrupt politics. Leisure, good manners, and the good way of life might again become ours.

DESPITE THEIR *addiction to the written word, the agrarians wrote very little about their own role in cultural history. One of the few exceptions to this general lack of primary historical material is Donald Davidson's essay summing up the causes and results of the publication of* I'll Take My Stand. *"Uppermost in our minds was our feeling of intense disgust with the spiritual disorder of modern life—its destruction of human integrity and its lack of purpose." The agrarians wanted a life which would naturally engender "order, leisure, character, stability, and that would also, in the larger sense, be aesthetically enjoyable." Out of these traditionally conservative concerns slowly developed the economic and political views ultimately expressed by the agrarians, most cogently in the preceding article by Frank Owsley. Thus, typically, nonpolitical concerns generated political positions, and the activities of government became important only insofar as they make possible other activities free from unnecessary interference.*

20. *I'll Take My Stand*: A History

By Donald Davidson

In the autumn of 1930 I was one of twelve Southerners who
made an avowal of their concern for the destiny of the South.
This avowal took the form of a book of essays, preceded by a
statement of principles, the whole under the title: *I'll Take My
Stand: The South and the Agrarian Tradition.* For certain obvious
reasons it seems proper to review the origin and history of this adventure in social criticism. Among those reasons is the desire—I trust,
a pardonable one—to have one true account of the book's history appear as a matter of record. It is with this purpose that I now write.
But it should be understood that my expression is not the result of
any new and systematic collaboration by the twelve original contributors. I am depending upon my own memory and am giving my own
interpretation. When I use the first person plural, I do so for convenience only, and no presumption is intended.

In publishing *I'll Take My Stand* we were hardly so aspiring as to
look for a great deal of support outside the South; but within our own
section we took for granted that we might speak as Southerners. We
thought that our fellow-Southerners would grasp without laborious
explanation the terms of our approach to Southern problems; and
that the argument, which was certain to follow, would proceed within
a range of assumptions understood and accepted by all. We welcomed
the argument, since we felt that all parties would benefit by a free
public discussion, of a sort unknown in the South since antebellum
days. Such a discussion has taken place.

Yet with due respect to the able critics, whether of South or North,
who have praised or blamed, seriously or jokingly, I beg leave to point
out that the discussion of *I'll Take My Stand*, although it has continued briskly over a period of nearly five years, has been somewhat
less profitable than it might have been, because the contending parties have too often argued in different terms. So far as the South was
concerned, we were not altogether right in assuming that we could
speak as Southerners to Southerners. For all that some of our critics
and we had in common in the way of premises, we might as well have
been addressing Mr. Henry Ford or Mr. Granville Hicks. No doubt we
should have spared ourselves many surprises if we had corrected our
manuscripts accordingly. But let that pass! Between these critics and

Note: Originally published in the *American Review* 5 (Summer 1935):
301–321.

ourselves is a gap of misunderstanding which in times like these ought not to be left yawning.

To our critics (if I may judge by their pronouncements), industrialism in 1930 was a foregone conclusion, an impregnable system moving inexorably on a principle of economic determinism and already dominating the United States and the South. It had evils, which might be softened by humanitarian devices; but its possibilities for good outbalanced the evil. Mr. Gerald Johnson, for one, spoke of "a glittering civilization" that ought to arise in an industrialized South. It is easy to imagine the pictures in his mind of a wealthy, urbanized South, plentifully equipped with machines, hospitals, universities, and newspaper literates as alert as he is. The pictures of agrarianism were correspondingly bleak. To such critics, agrarianism suggested doomed farmers eaten up with hookworm, brutal labour from sunrise to sunset, or at best an idealized plantation life vanishing or utterly gone; or, so far as agrarianism meant agriculture in the strict sense, it signified a snappy commercialized occupation, making large-scale use of machines and scientific agronomy. When we championed agrarianism, they were amused and incredulous, if not disgusted, and therefore the tone of their discussion was often one of scornful levity.

It was easy enough, and sometimes exciting, to meet such levity with the retort called for under the circumstances. It would be easy now to inquire in all seriousness whether industrial civilization still glitters. But since we, no less than our critics, underestimated the speed and the thoroughness of the industrial collapse, I put this question, too, aside. Such uncomplimentary exchanges get nowhere, since they leave the premises of argument untouched. We did not and we do not think of industrialism and agrarianism in the terms that our critics have used. For their part, they have been unable to see the purposes of *I'll Take My Stand* in the proper context. It is that context which I wish to describe.

I'll Take My Stand was intended to be a book of principles and ideas, offering, with whatever implications it might have for America in general, a philosophy of Southern life rather than a detailed programme. It was based upon historical analysis and contemporary observation. It was not a handbook of farming or economics. It was not a rhapsody on Pickett's Charge and the Old Plantation. It was first of all a book for mature Southerners of the late nineteen-twenties, in the so-called New South—Southerners who, we trusted, were not so far gone in modern education as to require, for the act of comprehension, coloured charts, statistical tables, graphs, and journalistic monosyllables, but were prepared to use intelligence and memory.

In so far as it might benefit by an historical approach, the book needs to be considered against the background of 1929 and the years previous when it was being germinated and planned, and not, as it has been interpreted, against the background of Mr. Hoover's failure, the depression, and the New Deal. If we could have foreseen these events, we would have contrived to make the essays point clearly the moral that was even then implicit in them. But we were not, like the Prophet Moses, aware of any impending plagues to which we could refer for confirmation. In those years industrial commercialism was rampant. In no section were its activities more blatant than in the South, where old and historic communities were crawling on their bellies to persuade some petty manufacturer of pants or socks to take up his tax-exempt residence in their midst. This industrial invasion was the more disturbing because it was proceeding with an entire lack of consideration for its results on Southern life. The rural population, which included at least two-thirds of the total Southern population, was being allowed to drift into poverty and was being viewed with social disdain. Southern opinion, so far as it was articulate, paid little serious attention to such matters. The older liberals of the Walter Hines Page school still believed in the easy humanitarianism of pre-World-War days. The younger liberals were damning the Fundamentalists, and rejoicing in the efforts of the sociological missionaries who were arriving almost daily from the slum-laboratories of Chicago and New York. The business interests were taking full advantage of the general dallying with superficial issues.

I do not know at what precise moment the men who contributed to *I'll Take My Stand* arrived at the notion of making their views public. I do know that as individuals, observing and thinking separately, they arrived at the same general conclusions at about the same time. Although some of us were intimate friends, we had recently been scattered and had been writing in widely different fields. I remember that we were greatly and very pleasantly surprised, when we first approached the Southern topic, to find ourselves in hearty agreement. Each had been cherishing his notions in solitude, hardly expecting them to win the approval of the determined moderns who were his friends. But if we who had been so far separated and so differently occupied could so easily reach an understanding, were there not many other Southerners, fully as apprehensive and discontented as ourselves, who would welcome a forthright assertion of principles? These must be Southern principles, we felt, for the only true salvation of the South had to come from within—there had been already too much parasitic reliance on external counsel. But the principles must also be relevant to the new circumstances. What were the right Southern principles in the late nineteen-twenties?

Of course we never imagined that Southern principles, once defined, would apply just as benevolently in New York City as some wise men thought that Eastern metropolitan principles would apply in the South. We never dreamed of carrying across the line some kind of Southern crusade to offset the Northern push which at our own doors was making noises like a Holy War. In only one contingency (which at that time seemed remote enough) could we possibly conceive that Southern principles might have a national meaning. Whoever or whatever was to blame for the condition of American civilization in those days—and there were malcontents even in the North who were asking such embarrassing questions—certainly the South was not in any responsible sense the author of that condition. The characteristic American civilization of the nineteen-twenties had been produced under Northern auspices. It was the result of a practically undisturbed control over American affairs that the North had enjoyed since its victory at Appomattox, and of a fairly deliberate and consistent exclusion of Southern views. If ever it should occur to the people of the North that that exclusion was a defect—if ever Southern opinions should again be as hospitably entertained as were Mr. Jefferson's and Mr. Madison's in other days, then Southern principles would again have a meaning beyond the borders of the South.

The idea of publishing a book dealing with the Southern situation went back perhaps as far as 1925 and certainly had begun to take shape by 1928. For it was American industrialism of the boom period that disturbed us, no less than the later spectacle of industrial disorder. Before even a prospectus could be outlined, a great deal of discussion and correspondence was necessary. A sketch of what we had been doing just before the publication of *I'll Take My Stand* may be worth noting, since it indicates the diversity of interests from which we were drawn to focus on a single project. Tate had been in France, finishing his biography of Jefferson Davis and writing poetry and literary criticism. Ransom had been at work upon *God Without Thunder*, a study of religion and science. Wade had been writing a biography of John Wesley. Owsley was continuing the historical research that grew out of his *State Rights in the Confederacy* and that was to lead to his *King Cotton Diplomacy*. Nixon, who had just left Vanderbilt for Tulane, had been studying the Populist movement and the problem of the tenant farmer. Warren was at Oxford; he had published a biography of John Brown. Lytle had been in the East, writing plays and acting. Lanier had been teaching at New York University and doing research in the psychology of race. Kline had just received a Master of Arts degree in English at Vanderbilt University. I was attempting to edit a book page and to follow the curious tergiversations that modernism produced among the rising Southern writers. As for the other two contributors (who were not of the "Nashville group"), Stark Young, in addition to dramatic criticism, had written some excellent novels on Southern themes which at that time were none too well appreciated; and John Gould Fletcher, in England, had turned to social criticism in *The Two Frontiers*, a comparative study of Russia and America.

Most of us had a good deal of cosmopolitanism in our systems, the result of travel or residence abroad or of prolonged absorption in literature, pedagogy, or technical research. Those of us who had written poetry and criticism were painfully aware of the harsh constriction that modern life imposes on the artist. We were rebellious that such

constriction should operate upon Southern artists—or, for that matter, upon any artist; and some of us had written essays asking why
this should be so. All of us, I think, were turning with considerable
relief from the shallow social criticism and tortured art of the
nineteen-twenties to the works of the new historians and biographers
who were somehow avoiding both the complaisance of the old
Southern liberals and the dissociated cynicism of the younger ones. In
their perfectly objective restatement of Southern history and American history we found new cause for our growing distrust of the scorn
that was being volleyed at the "backward" South. What the historians
said was in all really important points at startling variance with the
assumptions of social critics and the "social workers" whose procedure was based on big-city attitudes. Suddenly we realized to the full
what we had long been dimly feeling, that the Lost Cause might not
be wholly lost after all. In its very backwardness the South had clung
to some secret which embodied, it seemed, the precise elements out
of which its own reconstruction—and possibly even the reconstruction of America—might be achieved. With American civilization, ugly
and visibly bent on ruin, before our eyes, why should we not explore
this secret?

We were the more inclined to this course because of a natural loyalty to the South which the events of the nineteen-twenties had
warmed and quickened. This was our first and most enduring point of
agreement. That loyalty had both combative and sentimental aspects,
I am sure. We were and are devoted to the South in spite of its defects, because it is our country, as our mother is our mother. But we
have never been in the false and uncritical position attributed to us
by some interpreters, of invariably preferring Southern things merely
because they are Southern. For the record let it be noted that no more
drastic criticisms of Southern life and affairs, past and present, can
be found than in some of the books and essays of Owsley and Tate;
and they, with Wade and others, have on occasion been denounced by
Southern organizations for their "disloyalty." We never believed that
one could be a good Southerner by simply drinking mint-juleps or by
remarking sententiously on the admirable forbearance of Lee after
Appomattox.

Such were our guiding motives. The search for Southern principles
was a more deliberate affair, and doubtless had a good deal in it of
that rationalization which is so often condemned and so generally indulged in. I am sure that at first we did not do much thinking in
strictly economic terms. Uppermost in our minds was our feeling of
intense disgust with the spiritual disorder of modern life—its destruction of human integrity and its lack of purpose; and, with this, we had
a decided sense of impending fatality. We wanted a life which through
its own conditions and purposefulness would engender naturally
(rather than by artificial stimulation), order, leisure, character, stability, and that would also, in the larger sense, be aesthetically enjoy-

able. What history told us of the South, what we knew of it by experience, now freshened by conscious analysis, and what we remembered of the dignity and strength of the generation that fought the Confederate War (for most of us were old enough to have received indelible impressions from survivors who never in anything but a military sense surrendered)—all this drove us straight to the South and its tradition. The good life we sought was once embodied here, and it lingered yet. Even in its seeming decline it contrasted sharply with the mode of life that we feared and disliked. The pertinent essays and reviews which we wrote before the appearance of *I'll Take My Stand* all had this central theme. Readers who wish to look for them will find them in *Harper's Magazine*, *The Forum*, the *Sewanee Review*, the *Nation*, the *New Republic*, the *Mississippi Valley Historical Review*, and elsewhere.

As we thought and talked further, we realized that the good life of the Old South, in its best period, and the life of our own South so far as it was still characteristic, was not to be separated from the agrarian tradition which was and is its foundation. By this route we came at last to economics and so found ourselves at odds with the prevailing schools of economic thought. These held that economics determines life and set up an abstract economic existence as the governor of man's effort. We believed that life determines economics, or ought to do so, and that economics is no more than an instrument, around the use of which should gather many more motives than economic ones. The evil of industrial economics was that it squeezed all human motives into one narrow channel and then looked for humanitarian means to repair the injury. The virtue of the Southern agrarian tradition was that it mixed up a great many motives with the economic motive, thus enriching it and reducing it to a proper subordination.

Therefore the agrarian tradition was necessarily defined as "a way of life" from which originated, among other things, an economy. In *I'll Take My Stand* we did not enlarge upon the technical features of the economy, which could wait for a later description, but we treated other features of the Southern tradition at elaborate length and in broad contrast with the hostile industrial conceptions. The times seemed to call for just this emphasis, but I can see now that it puzzled our critics, who had somehow learned to think of "agrarian" in the strictly occupational terms used by newspapers and professional economists. Though it undoubtedly took too much for granted in our readers, the definition was sufficient for our immediate purposes. To us it signified a complete order of society based ultimately upon the land. It presupposed several kinds of farmers and endless varieties of other occupations. The elements of such a society had always existed in the South. They must now be used and improved upon if people were to remain their own masters and avoid the consequences of an industrial order which we could already see was headed toward communism or fascism.

The large-scale plantation had been an important part of the older Southern life, but we were rather critical of the plantation, both because we felt its rôle had been over-emphasized and sentimentalized, and because we were interested in correcting, for the modern South, the abuses of the plantation system. We thought the rôle of the small farmer, or yeoman farmer, had been very much underestimated. We were concerned with the fate of the tenant farmer, with rural towns and communities, and with their importance in setting the tone of Southern life, even in the cities. We wished that the greatest possible number of people might enjoy the integrity and independence that would come with living upon their own land. Therefore we tended to push the large plantation into the background of consideration and to argue the case of the yeoman farmer. In this we followed Jefferson; but where the political rôle of the South was concerned we followed Calhoun, for it was the obvious, if regrettable, duty of the South to continue to defend itself against an aggressive, exploiting North.

Yet undeniable as our nostalgia for old times may have been—and quite justified—we had no intention of drawing a mellow and pretty picture of an idealized past. We leaned rather far in the other direction. Certainly Lytle's essay, "The Hind Tit," was aimed to show the merits of an agrarian life, even in its roughest and most backwoodsy state. We were determined, furthermore, to make the broadest possible application of the general theory, and therefore we planned and secured essays that discussed religion, education, manners, the theory of progress, the race problem, the historical background, the arts, the problem of the college graduate. Only one of the essays dealt with economics specifically. One essay outlined the general argument of the book, and like several of the other essays included a close negative analysis of industrialism, which we took pains to define rather carefully. We did not, of course, mean that the term industrialism should include any and every form of industry and every conceivable use of machines; we meant giant industrialism, as a force dominating every human activity: as the book says, "the decision of society to invest its economic resources in the applied sciences."

From the outset we had to deal with the problem of who the contributors ought to be. This finally resolved itself into the problem of who could be trusted to approach the issues as we saw them. A few of us, at Nashville, had enjoyed the benefits of long friendship and much discussion. We knew each other's minds, but we needed help. A memorandum in my file indicates that we planned the volume to be "deliberately partisan" to an extent which would exclude certain kinds of contributors: "sentimental conservatives whose sectionalism is of an extreme type" and "progressives whose liberalism is of an 'uplift' type". My note further says: "The volume will emphasize trans-Appalachian Southern thought and will therefore have a minority of contributors (if any at all) from the Atlantic states". But the names of possible contributors as recorded in this prospectus suggest how catholic our intention, or how great our innocence of mind, was in those days. Besides some names of the actual contributors, it includes the following: William E. Dodd, Broadus Mitchell, Newbell Niles Puckett, W. W. Alexander, Julia Peterkin, G. B. Winton, Grover Hall, Louis Jaffee, Julian Harris, Judge Finis Garrett, Chancellor James H. Kirkland. To these were later added the names of Gerald Johnson, Stringfellow Barr, John Peale Bishop. But of the persons named only two were actually solicited—Gerald Johnson and Stringfellow Barr; and both declined, Mr. Johnson with a curt jocular quip, Mr. Barr after a friendly exchange of correspondence which seemed at first to indicate his adherence.

Perhaps these rebuffs discouraged us from a wider solicitation. At any rate the contributors finally agreed upon came into the book largely because, by reason of close acquaintance, this or that person felt they could be counted on and could presume to approach them. Even then, for the sake of unity, we felt obliged to draw up the "Statement of Principles" printed as an introduction. Each contributor was asked to approve these principles and to offer suggestions of his own. The "statement" was revised several times. Nearly all of the contributors had something to suggest, and most of the suggestions were duly embodied. Finally, it represented composite opinion, arrived at after much trouble. The actual phrasing was the work of Ransom, except for some passages and sentences here and there. I remember one last-minute change of wording. The second paragraph originally began: "Nobody now proposes for the South, or for any other community in this country, an independent political destiny. That idea was finished in 1865." The latter sentence was changed to read, "That idea *is thought to have been* finished in 1865."

There was no editor in the usual sense; the book was a joint undertaking. However, some of us at Nashville acted as an informal steering committee and were obliged to hold many consultations more or less editorial. One hotly argued editorial difficulty arose not long before the book was scheduled to appear. Tate, Warren, and Lytle held that the title ought to be changed from *I'll Take My Stand* to *A Tract Against Communism*. Over against this suggestion, which had good reason in it, was the embarrassing fact that the book was practically ready for issue. The following extract from a letter by Tate, written immediately after this incident, is prophetic of what was in store for us: "It is over now. Your title triumphs. And I observe that Alexander [of the Nashville *Tennessean*] today on the basis of the title defines our aims as an 'agrarian revival' and reduces our real aims to nonsense. These are, of course, an agrarian revival in the full sense, but by not making our appeal through the title to ideas, we are at the mercy of all the Alexanders—for they need only to draw portraits of us plowing or cleaning the spring to make hash of us before we get a hearing."

Tate was exactly right as to what would happen, though he now says: "It would have happened anyway." In the contentious months that followed, when we argued with all objectors who were worth arguing with, such portraits or far worse ones were drawn. We had virtually dared our contemporaries to debate with us the question, then more or less tabooed, of whether the new industrialism was as good for the South as was claimed. With due allowance for various friendly receptions and a generous allotment of newspaper space which certainly gave us a hearing of a sort, it seems worth while to record a few samples of the raillery, not always good-humoured, with which our contemporaries greeted us. They begged to remind us of ox-carts and outdoor privies, and inquired whether we ever used porcelain bathtubs. If we admired agrarianism, what were we doing in libraries, and why were not out gee-hawing? Had we ever tried to "make money" on a farm? Did we want to "turn the clock back" and retreat into "a past that never was"?

The Chattanooga *News*, although it complimented us with a series of very lengthy editorials, dubbed us "the Young Confederates," smiled indulgently over our "delightful economic absurdities," and said: "This quixotic tilting of literary lances against industrialization smacks of the counsel of despair." The Macon *Telegraph*, famous liberal newspaper that carries on its masthead a quotation from Mill's "Essay on Liberty," tore into the book, even before it was published, with all the savagery of the Chicago *Tribune*'s best South-baiting editorials. Under the sarcastic title, "Lee, We Are Here!" the *Telegraph* began its insinuations thus: "One of the strangest groups to flourish in the South is the Neo-Confederates. This socially reactionary band does not come out of Atlanta—hatch of the Ku Klux Klan and the Supreme Kingdom—but appears to have its headquarters in Nashville." Later, with the book in hand, the *Telegraph* represented it as "a nostalgia cult owning a basis no more serious than sentiment," "an amusing patter-song," "a high spot in the year's hilarity." The New Orleans *Tribune* quoted with avowed relish some phrases which the New York *Times* had editorially applied to the book: "a boy's Froissart of tales," "twelve Canutes," worn-out romanticism."

A few critics, but only a very few, were more serious-minded and friendly. Some of these, oddly enough, were Eastern critics, who had lived at close quarters with industrialism and learned to dislike it; and in the end an Eastern magazine, THE AMERICAN REVIEW, gave us both understanding and hospitality of a sort we have never received, for example, from the *Virginia Quarterly Review*. And among Southern critics, it was a notable fact that our most consistent newspaper support came from Birmingham, the South's most highly industrialized city; from John Temple Graves II, of the Birmingham *News*.

Since we are not thin-skinned, we have managed to survive a curious notoriety of the sort that tempts friends to smile askance and tap their foreheads significantly. But our publishers practically dropped the book, no sooner than it was issued.

To the more sober charge that the agrarian proposals were not accompanied by a specific programme we have not always been disposed to give heed. We had not attempted to frame any positive set-up for industry under an agrarian economy, and even our programme for the farm was not much particularized in the book itself. To an eminent and friendly Tennessean, who deprecated our lack of a political programme, one of us answered that we represented "a body of principles looking for a party," and he was thereupon invited to run for Governor on an agrarian ticket. The truth is that *I'll Take My Stand* was by necessity a general study, preliminary to a specific application which we hoped the times would permit us, with others, to work out slowly and critically. The emergencies of 1930 and later years made such deliberate procedure impossible. But even when the book was in press we should have been pleased to add the very specific proposals which were, in fact, made public during the debates sponsored by various newspapers and educational institutions. Ransom, for example, through 1930 and 1931 argued for a kind of subsistence farming (hardly of the later Rooseveltian model) and for government policies which would bring about a wide distribution of owned land. He has later developed these proposals in magazine articles and pamphlets. In fact most of the contributors, through whatever media have been open to them, in recent years have pushed the principles of agrarianism far beyond the point represented in *I'll Take My Stand* and have made proposals about as specific as could be expected from men who do not have the good fortune to be members of Congress or of the Brain Trust. These may be viewed as a substitute, however inadequate, for a second volume of *I'll Take My Stand*, which through causes beyond our control we have not been able to publish.

Since my purpose here is expository rather than argumentative, I will do no more than indicate the direction of agrarian proposals. Most of them have been fully stated by Frank Owsley in his recent article, "The Pillars of Agrarianism" (THE AMERICAN REVIEW, March 1935). We consider the rehabilitation of the farmer as of first importance to the South, the basis of all good remedial procedure; and we therefore favour a definite policy of land conservation, land distribution, land ownership. At the risk of appearing socialistic to the ignorant, we favour legislation that will deprive the giant corporation of its privilege of irresponsibility, and that will control or prevent the socially harmful use of labour-saving (or labour-evicting) machinery. We advocate the encouragement of handicrafts, or of modified handicrafts with machine tools. In this connection, we believe that the only kind of new industry the South can now afford to encourage is the small industry which produces fine goods involving craftsmanship and art. We oppose the introduction of "mass-producing" industries that turn out coarse goods and cheap gadgets. We favour the diversion of public and private moneys from productive to non-productive uses—as for example to the arts—that over-accumulation of invested capital

may be forestalled. We hold very strongly for a revision of our political framework that will permit regional governments to function adequately; and that will enable the national government to deal sensibly
with issues in which the interests of regions are irreconcilable, or prevent the kind of regional exploitation, disguised as paternalism, now
being practised on the South. That is to say, we favour a true Feder-
alism and oppose Leviathanism, as ruinous to the South and eventually fatal to the nation.

It may be said of such proposals that they are not at all points peculiar to the Southern Agrarians, but are held by persons of various
bias, some of whom may lean to an industrial point of view. I am
sure this observation would be correct. The so-called Agrarians are not
a neatly organized band of conspirators. They are individuals united
in a common concern but differing among themselves as to ways and
means. They hope that their concern for the South, and to some extent their approach to Southern problems, is shared by many persons.
They are conscious that many other minds than theirs are busy with
these problems. They would be glad, as the book states, to be counted
as members of a national agrarian movement.

Nevertheless, it is fair to emphasize at least two points of fundamental difference between the agrarian approach and others. We are
interested in a way of life that will restore economics, among other
things, rather than in an economics that promises merely to restore
bare security, on hazardous terms, while leaving untouched the deep
corruptions that render the security hardly capable of being enjoyed
or nobly used. For this reason we are obliged to regard the Roosevelt
Administration with a mixture of approval and distrust, for its approach, to the Southern situation especially, is too much of the latter
order. At times President Roosevelt and his advisers seem to be governed by only two motives: the economic and the humanitarian. They
propose to repair our faltering economic system and to guarantee a
modicum of comfort to the human casualties of our false way of life.
But they are doing nothing to repair the false way of life. Rather they
seem to want to crystallize it in all its falsity. We believe that no
permanent solution of our troubles can be found in that way. Complication will be heaped upon complication, until we shall be destroyed in the end from sheer moral impotence. But that is hard to
explain to people who insist in believing that labour can be benefited
only by the invention of machinery and the promotion of labour un-
ions, or who do not admit that the same human will which builds
skyscrapers can also abandon them.

The second point of difference is one on which we would make few
concessions, or none. Undoubtedly the South is a part of modern economy. Who could deny that? We should nevertheless insist that the
South still has liberty to determine what its rôle will be with relation
to that economy; and that that liberty ought not to be abrogated by

the South or usurped by others. Unless the South can retain that power of decision, it can retain little of what may be, in any good sense, Southern. Above all, it cannot keep its self-respect or ever have the confidence in its own genius which is the greatest moral necessity of a living people.

VI. Politics Is the Enemy

IT MAY SEEM to be an overly sweeping generalization, but I think that it is basically true that cultural conservatives do not really understand political activity. Like their beloved Jefferson, they are against political activity, and thus they find it difficult to use or to analyze clearly. Their first instinct when given power is to shrink government activity, in effect to abdicate responsibility, to stall, temporize, and hope that private solutions to problems can be found before things get so serious that the government can no longer ignore them. One obvious result of this stance is that cultural conservatives have written very little directly concerning politics—indeed, after the great outburst of conservative political thought between 1770 and 1810, very little conservative political science of any kind has appeared, and although occasional partisans appear to praise the writings of a John C. Calhoun or a William Graham Sumner, no one pays serious attention for very long except for historical reasons.

This pattern is especially striking in the work of cultural conservatives during the first half of the twentieth century. Many of them did write a large number of words on political subjects, often tinged with sarcasm, cynicism, and even hatred. They often made excellent debating points in the process, but they were generally and perhaps rightly ignored by most Americans because what they said often had little bearing on the actual daily processes of government. Conservatism had little to say to politicians that they could use in framing legislation. All it seemed to counsel was a sweeping No! to the proposals of others. Even when this advice was sound, it had little political appeal and thus could not have much impact. Whether they liked it or not, the conservatives lived in a democracy and had to take public opinion and voting behavior into account if they ever wanted to "matter."

The first selection in this section illustrates these contentions. As Irving Babbitt argues in his opening paragraph, "when studied with any degree of thoroughness, the economic problem will be found to run into the political problem, the political problem in turn into the philosophical problem, and the philosophical problem itself to be almost indissolubly bound up at last with the religious problem." He then quickly slides into his usual stance as an opponent of modernism and naturalism, and much of the rest of the book reads like a study of the political implications of comparative literary study. One can scarcely imagine what a politician, or even a professor of government, could ever do with it.

21. Democracy and Leadership

By Irving Babbitt

According to Mr. Lloyd George, the future will be even more exclusively taken up than is the present with the economic problem, especially with the relations between capital and labor. In that case, one is tempted to reply, the future will be very superficial. When studied with any degree of thoroughness, the economic problem will be found to run into the political problem, the political problem in turn into the philosophical problem, and the philosophical problem itself to be almost indissolubly bound up at last with the religious problem. This book is only one of a series in which I have been trying to bring out these deeper implications of the modern movement. Though devoted to different topics, the volumes of the series are yet bound together by their common preoccupation with the naturalistic trend, which goes back in some of its main aspects at least as far as the Renaissance, but which won its decisive triumphs over tradition in the eighteenth century. Among the men of the eighteenth century who prepared the way for the world in which we are now living I have, here as elsewhere in my writing, given a preëminent place to Rousseau. It is hard for any one who has investigated the facts to deny him this preëminence, even though one should not go so far as to say with Lord Acton that "Rousseau produced more effect with his pen than Aristotle, or Cicero, or Saint Augustine, or Saint Thomas Aquinas, or any other man who ever lived."[1] The great distinction of Rousseau in the history of thought, if my own analysis be correct, is that he gave the wrong answers to the right questions. It is no small distinction even to have asked the right questions.

Rousseau has at all events suggested to me the terms in which I have treated my present topic. He is easily first among the theorists of radical democracy. He is also the most eminent of those who have attacked civilization. Moreover, he has brought his advocacy of democracy and his attack upon civilization into a definite relationship with one another. Herein he seems to go deeper than those who relate democracy, not to the question of civilization versus barbarism, but to the question of progress versus reaction. For why

Note: Originally published in *Democracy and Leaderhip* (Boston: Houghton Mifflin, 1924), pp. 1–4, 5–7, 22–26, 200–207. Reprinted by permission of Edward S. Babbitt.

1. See *Letters of Lord Acton to Mary Gladstone*, p. xii.

should men progress unless it can be shown that they are progressing toward civilization; or of what avail, again, is progress if barbarism is, as Rousseau affirms, more felicitous? If we thought
clearly enough, we should probably dismiss as somewhat old-
fashioned, as a mere survivor of the nineteenth century, the man who
puts his primary emphasis on the contrast between the progressive
and the reactionary, and turn our attention to the more essential contrast between the civilized man and the barbarian. The man of the
nineteenth century was indeed wont to take for granted that the type
of progress he sought to promote was a progress towards civilization.
Some persons began to have doubts on this point even before the War,
others had their doubts awakened by the War itself, and still others
have been made doubtful by the peace. An age that thought it was
progressing towards a "far-off divine event," and turned out instead
to be progressing towards Armageddon, suffered, one cannot help sur-
mising, from some fundamental confusion in its notions of progress.
One may be aided in detecting the nature of this confusion by the
Emersonian distinction of which I have made considerable use in my
previous writing—the distinction, namely, between a "law for man"
and a "law for thing." The special praise that Confucius bestowed on
his favorite disciple was that he was "always progressing and never
came to a standstill." What Confucius plainly had in mind was progress according to the human law. What the man of the nineteenth
century meant as a rule by the term was no less plainly material progress. He seems to have assumed, so far as he gave the subject any
thought at all, that moral progress would issue almost automatically
from material progress. In view of the duality of human experience,
the whole question is, however, vastly more complex than the ordinary
progressive has ever suspected. Progress according to the natural law
must, if it is to make for civilization, be subordinated to some adequate end; and the natural law does not in itself supply this end. As a
result of the neglect of this truth, we have the type of man who deems
himself progressive and is yet pursuing power and speed for their own
sake, the man who does not care where he is going, as some one has
put it, provided only he can go there faster and faster.

If progress and civilization do not mean more than this, one might
be justified in sharing Rousseau's predilection for barbarism. The reason he gives for preferring the barbaric to the civilized state is in itself
extremely weighty: the barbaric state is, he maintains, the more fraternal. The fraternal spirit is the fine flower, not merely of genuine
philosophy, but of genuine religion. One should be ready to make almost any sacrifice in order to attain it. My endeavor has, however,
been to show that Rousseau's fraternity is only a sentimental dream.
The psychic impossibility involved in this dream is obvious, one may
even say, glaring. For example, Walt Whitman, one of the chief of
Rousseau's American followers, preaches universal brotherhood

among men each one of whom is, like himself, to "permit to speak at every hazard, Nature without check with original energy";[2] in other words, Whitman proposes to base brotherhood, a religious virtue, on expansive appetite.

. . . .

In any case the assertion that one attains to more abundant life (in the religious sense) by getting rid of the don'ts sums up clearly, even though in an extreme form, the side of the modern movement with which I am taking issue. This book in particular is devoted to the most unpopular of all tasks—a defence of the veto power. Not the least singular feature of the singular epoch in which we are living is that the very persons who are least willing to hear about the veto power are likewise the persons who are most certain that they stand for the virtues that depend upon its exercise—for example, peace and brotherhood. As against the expansionists of every kind, I do not hesitate to affirm that what is specifically human in man and ultimately divine is a certain quality of will, a will that is felt in its relation to his ordinary self as a will to refrain. The affirmation of this quality of will is nothing new: it is implied in the Pauline opposition between a law of the spirit and a law of the members. In general, the primacy accorded to will over intellect is Oriental. The idea of humility, the idea that man needs to defer to a higher will, came into Europe with an Oriental religion, Christianity. This idea has been losing ground in almost exact ratio to the decline of Christianity. Inasmuch as the recognition of the supremacy of will seems to me imperative in any wise view of life, I side in important respects with the Christian against those who have in the Occident, whether in ancient or modern times, inclined to give the first place either to the intellect or the emotions. I differ from the Christian, however, in that my interest in the higher will and the power of veto it exercises over man's expansive desires is humanistic rather than religious. I am concerned, in other words, less with the meditation in which true religion always culminates, than in the mediation or observance of the law of measure that should govern man in his secular relations. Moreover, I am for coming at my humanism in a positive and critical rather than in a merely traditional manner. To this extent I am with the naturalists, who have from the start been rejecting outer authority in favor of the immediate and experimental. One should have only respect for the man of science in so far as he deals in this critical fashion with the natural law—and no small part of human nature itself comes under the natural law. The error begins when an attempt is made to extend this law to cover the whole of human nature. This is to deny not merely outer authority, but something that is a matter of immediate experience, the opposition, namely, of which the individual is conscious in himself, between

2. See *Song of Myself*.

a law of the spirit and a law of the members. Deny or dissimulate
this opposition and the inner life tends in the same measure to disappear. Carlyle's contrast between the Rousseauism of the French Revolution and true Christianity is also the contrast between humanitarianism in general, in either its sentimental or its utilitarian form, and
any doctrine that affirms the higher will. "Alas, no, M. Roux!" Carlyle
exclaims. "A Gospel of Brotherhood not according to any of the four
old Evangelists and calling on men to repent, and amend *each his
own* wicked existence, that they might be saved; but a Gospel rather,
as we often hint, according to a new fifth Evangelist Jean-Jacques,
calling on men to amend *each the whole world's* wicked existence and
be saved by making the Constitution. A thing different and distant
toto coelo."

.   .   .   .

I wish also to say a few words at the outset regarding certain possible misapprehensions of my method. The most serious of these misapprehensions may arise if one looks either in this volume or in the
previous volumes of the series (with the partial exception of "The
Masters of Modern French Criticism") for rounded estimates of individuals. I have not attempted such estimates. Still less have I attempted rounded estimates of historical epochs—for example, of the nineteenth century. It is even less sensible, perhaps to indict a whole century than it is, according to Burke, to indict a whole people. I am at-
tacking, not the nineteenth century in general, but the naturalistic
nineteenth century and its prolongation into the twentieth century,
along with the tendencies in the previous centuries, from the Renaissance down, that prepared the way for naturalism. My treatment of
this whole naturalistic trend has seemed, even to critics who are not
altogether unfriendly, to be negative, extreme, and one-sided. I hope
I may be pardoned if I reply briefly to each of these three charges.

As to the charge that my treatment of naturalism is one-sided, there
is a sense, it must be admitted, in which it is not only one-sided, but
one-sided to the last degree. There is, however, a humanistic intention
even in the one-sidedness. I dwell persistently on the aspect of human
nature that the naturalists have no less persistently neglected in the
hope that the way may thus be opened for a more balanced view.
Moreover, what the naturalists have neglected is not something that
is on the fringe or outer rim of human experience, but something, on
the contrary, that is very central. The naturalistic effort during the
past century or more has resulted in an immense and bewildering
peripheral enrichment of life—in short, in what we are still glorifying
under the name of progress. I have no quarrel with this type of progress in itself, I merely maintain that no amount of peripheral enrichment of life can atone for any lack at the centre. Furthermore, though
I assail the naturalists for what seems to me a vital oversight, I have,
let me repeat, at least one trait in common with them—I desire to be

experimental. I seek to follow out the actual consequences of this oversight, to deal with it, not abstractly, but in its fruits. If certain readers have persisted in seeing in my books something that I myself have not sought to put there, namely, rounded estimates of individuals and historic epochs, the misapprehension has no doubt arisen from the very abundance of my concrete illustrations.

As to the charge that I am negative, I have already said that the element in man that has been overlooked by naturalistic psychology is felt in relation to his ordinary self negatively. If instead of taking the point of view of one's ordinary self, one heeds the admonitions of the inner monitor, the result is two of the most positive of all things: character and happiness. This is the great paradox of life itself. For being negative in this sense I am not in the least apologetic. There is, however, another sense in which I may seem negative and about this I feel somewhat differently. The type of criticism that prevailed about the beginning of the nineteenth century proposed to substitute the "fruitful criticism of beauties for the barren criticism of faults." I may be accused of reversing too sharply this maxim even by some who admit that the proper remedy for the lax appreciativeness of the modern movement is a criticism that displays a tonic astringency. I am constantly calling attention to the defects of certain eminent personalities, it may be urged, and at the same time have little or nothing to say of their virtues. My method is even in this respect, I believe, legitimate, provided that it be properly understood, though I myself cannot help regretting that it should make me appear so constantly unamiable.

The charge that I am extreme touches me even more nearly than the charge that I am negative and one-sided; for I aim to be a humanist and the essence of humanism is moderation. There is, however, much confusion on the subject of moderation. A man's moderation is measured by his success in mediating between some sound general principle and the infinitely various and shifting circumstances of actual life. The man who is thus rightly mediatory attains to one of the most precious of virtues—urbanity; though one must add that probably no virtue has been more frequently counterfeited. When an intellectually and spiritually indolent person has to choose between two conflicting views he often decides to "split the difference" between them; but he may be splitting the difference between truth and error, or between two errors. In any case, he must dispose of the question of truth or error before he can properly begin to mediate at all. Otherwise he will run the risk of resembling the English statesman of whom it was said that he never deviated from the straight and narrow path between right and wrong. Some of the casuists whom Pascal attacked had managed to assume a moderate attitude towards murder! One may fancy oneself urbane when in reality one is in danger of being numbered with the immense multitude that Dante saw in the vestibule of Hell—the multitude of those who are equally "displeasing to God and to the enemies of God." To be sure, it is not always easy in any particular instance to distinguish between the humanist and the mere Laodicean. Thus Luther denounced Erasmus as a Laodicean, whereas to us he seems rather to have shown real poise and urbanity in his dealings with the religious and other extremists of his time.

At all events the differences of doctrine I debate in the following pages are of a primary nature and so not subject to mediation. Between the man who puts his main emphasis on the inner life of the individual and the man who puts this emphasis on something else— for example, the progress and service of humanity—the opposition is one of first principles. The question I raise, therefore, is not whether one should be a moderate humanitarian, but whether one should be a humanitarian at all. In general I commit myself to the position that we are living in a world that in certain important respects has gone wrong on first principles; which will be found to be only another way of saying that we are living in a world that has been betrayed by its leaders. On the appearance of leaders who have recovered in some form the truths of the inner life and repudiated the errors of naturalism may depend the very survival of Western civilization. The truths of the inner life may be proclaimed in various forms, religious and humanistic, and have actually been so proclaimed in the past and justified in each case by their fruits in life and conduct. It is because I am unable to discover these truths in any form in the philosophies now fashionable that I have been led to prefer to the wisdom of the age the wisdom of the ages.

.   .   .   .

Perhaps, indeed, the meddling and the muddling are not quite so widespread as one is at times tempted to suppose. There are probably still a few persons left who realize the importance of minding their own business, even though not in the full Platonic or Confucian sense. There is probably an element of exaggeration in a recent assertion that to the question, "Am I my brother's keeper?" the whole American people had replied in an "ecstatic affirmative." One should note in passing the intolerable dilution of the principle of obligation that is implied in extending to men indiscriminately what one owes to one's own brother. At all events, no small issues are involved in the question whether one should start with an expansive eagerness to do something for humanity or with loyalty to one's self. There may be something after all in the Confucian idea that if a man only sets himself right, the rightness will extend to his family first of all, and finally in widening circles to the whole community.

One's definition of work and of justice in terms of work will be found to be inseparably bound up with one's definition of liberty. The only true freedom is freedom to work. All the evidence goes to show that there is no safety in the nature of things for the idler and that the most perilous of all forms of idling is spiritual idling. The failure to take account of the subtler forms of working is what vitiates the attempts of the utilitarian to define liberty—for example, the attempt of J. S. Mill. If a man is only careful not to injure his fellow men, he should then, according to Mill, be free to cultivate his idiosyncrasy. One cannot grant in the first place that any such sharp division between the altruistic and the self-regarding elements in human nature is possible; and even if one did grant it, one should have to insist that the self-regarding virtues are the most important even from the point of view of society; for it is only by the exercise of these virtues that one becomes exemplary and so, as I have tried to show, truly helpful to others.

If society should in its own interests encourage those who work with their minds as compared with those who work with their hands, how much more should it give recognition to those who are engaged in a genuinely ethical working. It is in fact the quality of a man's work that should determine his place in the hierarchy that every civilized society requires. In short, from the positive point of view, work is the only justification of aristocracy. "By work," says Buddha, "a man is noble, by work he is an outcast."[3] The principle, though sound, is not, one must confess, altogether easy to apply. Though justice require that every man receive according to the quantity and quality of his work, there is in this competition a manifest inequality from the start. One man has an innate capacity that another cannot acquire by any amount of effort. God, according to the Platonic myth, has mingled lead with the nature of some and with the nature of others silver and gold. Stress unduly the initial differences between men and one will tend to fall into some system of caste, as Plato himself tends to do, or else one will incline to fatalism, whether naturalistic or predestinarian. On the other hand, deny these differences in favor of some equalitarian theory and one runs counter to the most palpable facts. Genuine justice seems to demand that men should be judged, not by their intentions or their endeavors, but by their actual performance; that in short the natural aristocrat, as Burke terms him, should receive his due reward, whether one attribute his superiority, with the man of science, to heredity, or, with the Christian, to grace, or, with the Buddhist, to his past working.

One's view of work and of the rewards that it deserves will determine necessarily one's attitude towards property. From the point of view of civilization, it is of the highest moment that certain individuals should in every community be relieved from the necessity of working with their hands in order that they may engage in the higher forms of working and so qualify for leadership. If the civilization is to be genuine, it must have men of leisure in the full Aristotelian sense. Those who in any particular community are allowed to enjoy property that is not the fruit of their own outer and visible toil cannot, therefore, afford to be idlers and parasites. An aristocratic or leading class,

3. *Sutta-Nipâta,* v. 135.

however the aristocratic principle is conceived, must, if it hopes in the long run to preserve its property and privileges, be in some degree exemplary. It is only too clear that the members of the French aristocracy of the Old Régime failed, in spite of many honorable exceptions, to measure up to this test. Some have argued from the revelations of recent writers like Colonel Repington and Mrs. Asquith that the English aristocracy is also growing degenerate. People will not consent in the long run to look up to those who are not themselves looking up to something higher than their ordinary selves. A leading class that has become Epicurean and self-indulgent is lost. Above all it cannot afford to give the first place to material goods. One may, indeed, lay down the principle that, if property as a means to an end is the necessary basis of civilization, property as an end in itself is materialism. In view of the natural insatiableness of the human spirit, no example is more necessary than that of the man who is setting limits to his desire for worldly possessions. The only remedy for economic inequality, as Aristotle says, is "to train the nobler sort of natures not to desire more";[4] this remedy is not in mechanical schemes for dividing up property; "for it is not the possessions but the desires of mankind which require to be equalized."[5] The equalization of desire in the Aristotelian sense requires on the part of individuals a genuinely ethical or humanistic working. To proclaim equality on some basis that requires no such working will result ironically. For example, this country committed itself in the Declaration of Independence to the doctrine of natural equality. The type of individualism that was thus encouraged has led to monstrous inequalities and, with the decline of traditional standards, to the rise of a raw plutocracy. A man who amasses a billion dollars is scarcely exemplary in the Aristotelian sense, even though he then proceeds to lay out half a billion upon philanthropy. The remedy for such a failure of the man at the top to curb his desires does not lie, as the agitator would have us believe, in inflaming the desires of the man at the bottom; nor again in substituting for real justice some phantasmagoria of social justice. As a result of such a substitution, one will presently be turning from the punishment of the individual offender to an attack on the institution of property itself; and a war on capital will speedily degenerate, as it always has in the past, into a war on thrift and industry in favor of laziness and incompetence, and finally into schemes of confiscation that profess to be idealistic and are in fact subversive of common honesty. Above all, social justice is likely to be unsound in its partial or total suppression of competition. Without competition it is impossible that the ends of true justice should be fulfilled—namely, that every man should receive according to his works. The principle of competition is, as Hesiod pointed out long ago, built into the very roots of the

4. *Politics*, 1267b.
5. *Ibid.*, 1266b.

world;[6] there is something in the nature of things that calls for a real
victory and a real defeat. Competition is necessary to rouse man from
his native indolence; without it life loses its zest and savor. Only, as
Hesiod goes on to say, there are two types of competition—the one that
leads to bloody war and the other that is the mother of enterprise and
high achievement. He does not perhaps make as clear as he might how
one may have the sound rivalry and, at the same time, avoid the type
that degenerates into pernicious strife. But surely the reply to this question is found in such sentences of Aristotle as those I have just been
quoting. The remedy for the evils of competition is found in the moderation and magnanimity of the strong and the successful, and not in
any sickly sentimentalizing over the lot of the underdog. The mood
of unrest and insurgency is so rife to-day as to suggest that our leaders, instead of thus controlling themselves, are guilty of an extreme
psychic unrestraint.

One should note a certain confusion on the part of the advocates of
social justice as to the nature of capital. Dr. Johnson is reported to
have said at the sale of Thrale's brewery: "We are not here to sell a
parcel of boilers and vats, but the potentiality of growing rich beyond
the dreams of avarice." The realizing of the potentiality depended, of
course, on the ability of the management, and this ability was not
only a part, but the essential part of the capital of the brewery. It is
being assumed at present that the capital invested in our railways may
be measured by what one may term their junk value. As a result of
this and similar fallacies, both the owners and managers of the railways have been so treated of recent years as to discourage enterprise
in this field of industry. It seems easy to convince the public that the
railways are suffering from watered stock when what they are really
suffering from is watered labor. If our apostles of service and social
justice have their way, that considerable portion of the savings of the
middle class that is now invested in the railways, either directly or indirectly through the insurance companies and savings banks, may
undergo partial or total confiscation.

Every form of social justice, indeed, tends to confiscation and confiscation, when practised on a large scale, undermines moral standards and, in so far, substitutes for real justice the law of cunning and
the law of force. To be on one's guard against these perils of social
justice, one needs that coöperation of keen analysis and imagination
that can alone produce genuine vision; whereas a great number of
persons are weak in analysis, and idyllic rather than ethical in their
imagining. Not being able, as a result, to get at underlying causes,
they are prone to doctor symptoms and to resort to what Burke calls
"tricking short-cuts, and little fallacious facilities." The apparent good
turns out to be evil in its secondary consequences, and the apparent
evil turns out to be the necessary condition of some good. Things often

6. See beginning of *Works and Days*.

change their aspect, not once but several times, when thus traced in their ultimate effects. The ordinary laboring man, for instance, may not be able to see that the "levy upon capital," for which he is urged to vote in the name of social justice, will finally recoil upon himself. It is not yet clear that it is going to be possible to combine universal suffrage with the degree of safety for the institution of property that genuine justice and genuine civilization both require. Taxation without representation was the main grievance of the American revolutionists; but that is precisely what an important section of the community has to submit to to-day. Can those who tax in the name of the sovereign people be counted on to tax more equitably than those who alleged the royal prerogative?

THE CONSERVATIVE *who had the largest audience during this period was probably H. L. Mencken, although his appeal to that audience was never primarily political. Mencken's political writing usually concentrated on the basic assumptions of liberal democracy and the cant that all too frequently went with them. For Mencken people simply were not equal in any meaningful sense, and the liberal assumption that they were led to the countless amusements and frustrations of American politics. Nock, Cram, and Babbitt frequently worked themselves up to high levels of indignation on this subject, as previous documents have demonstrated, but none of them really equaled the exuberant scorn which Mencken could generate during an election campaign.*

Yet even when he attempted more detached and serious writing, Mencken's work hardly rates as good political science. Too often, he settles for the assertion of opinion; he rarely conveys research, concrete proposals, or any sense of what should be possible for a good and decent government to do. If people are incompetent and politicians frauds, the fact remains that life must go on and government must function, and contempt is not an adequate program of action for a head of state. Mencken's frequently hilarious journalism is available in numerous reprints, and I have omitted it here. The selection below is reasonably typical of his more serious efforts, and with a few changes in language and tone it could have been written by several of the other men in this book.

22. Notes on Democracy

By Henry Louis Mencken

Democracy came into the Western World to the tune of sweet, soft music. There was, at the start, no harsh bawling from below; there was only a dulcet twittering from above. Democratic man thus began as an ideal being, full of ineffable virtues and romantic wrongs—in brief, as Rousseau's noble savage in smock and jerkin, brought out of the tropical wilds to shame the lords and masters of the civilized lands. The fact continues to have important consequences to this day. It remains impossible, as it was in the Eighteenth Century, to separate the democratic idea from the theory that there is a mystical merit, an esoteric and ineradicable rectitude, in the man at the bottom of the scale—that inferiority, by some strange magic, becomes a sort of superiority—nay, the superiority of superiorities. Everywhere on earth, save where the enlightenment of the modern age is confessedly in transient eclipse, the movement is toward the completer and more enamoured enfranchisement of the lower orders. Down there, one hears, lies a deep, illimitable reservoir of righteousness and wisdom, unpolluted by the corruption of privilege. What baffles statesmen is to be solved by the people, instantly and by a sort of seraphic intuition. Their yearnings are pure; they alone are capable of a perfect patriotism; in them is the only hope of peace and happiness on this lugubrious ball. The cure for the evils of democracy is more democracy!

This notion, as I hint, originated in the poetic fancy of gentlemen on the upper levels—sentimentalists who, observing to their distress that the ass was over-laden, proposed to reform transport by putting him into the cart. A stale Christian bilge ran through their veins, though many of them, as it happened, toyed with what is now called Modernism. They were the direct ancestors of the more saccharine Liberals of to-day, who yet mouth their tattered phrases and dream their preposterous dreams. I can find no record that these phrases, in the beginning, made much impression upon the actual objects of their rhetoric. Early democratic man seems to have given little thought to the democratic ideal, and less veneration. What he wanted was something concrete and highly materialistic—more to eat, less work, higher

Note: Originally published in *Notes on Democracy*, by H. L. Mencken (New York: Knopf, 1926), pp. 3–15, 99–106. Copyright © 1926 by Alfred A. Knopf, Inc., and renewed 1954 by H. L. Mencken. Reprinted by permission of Alfred A. Knopf, Inc.

wages, lower taxes. He had no apparent belief in the acroamatic virtue
of his own class, and certainly none in its capacity to rule. His aim
was not to exterminate the baron, but simply to bring the baron back
to a proper discharge of baronial business. When, by the wild shooting
that naturally accompanies all mob movements, the former end was
accidentally accomplished, and men out of the mob began to take on
baronial airs, the mob itself quickly showed its opinion of them by
butchering them deliberately and in earnest. Once the pikes were out,
indeed, it was a great deal more dangerous to be a tribune of the
people than to be an ornament of the old order. The more copiously
the blood gushed, the nearer that old order came to resurrection. The
Paris proletariat, having been misled into killing its King in 1793,
devoted the next two years to killing those who had misled it, and by
the middle of 1796 it had another King in fact, and in three years
more he was King *de jure*, with an attendant herd of barons, counts,
marquises and dukes, some of them new but most of them old, to
guard, symbolize and execute his sovereignty. And he and they were
immensely popular—so popular that half France leaped to suicide
that their glory might blind the world.

Meanwhile, of course, there had been a certain seeping down of
democratic theory from the metaphysicians to the mob—obscured by
the uproar, but still going on. Rhetoric, like a stealthy plague, was
doing its immemorial work. Where men were confronted by the harsh,
exigent realities of battle and pillage, as they were everywhere on the
Continent, it got into their veins only slowly, but where they had time
to listen to oratory, as in England and, above all, in America, it
fetched them more quickly. Eventually, as the world grew exhausted
and the wars passed, it began to make its effects felt everywhere.
Democratic man, contemplating himself, was suddenly warmed by
the spectacle. His condition had plainly improved. Once a slave, he
was now only a serf. Once condemned to silence, he was now free to
criticize his masters, and even to flout them, and the ordinances of
God with them. As he gained skill and fluency at that sombre and
fascinating art, he began to heave in wonder at his own merit. He was
not only, it appeared, free to praise and damn, challenge and remon-
strate; he was also gifted with a peculiar rectitude of thought and
will, and a high talent for ideas, particularly on the political plane. So
his wishes, in his mind, began to take on the dignity of legal rights,
and after a while, of intrinsic and natural rights, and by the same
token the wishes of his masters sank to the level of mere ignominious
lusts. By 1828 in America and by 1848 in Europe the doctrine had
arisen that all moral excellence, and with it all pure and unfettered
sagacity, resided in the inferior four-fifths of mankind. In 1867 a philosopher out of the gutter pushed that doctrine to its logical conclusion. He taught that the superior minority had no virtues at all, and
hence no rights at all—that the world belonged exclusively and absolutely to those who hewed its wood and drew its water. In less than

half a century he had more followers in the world, open and covert, than any other sophist since the age of the Apostles.

Since then, to be sure, there has been a considerable recession from that extreme position. The dictatorship of the proletariat, tried here and there, has turned out to be—if I may venture a prejudiced judgment—somewhat impracticable. Even the most advanced Liberals, observing the thing in being, have been moved to cough sadly behind their hands. But it would certainly be going beyond the facts to say that the underlying democratic dogma has been abandoned, or even appreciably overhauled. To the contrary, it is now more prosperous than ever before. The late war was fought in its name, and it was embraced with loud hosannas by all the defeated nations. Everywhere in Christendom it is now official, save in a few benighted lands where God is temporarily asleep. Everywhere its fundamental axioms are accepted: (a) that the great masses of men have an inalienable right, born of the very nature of things, to govern themselves, and (b) that they are competent to do it. Are they occasionally detected in gross and lamentable imbecilities? Then it is only because they are misinformed by those who would exploit them: the remedy is more education. Are they, at times, seen to be a trifle naughty, even swinish? Then it is only a natural reaction against the oppressions they suffer: the remedy is to deliver them. The central aim of all the Christian governments of to-day, in theory if not in fact, is to further their liberation, to augment their power, to drive ever larger and larger pipes into the great reservoir of their natural wisdom. That government is called good which responds most quickly and accurately to their desires and ideas. That is called bad which conditions their omnipotence and puts a question mark after their omniscience.

So much for the theory. It seems to me, and I shall here contend, that all the known facts lie flatly against it—that there is actually no more evidence for the wisdom of the inferior man, nor for his virtue, than there is for the notion that Friday is an unlucky day. There was, perhaps, some excuse for believing in these phantasms in the days when they were first heard of in the world, for it was then difficult to put them to the test, and what cannot be tried and disproved has always had a lascivious lure for illogical man. But now we know a great deal more about the content and character of the human mind than we used to know, both on high levels and on low levels, and what we have learned has pretty well disposed of the old belief in its congenital intuitions and inherent benevolences. It is, we discover, a function, at least mainly, of purely physical and chemical phenomena, and its development and operation are subject to precisely the same natural laws which govern the development and operation, say, of the human nose or lungs. There are minds which start out with a superior equipment, and proceed to high and arduous deeds; there are minds which never get any further than a sort of insensate sweating, like that of a kidney. We not only observe such differences; we also begin to chart them with more or less accuracy. Of one mind we may say with some confidence that it shows an extraordinary capacity for function and development—that its possessor, exposed to a suitable process of training, may be trusted to acquire the largest body of knowledge and the highest skill at ratiocination to which *Homo sapiens* is adapted. Of another we may say with the same confidence that its abilities are sharply limited—that no conceivable training can move it beyond a certain point. In other words, men differ inside their heads as they differ outside. There are men who are naturally intelligent and can learn, and there are men who are naturally stupid and cannot.

Here, of course, I flirt with the so-called intelligence tests, and so bring down upon my head that acrid bile which they have set to flowing. My plea in avoidance is that I have surely done my share of damning them: they aroused, when they were first heard of, my most brutish passions, for pedagogues had them in hand. But I can only say that time and experience have won me to them, for the evidence in favor of them slowly piles up, pedagogues or no pedagogues. In other words, they actually work. What they teach is borne out by immense accumulations of empiric corroboration. It is safe, nine times out of ten, to give them credence, and so it seems to me to be safe to generalize from them. Is it only a coincidence that their most frantic critics are the Liberals, which is to say, the only surviving honest believers in democracy? I think not. These Liberals, whatever their defects otherwise, are themselves capable of learning, and so they quickly mastered the fact that MM. Simon and Binet offered the most dangerous menace to their vapourings ever heard of since the collapse of the Holy Alliance. Their dudgeon followed. In two ways the tests give aid and comfort to their enemies. First, they provide a more or less scientific means of demonstrating the difference in natural intelligence between man and man—a difference noted ages ago by common observation, and held to be real by all men save democrats, at all times and everywhere. Second, they provide a rational scale for measuring it and a rational explanation of it. Intelligence is reduced to levels, and so given a reasonable precision of meaning. An intelligent man is one who is capable of taking in knowledge until the natural limits of the species are reached. A stupid man is one whose progress is arrested at some specific time and place before then. There thus appears in psychology—and the next instant in politics—the concept of the unteachable. Some men can learn almost indefinitely; their capacity goes on increasing until their bodies begin to wear out. Others stop in childhood, even in infancy. They reach, say, the mental age of ten or twelve, and then they develop no more. Physically, they become men, and sprout beards, political delusions, and the desire to propagate their kind. But mentally they remain on the level of schoolboys.

The fact here is challenged sharply by the democrats aforesaid, but

certainly not with evidence. Their objection to it is rather of a meta-
physical character, and involves gratuitous, transcendental assumptions as to what ought and what ought not to be true. They echo also,
of course, the caveats of other and less romantic critics, some of them
very ingenious; but always, when hard pressed, they fall back pathetically upon the argument that believing such things would be in
contempt of the dignity of man, made in God's image. Is this argument sound? Is it, indeed, new? I seem to have heard it long ago,
from the gentlemen of the sacred faculty. Don't they defend the rubbish of Genesis on the theory that rejecting it would leave the rabble
without faith, and that without faith it would be one with the brutes,
and very unhappy, and, what is worse, immoral? I leave such contentions to the frequenters of Little Bethel, and pause only to observe
that if the progress of the human race had depended upon them we'd
all believe in witches, ectoplasms and madstones to-day. Democracy,
alas, is also a form of theology, and shows all the immemorial stigmata. Confronted by uncomfortable facts, it invariably tries to dispose
of them by appeals to the highest sentiments of the human heart. An
anti-democrat is not merely mistaken; he is also wicked, and the more
plausible he is the more wicked he becomes. As I have said, the earliest of modern democrats were full of Christian juices. Their successors never get very far from Genesis i, 27. They are Fundamentalists
by instinct, however much they may pretend to a mellow scepticism.

One undoubted fact gives them a certain left-handed support,
though they are far too discreet to make use of it. I allude to the fact
that man on the lower levels, though he quickly reaches the limit of
his capacity for taking in actual knowledge, remains capable for a
long time thereafter of absorbing delusions. What is true daunts him,
but what is *not* true finds lodgment in his cranium with so little resistance that there is only a trifling emission of heat. I shall go back
to this singular and beautiful phenomenon later on. It lies at the heart
of what is called religion, and at the heart of all democratic politics
no less. The thinking of what Charles Richet calls *Homo stultus* is almost entirely in terms of palpable nonsense. He has a dreadful capacity for embracing and cherishing impostures. His history since the
first records is a history of successive victimizations—by priests, by
politicians, by all sorts and conditions of quacks. His heroes are always frauds. In all ages he has hated bitterly the men who were labouring most honestly and effectively for the progress of the race.
What such men teach is beyond his grasp. He believes in consequence
that it is unsound, immoral and of the devil.

.   .   .   .

I find myself quoting yet a third German: he is Professor Robert
Michels, the economist. The politician, he says, is the courtier of
democracy. A profound saying—perhaps more profound than the
professor, himself a democrat, realizes. For it was of the essence of

the courtier's art and mystery that he flattered his employer in order
to victimize him, yielded to him in order to rule him. The politician
under democracy does precisely the same thing. His business is never
what it pretends to be. Ostensibly he is an altruist devoted whole-
heartedly to the service of his fellow-men, and so abjectly public-
spirited that his private interest is nothing to him. Actually he is a
sturdy rogue whose principal, and often sole aim in life is to butter
his parsnips. His technical equipment consists simply of an arma-
mentarium of deceits. It is his business to get and hold his job at all
costs. If he can hold it by lying, he will hold it by lying; if lying peters
out he will try to hold it by embracing new truths. His ear is ever close
to the ground. If he is an adept he can hear the first murmurs of popular clamour before even the people themselves are conscious of them.
If he is a master he detects and whoops up to-day the delusions that
the mob will cherish next year. There is in him, in his professional aspect, no shadow of principle or honour. It is moral by his code to get
into office by false pretences, as the late Dr. Wilson did in 1916. It is
moral to change convictions overnight, as multitudes of American politicians did when the Prohibition avalanche came down upon them.
Anything is moral that furthers the main concern of his soul, which is
to keep a place at the public trough. That place is one of public honour, and public honour is the thing that caresses him and makes him
happy. It is also one of power, and power is the commodity that he
has for sale.

I speak here, of course, of the democratic politician in his rôle of
statesman—that is, in his best and noblest aspect. He flourishes also
on lower levels, partly subterranean. Down there public honour would
be an inconvenience, so he hawks it to lesser men, and contents himself with power. What are the sources of that power? They lie, obviously, in the gross weaknesses and knaveries of the common people
—in their inability to grasp any issues save the simplest and most
banal, in their incurable tendency to fly into preposterous alarms, in
their petty self-seeking and venality, in their instinctive envy and
hatred of their superiors—in brief, in their congenital incapacity for
the elemental duties of citizens in a civilized state. The boss owns
them simply because they can be bought for a job on the street or a
load of coal. He holds them, even when they pass beyond any need
of jobs or coal, by his shrewd understanding of their immemorial
sentimentalities. Looking at Thersites, they see Ulysses. He is the state
as they apprehend it; around him clusters all the romance that used
to hang about a king. He is the fount of honour and the mould of
form. His barbaric code, framed to fit their gullibility, becomes an
example to their young. The boss is the eternal *reductio ad absurdum*
of the whole democratic process. He exemplifies its reduction of all
ideas to a few elemental wants. And he reflects and makes manifest
the inferior man's congenital fear of liberty—his incapacity for even

the most trivial sort of independent action. Life on the lower levels is life in a series of interlocking despotisms. The inferior man cannot imagine himself save as taking orders—if not from the boss, then from the priest, and if not from the priest, then from some fantastic drill-sergeant of his own creation. For years the reformers who flourished in the United States concentrated their whole animus upon the boss: it was apparently their notion that he had imposed himself upon his victims from without, and that they could be delivered by destroying him. But time threw a brilliant light upon that error. When, as and if he was overthrown there appeared in his place the prehensile Methodist parson, bawling for Prohibition and its easy jobs, and behind the parson loomed the grand goblin, natural heir to a long line of imperial worthy potentates of the Sons of Azrael and sublime chancellors of the Order of Patriarchs Militant. The winds of the world are bitter to *Homo vulgaris*. He likes the warmth and safety of the herd, and he likes a bell-wether with a clarion bell.

The art of politics, under democracy, is simply the art of ringing it. Two branches reveal themselves. There is the art of the demagogue, and there is the art of what may be called, by a shot-gun marriage of Latin and Greek, the demaslave. They are complementary, and both of them are degrading to their practitioners. The demagogue is one who preaches doctrines he knows to be untrue to men he knows to be idiots. The demaslave is one who listens to what these idiots have to say and then pretends that he believes it himself. Every man who seeks elective office under democracy has to be either the one thing or the other, and most men have to be both. The whole process is one of false pretences and ignoble concealments. No educated man, stating plainly the elementary notions that every educated man holds about the matters that principally concern government, could be elected to office in a democratic state, save perhaps by a miracle. His frankness would arouse fears, and those fears would run against him; it is his business to arouse fears that will run in favour of him. Worse, he must not only consider the weaknesses of the mob, but also the prejudices of the minorities that prey upon it. Some of these minorities have developed a highly efficient technique of intimidation. They not only know how to arouse the fears of the mob; they also know how to awaken its envy, its dislike of privilege, its hatred of its betters. How formidable they may become is shown by the example of the Anti-Saloon League in the United States—a minority body in the strictest sense, however skillful its mustering of popular support, for it nowhere includes a majority of the voters among its subscribing members, and its leaders are nowhere chosen by democratic methods. And how such minorities may intimidate the whole class of place-seeking politicians has been demonstrated brilliantly and obscenely by the same corrupt and unconscionable organization. It has filled all the law-making bodies of the nation with men who have got into office by submitting cravenly to its dictation, and it has filled thousands of administrative posts, and not a few judicial posts, with vermin of the same sort.

Such men, indeed, enjoy vast advantages under democracy. The mob, insensitive to their dishonour, is edified and exhilarated by their success. The competition they offer to men of a decenter habit is too powerful to be met, so they tend, gradually, to monopolize all the public offices. Out of the muck of their swinishness the typical American law-maker emerges. He is a man who has lied and dissembled, and a man who has crawled. He knows the taste of boot-polish. He has suffered kicks in the tonneau of his pantaloons. He has taken orders from his superiors in knavery and he has wooed and flattered his inferiors in sense. His public life is an endless series of evasions and false pretences. He is willing to embrace any issue, however idiotic, that will get him votes, and he is willing to sacrifice any principle, however sound, that will lose them for him. I do not describe the democratic politician at his inordinate worst; I describe him as he is encountered in the full sunshine of normalcy. He may be, on the one hand, a cross-roads idler striving to get into the State Legislature by grace of the local mortgage-sharks and evangelical clergy, or he may be, on the other, the President of the United States. It is almost an axiom that no man may make a career in politics in the Republic without stooping to such ignobility: it is as necessary as a loud voice. Now and then, to be sure, a man of sounder self-respect may make a beginning, but he seldom gets very far. Those who survive are nearly all tarred, soon or late, with the same stick. They are men who, at some time or other, have compromised with their honour, either by swallowing their convictions or by whooping for what they believe to be untrue. They are in the position of the chorus girl who, in order to get her humble job, has had to admit the manager to her person. And the old birds among them, like chorus girls of long experience, come to regard the business resignedly and even complacently. It is the price that a man who loves the clapper-clawing of the vulgar must pay for it under the democratic system. He becomes a coward and a trimmer *ex officio*. Where his dignity was in the days of his innocence there is now only a vacuum in the wastes of his subconscious. Vanity remains to him, but not pride.

DONALD DAVIDSON *rarely wrote directly on political subjects. When he did so he appeared to be a conventional Southern Democrat, hostile to northern capitalism and governmental centralization of power and defensive of the South and its right as a distinctive region to go its own agrarian and idiosyncratic way. Sitting in Nashville, he received Mencken's* Notes on Democracy *with the amusement he expressed below. Mencken was an incomparable humorist, but loose with facts and of little use for changing democracy in any practical way. Davidson himself did nothing constructive for political science, however often he might repeat words like "agrarian," "the South," and "regionalism," but his measured response helped fill in the conservative political position and put Mencken into a sensible perspective.*

23. H. L. Mencken

By Donald Davidson

When I had finished H. L. Mencken's new book, *Notes on Democracy*, I looked out of the window with a sort of halfway vague expectation that I would find tottering buildings, rows of groveling sinners, and other Judgment Day effects. But nothing had happened. All the inhabitants of the Mencken universe—the Boobs, the Morons, and the Yokels—were calmly and even gaily going about their business, totally unaware of large volcanic disturbances in the region of New York. Streetcars were running. A new building was going up across the street. The brick-layers' cars were parked at the curb. A billboard announced that Chesterfields satisfy. The clouds were ambling northward in a gentle southern sky. All was as usual. There were no signs of crumbling civilization, or even of a penitent civilization.

After all, I thought, until Mr. Mencken convinces the Morons that they are Morons and should hence be submissive, how is he going to do the world much good? And since the Morons naturally haven't gumption enough to read his books, much less understand them, how is the convincing to be accomplished? Perhaps, however, he had no persuasive intentions. Let me try to understand Mr. Mencken, not to worship him or abuse him. After just consideration, I arrive at two possible views of his activity, as illustrated especially in his recent book. In one view he appears as a social philosopher or critic indulging in a rather destructive analysis but, unlike the giddy reformers, proposing no panaceas; and in this view he must be taken seriously. The other view puts him up as a gargantuan humorist with an immense capacity for invective and ridicule; and this view requires him to be enjoyed for his own sake, like any other writer who knows the pyrotechnic possibilities of language.

Taking first the serious view, I must offer the opinion that in *Notes on Democracy* Mr. Mencken deals with the weightiest subject he has yet approached. And, although the book is to a certain extent a restatement of his now familiar ideas, it is, on the whole, new material. He divides his *Notes* into three principal sections: "Democratic Man," "The Democratic State," "Democracy and Liberty." There is also a "Coda," in which, surveying the general destruction, he disclaims any knowledge of the future and declares that he enjoys de-

Note: Originally published in the *Nashville Tennessean*, December 12, 1926. Reprinted by permission of the *Nashville Tennessean*.

mocracy immensely because "it is incomparably idiotic, and hence incomparably amusing." The treatment of these various topics is not very systematic. Each Note is of course a denunciation; but each denunciation is a separate volcano, erupting lava like its neighbors, but disposed and erected by whim rather than geometry or logic. There is some overlapping and likewise some contradiction, as is usual in Mr. Mencken's writings. But there is no careful symmetrical arrangement, no neatly marching parade of thesis—data—proof—conclusion.

Mr. Mencken sets up in his first section the idea that democratic man, considered in the mass, is a congenital moron incapable of an intelligent act. He admits that there are a few superior beings, but most minds are capable only "of a sort of insensate sweating, like a kidney." This view of the mob he bolsters up with the intelligence tests, which he sees as outlining intellectual levels beyond which no advance can be made. Therefore education offers no hope, because the Moron mob, which has a low "I.Q.," cannot be educated. Thus he knocks over the foundation of democratic theory which attributes some sort of mysterious (and Mencken would say, bogus) wisdom to the masses and exalts the Will of the People. The Will of the People, in his opinion, signifies simply the triumph of inferiority. And, since the mob is animated only by the savage motives of fear and envy, a government based on intelligence becomes an impossibility, for the masses are so stupid that they will oppose, and always have opposed, even sensible efforts to better their lumpish and besotted condition.

Furthermore, the democratic state, in Mr. Mencken's survey, becomes a travesty, simply because it is so thoroughly and nauseously democratic. The will of the people, if exerted, can accomplish any fool thing. The democratic mob "could extend the term of the president to life, or they could reduce it to one year, or even to one day. They could provide that he must shave his head, or that he must sleep in his underclothes." Politics, instead of a science, becomes a "combat between jackals and jackasses." Only demagogues can rule. Gentlemen stay out of politics. Instead we have a Harding, whose "notion of a good time was to refresh himself in the manner of a small-town Elk," or a Coolidge, of whom Mr. Mencken says: "There is no evidence that he is acquainted with a single intelligent man." The typical senator is "simply a party hack. . . . His backbone has a sweet resiliency. . . . it is quite impossible to forecast his action, even on a matter of the highest principle, without knowing what rewards are offered by the rival sides." Bribery and corruption are the order of the day. Public servants become cowards.

And then the fair principle of liberty, what of that? Democratic man, says Mr. Mencken, doesn't want it. He wants only safety and peace: "The peace of a trusty in a well-managed penitentiary." He wants laws, and especially laws that protect him against himself. Democracy "kills the thing it loves." It applauds mediocrity and pulls down superiority. Therefore puritanism is a natural accompaniment of democracy. For the puritan wants (1) "to punish the other fellow for having a better time;" (2) "to bring the other fellow down to his own unhappy level." It is typical of democracy that "Every district attorney goes to his knees each night to ask God to deliver a Thaw or a Fatty Arbuckle into his hands"—all because the mob delights in seeing rich persons browbeaten.

Thus Mencken! I have quoted freely but not as freely as I would like to, for every page is thickly sown with verbal torpedoes, exciting for their explosive vehemence, however questionable their direction and effect. But how shall Mr. Mencken's criticism of democracy be criticized? Mr. Mencken, who uses the South as the butt of his jokes and represents it as totally intolerant, would perhaps think that I would be in danger of assassination if I ventured to express any agreement with his ideas. But I do so venture, with a feeling of complete safety. The truth is that most of his excoriation of democracy is old stuff—at least as old as Thomas Carlyle, who also asserted that democracy sabotaged the superior man. Even the most ardent democrats must admit—and can admit with a tolerant smile—the bulk of Mr. Mencken's charges as to democracy's shortcomings. Furthermore, the influence Mr. Mencken wields and the whole secret of his method lie in the fact that he turbulently overstates what everybody knows. Nowhere, except in political editorials and the platitudes of orators, both of which are pretty generally received with skepticism, will you find the view that our present democracy is the absolute "summum bonum." Mr. Mencken's criticisms of democracy are paralleled by the jokes of Will Rogers, the bitingly satirical comic strips, and vaudeville patter, all of which we absorb with enormous gusto. Andy Gump's political campaign went over with a bang; but it was in its implication as destructively critical as *Notes on Democracy*. Goldberg's boobs are as savagely treated as Mencken's boobs. But this is true, also, that Mr. Mencken exceeds other critics in his ferocity and unscrupulousness. His exaggerations are not simply exaggerations; they are often studied distortions at plain variance with the truth; in fact, Mr. Mencken, who is as poetic as a tale-bearing child, cannot always be trusted to give the correct facts. In spite of his really powerful intellectual equipment, he often draws on himself the just charge of malice because he is either too lazy or too prejudiced to separate truth from falsehood.

His criticism of democracy is, of course, full of holes and non sequiturs. We have not merely to make the charge that Mr. Mencken views democracy everywhere at its worst. His major premise, based on modern biology, behavioristic psychology, and the like, serves his purpose, but is shaky in its claim that inferior men can never become superior men. Mr. Mencken admits that some men are superior; he does not admit that the class can be enlarged; the best democratic theory might say that it could be. Furthermore, though Mr. Mencken makes much of the gullibility of the mob, he refuses to admit that superior men can do the gulling; and though he is raucously tolerant of biological evolution, he is quite intolerant of the idea of political evolution. In fact, his opinions drive him, as he is frank enough to admit, directly toward anarchy; and in essence, we are forced to conclude that Mr. Mencken is sorry he was born, and that life offers him no pleasure except an occasional tickling, a sensual excitement, or sardonic laughter at the ridiculousness of the world. Even so, though Mr. Mencken may be sorry he was born, it is fortunate that he was born in the United States, which, with England, is the only country democratic enough to permit a confirmed and lowly misanthrope to rise to his present position of honor, wealth, and power, or to tolerate his persistent rowdyism after he has arrived.

So, Mencken, the destroyer, necessary as he may be in his role as an occasional stimulant or a gadfly, is not to be trusted as a purveyor of ideas. Mencken as humorist is another thing. Others may imitate, but none can approach the vivacity and brilliance of his style: the sentences that crack like a whip, the phrases that fall and rebound like Thor's hammer, the surly laughter that revels in well-seasoned colloquialisms, ridiculous incongruities, sudden and vulgar paradoxes. Read Mr. Mencken for his ideas, and you will only hug the viper of melancholy to your bosom. Read him as you would read Mark Twain, you will not only escape the virus, but you will have a rare, indeed a unique, entertainment. You will have also the democratic (according to Mencken) pleasure of seeing the mighty ones biffed soundly; and you will only spoil the joke if you get angry because you are biffed yourself.

THE ONE *genuinely significant exception to the strong criticism I have made about conservative political writing is Walter Lippmann's* The Good Society. *Written in the depths of the depression by a former socialist and prophet of modernism, it expresses a number of viewpoints that set it and its author somewhat apart from the other men in this book. Lippmann (1889–1974), alone among the authors in this book, was of Jewish background, and he therefore escaped the sometimes oppressive concerns of a dying Protestantism that so often seemed to obsess the cultural conservatives. Only a Spanish Catholic like Santayana could be quite as detached as Lippmann from the dominant concerns of the culture in which he lived and which he criticized. Except for a few brief stints in both local and national governments, Lippmann spent his life as an enormously productive journalist, writing both columns and books for sixty years. His work covered an extraordinary number of subjects, from personal morals to foreign policy; however, there is no space to analyze it here.*

During Woodrow Wilson's presidency, Lippmann had played a role as an adviser in the Versailles peace conference. The failure of Wilsonian idealism helped destroy his faith in the possibilities of governmental intervention, and the rise of totalitarian regimes in Europe completed the job by sending him publicly to a conservative position defensive of natural law, human rights, and the mechanisms of capitalism and the free market. Unlike Babbitt, Lippmann was never a man of the academy; unlike Nock, Cram, and Mencken, he did not scorn human nature or the democratic individual. He was instead a man sympathizing with the masses and in daily contact with actual political processes. He knew of the failures of government at first hand, and he thought he knew things which would actually help governmental officials formulate constructive policies.

The Good Society is a long and complex book, and even so it needs supplementing with Lippmann's daily journalism for a full capturing of his constructive conservative alternative to statism and the New Deal. Basically, the position which he adopts, and which he persists in calling "liberal" in spite of the changing meanings of that term, stresses the value of the human personality, its need to develop its innate faculties to the fullest, and the appropriateness of the capitalist market model for the achievement of this goal. The proponents of extensive state planning, he asserts, have not adequately understood either human nature or the workings of the marketplace, and until they do they will forever get in the way of productively led lives. In addition, collectivists need a new understanding of the law and of the necessity for an end to arbitrary governmental activity. On these two pillars, the market and the legal system, Lippmann elaborated his defense of the conservative position. A thinker could not plan the Good Society; he could only allow all individuals to pursue their own valid ends and keep the channels of market and court open to them for their protection. Human nature was too varied and life too complex to attempt anything more. In effect, he brought Jefferson up to date and provided conservatism with the closest thing it had in this period to a mature political science.

24. The Good Society

By Walter Lippmann

We are now in a position to see that collectivism and liberalism are different ways of answering the paramount technical and human questions which have been posed by the division of labor. Abstractly the question is how the allocation of capital and labor shall be determined. In human and concrete terms it is the question of where savings shall be invested and at what jobs men shall work and what goods they shall be able to consume. Here, obviously, is the greatest of all social questions, for in determining what goods shall be produced, at what places, of what quality and quantities, the whole worldly existence of men and of their communities is decided. To regulate the division of labor is to determine whether men shall work on farms or in factories, whether particular regions shall be agricultural or industrial, what opportunities shall be offered to individuals, what standard of life they may expect.

The collectivist method is to have these questions answered by a planning board and to have its decisions enforced by the coercive authority of the state. Under gradual collectivism, the authority of the state or the private power of vested interests is used to resist or to dominate the decisions of the market. Though the market is not abolished, it is not allowed to function wherever there is an organized interest strong enough to interfere with it. In any complete collectivism—in war time everywhere and in peaceful periods in the totalitarian states—the market as the regulator of the division of labor is abolished and supplanted by government bureaus. Officials then direct production by conscripting labor and savings and by rationing goods for consumption.

The first principle of liberalism, on the contrary, is that the market must be preserved and perfected as the prime regulator of the division of labor. It was the historic mission of liberalism to discover the significance of the division of labor; its uncompleted task is to show how law and public policy may best be adapted to this mode of production which specializes men's work, and thereby establishes an increasingly elaborate interdependence among individuals and their communities

Note: From *The Good Society*, by Walter Lippmann (Boston: Little, Brown, 1943), pp. 173–176, 344–348, 362–368. Copyright © 1936, 1937, 1943, by Walter Lippmann. Reprinted by permission of Little, Brown & Co., in association with the Atlantic Monthly Press.

throughout the world. The liberal philosophy is based on the conviction that, except in emergencies and for military purposes, the division of labor cannot be regulated successfully by coercive authority, whether it be public or private; that the mode of production which mankind generally began to adopt about a hundred and fifty years ago is in its essence a market economy, and that, therefore, the true line of progress is not to impair or to abolish the market, but to maintain and improve it.

The liberal conviction that there can be no other satisfactory regulator of work, investment, and consumption rests on the realization that when men specialize their labor, they must live by exchanging the product. If they are to exchange their own product for another product that they need, they must make a product that some other specialist needs. So there must be a place where the things they can and are willing to make are matched with the things that other men need or would like to have. That place is the market place. When the collectivist abolishes the market place, all he really does is to locate it in the brains of his planning board. Somehow or other these officials are supposed to know, by investigation and calculation, what everyone can do and how willing he is to do it and how well he is able to do it and, also, what everyone needs and how he will prefer to satisfy his needs. From the liberal point of view it is naïve to suppose that any body of officials could perform that function in time of peace and in an economy of abundance and for the whole wide world.

If a planning board announced that, henceforth, machines in factories would be run not by electrical power generated in dynamos but by decrees issued by public officials, it would sound absurd. Yet the pretension to regulate the division of labor by abolishing the market and substituting authoritative planners is an idea of the same order. For what placed those dynamos in those particular factories and dedicated that much capital and labor to that particular kind of production was a calculation based on data furnished by the markets. Only when a nation is devoting all its energies to some specific task like mobilizing for war or satisfying elementary human needs in time of dire emergency is there any way of directing production without the regulatory guidance of the market. So the market is as integral a part of the system of production as the machinery, the labor, and the materials. There is no other conceivable way in which the infinitely varied ambitions and capacities of men can be matched with their infinitely varied needs and tastes. The totalitarian state merely suppresses this infinite variety of capacity and choice by the rationing of standardized goods and the conscription of standardized labor.

The market is not something invented by businessmen and speculators for their profit, or by the classical economists for their intellectual pleasure. The market is the only possible method by which labor that has been analyzed into separate specialties can be synthesized into useful work. The wheat farmer would die for want of a crust of bread, the cotton planter would go naked, the carpenter would have to live in a cave, if markets did not bring together wheat farmers, millers, and bakers, cotton planters, spinners, weavers, and clothiers, lumbermen and carpenters. This bringing together at the right time, in the right quantities, in accordance with the ability to produce and the desire to consume, cannot be organized and administered from above by any human power. It is an organic, not a fabricated, synthesis which can be effected only by the continual matching of bids and offers. For the division of labor and its regulation in markets are two inseparable aspects of the same process of producing wealth, and the failure to understand that truth is a sure sign of a failure to understand the technical principle of production in the modern world.

. . . .

It will now be profitable, I think, to scrutinize more closely the postulates upon which Coke and Selden based their claim that the King was under God and the law. For the law which they made supreme over the King was the English common law developed by the courts out of immemorial custom. Thus Selden construed the right affirmed in the Magna Carta that "no freeman shall be imprisoned without due course of law" as meaning exactly what it said. The villeins, who were bound to the soil under feudal law, did not possess this right. They could be imprisoned at the will of their lords or of the King, and they had no remedy.

Now obviously if the higher law of the state is simply the traditional law as it has evolved in the course of history, to insist upon its supremacy is to put the living under the dominion of the dead, and to deny to them the power to remedy injustice and improve their condition. The attack which Bentham made upon Blackstone was the forerunner of the popular hostility in the United States to the judges and lawyers who identified the English common law not only with the Constitution but with the higher law of the Universe, and then opposed the redress of grievances. Thus while it was undoubtedly a great achievement to bring the King under the English common law, the attempt to keep the newly enfranchised people under this same traditional law appeared to them what in effect it was—an attempt to deprive them of their right to reform traditional privileges and immunities.

That, as we have already seen, was the reason why the progressive thinkers of the nineteenth century rejected the supremacy of law and poured contempt and ridicule upon the conception of a higher law. They had found that in practice the higher law meant either the traditional law, with all its historic injustices, or the vague, subjective, and irresponsible fantasies of doctrinaires agitating the crowd. The traditional law was in many vital respects intolerably unsuited to the modern world. The doctrinaires, when they appealed to the supposedly universal law, were observed to be violently unable to agree on what it was. Thus the whole conception was lost, and by the twentieth century political thinking had ceased to have any criteria beyond those of immediate expediency, self-assertiveness, and momentary success.

The rediscovery and the reconstruction of general political standards can be carried forward only, I believe, by developing the abiding truth of the older liberalism after purging it of the defects which destroyed it. The pioneer liberals vindicated the supremacy of law over the arbitrary power of men. That is the abiding truth which we inherit from them. But the law which they vindicated was in many respects the mere defense of ancient privileges and immunities. Thus they made it easy to invoke the supremacy of the law in order to prohibit the improvement of human affairs. In the decadence of liberalism the conception of higher law was used to defend vested rights and obstruct reform. That was its fatal defect and the cause of its downfall. But in the debacle there was swept away not only the mistaken insistence upon the supremacy of the traditional law, but the nobler intuition that liberty and human dignity depend upon the supremacy of the spirit of law.

We can, and I believe that we must, disentangle the general theory of liberalism from its historic identification with the common-law rights and privileges and immunities enjoyed by Englishmen and Americans in the nineteenth century. When Coke told James I that the King was under God and the law, the enduring part of the reply is not to be found in any pretension that the law itself as it happens to be is perfect and immutable; that, for example, the lawful right of the lord of the manor arbitrarily to imprison the villein is not to be challenged. The essential and enduring part of Coke's reply is the denial that the King may act arbitrarily. The denial that men may be arbitrary in human transactions *is* the higher law.

That is the substance of the higher law. That is the spiritual essence without which the letter of the law is nothing but the formal trappings of vested rights or the ceremonial disguise of caprice and willfulness. Constitutional restraints and bills of rights, the whole apparatus of responsible government and of an independent judiciary, the conception of due process of law in courts, in legislatures, among executives, are but the rough approximations by which men have sought to exorcise the devil of arbitrariness in human relations. Among a people which does not try to obey this higher law, no constitution is worth the paper it is written on: though they have all the forms of liberty, they will not enjoy its substance. The laws depend upon moral commitments which could never possibly be expressly stated in the laws themselves: upon a level of truthfulness in giving testimony, of reasonableness in argument, of trust, confidence, and good faith in transactions; upon a mood of disinterestedness and justice, far above anything that the letter of the law demands. It is not enough that men should be as truthful as the laws against perjury require and as reasonable as the rules of evidence compel a clever lawyer to be. To maintain a constitutional order they must be much more truthful, reasonable, just, and honorable than the letter of the laws. There must be more than legal prohibition against arbitrariness, against overreaching, deception, and oppression. There must be an habitual, confirmed, and well-nigh intuitive dislike of arbitrariness; a quick sensitiveness to its manifestations and a spontaneous disapproval and resistance. For only by adhering to this unwritten higher law can they make actual law effective or have criteria by which to reform it.

By this higher law all formal laws and all political behavior are judged in civilized societies. When the principle which Coke affirmed against the King is recognized, then the privileges of the lord of the manor no longer stand impervious to criticism and to reform. If the sovereign himself may not act willfully, arbitrarily, by personal prerogative, then no one may. His ministers may not. The legislature may not. Majorities may not. Individuals may not. Crowds may not. The national state may not. This law which is the spirit of law is the opposite of an accumulation of old precedents and new fiats. By this higher law, that men must not be arbitrary, the old law is continually tested and the new law reviewed.

To those who ask where this higher law is to be found, the answer is that it is a progressive discovery of men striving to civilize themselves, and that its scope and implications are a gradual revelation that is by no means completed. In the beginning of law men could aim no higher than to keep the peace. They had made a great advance when the injured man agreed to take in vengeance no more than an eye for an eye. They advanced further when the dominion of the strong over the weak was legalized as caste, and bounds were put on their superior strength. They advanced still further when the masters had duties towards as well as rights over their subjects. The advance continued as the rights of the masters were progressively checked and liquidated as having no intrinsic justification.

The development of human rights is simply the expression of the higher law that men shall not deal arbitrarily with one another. Human rights do not mean, as some confused individualists have supposed, that there are certain sterile areas where men collectively may not deal at all with men individually. We are in truth members of one another, and a philosophy which seeks to differentiate the community from the persons who belong to it, treating them as if they were distinct sovereignties having only diplomatic relations, is contrary to fact and can lead only to moral bewilderment. The rights of man are not the rights of Robinson Crusoe before his man Friday appeared. They stem from the right not to be dealt with arbitrarily by anyone else, and the inescapable corollary of the rights of man is the duty of man not to deal arbitrarily with others.

The gradual encroachment of true law upon willfulness and caprice is the progress of liberty in human affairs. That is how the emancipation of mankind has been begun and must be continued. As those who have the power to coerce lose the authority to rule by fiat, liberty advances. It advances by the continual struggle of men against the possessors of arbitrary power.

.   .   .   .

This truth our contemporary authoritarians, whether of the left or of the right, have failed to grasp. They look upon the great sprawling complex of transactions by which mankind lives; seeing that these transactions are in large part still unregulated by law, and that therefore there is much confusion and injustice, they have turned their backs upon the task of regulation by law and have beguiled themselves with the notion that they can plan this economy systematically and administer it rationally. The exact contrary is the truth. The modern economy is perhaps the least systematic of any that has ever existed. It is world-wide, formless, vast, complicated, and, owing to technological progress, in constant change. For that reason it is incapable of being conceived as a system, or of being replaced by another system, or of being managed as an administrative unit.

The hankering for schemes and systems and comprehensive organization is the wistfulness of an immature philosophy which has not come to terms with reality, no less when the conservators of vested interests would stabilize the modern economy in statu quo by protective laws and monopolistic schemes than when the revolutionist makes blueprints of a world composed of planned national economies "coördinated" by a world-planning authority. Neither takes any more account of reality than if he were studying landscape architecture with a view to making a formal garden out of the Brazilian jungle.

For the greater the society, the higher and more variable the standards of life, the more diversified the energies of its people for invention, enterprise, and adaptation, the more certain it is that the social order cannot be planned ex cathedra or governed by administrative command. We live in such an immensely diversified civilization that the only intelligible criterion which political thinkers can entertain in regard to it, the only feasible goal which statesmen can set themselves in governing it, is to reconcile the conflicts which spring from this diversity. They cannot hope to comprehend it as a system. For it is not a system. They cannot hope to plan and direct it. For it is not an organization. They can hope only to dispense lawful justice among individuals and associations where their interests conflict, to mitigate the violence of conflict and competition by seeking to make lawful justice more and more equitable.

It requires much virtue to do that well. There must be a strong desire to be just. There must be a growing capacity to be just. There must be discernment and sympathy in estimating the particular claims of divergent interests. There must be moral standards which discourage the quest of privilege and the exercise of arbitrary power. There must be resolution and valor to resist oppression and tyranny. There must be patience and tolerance and kindness in hearing claims, in argument, in negotiation, and in reconciliation.

But these are human virtues; though they are high, they are within the attainable limits of human nature as we know it. They actually exist. Men do have these virtues, all but the most hopelessly degenerate, in some degree. We know that they can be increased. When we talk about them we are talking about virtues that have affected the course of actual history, about virtues that some men have practised more than other men, and no man sufficiently, but enough men in great enough degree to have given mankind here and there and for varying periods of time the intimations of a Good Society.

But the virtues that are required for the overhead administration of a civilization are superhuman; they are attributes of Providence and not of mortal men. It is true that there have been benevolent despots and that for a little while in a particular place they have made possible a better life than their subjects were able to achieve without the rule of a firm and authoritative guardian. And no doubt it is still true that a community which does not have the essential discipline of liberty can choose only among alternative disciplines by authority. But if a community must have such a guardian, then it must resign itself to living a simple regimented existence, must entertain no hopes of the high and diversified standard of life which the division of labor and modern technology make possible. For despots cannot be found who could plan, organize, and direct a complex economy.

To do that would require a comprehensive understanding of the life and the labor and the purposes of hundreds of millions of persons, the gift of prophesying their behavior and omnipotence to control it. These faculties no man has ever possessed. When in theorizing we unwittingly postulate such faculties, we are resting our hopes on a conception of human nature which has no warrant whatever in any actual experience. The collectivist planners are not talking about the human race but about some other breed conceived in their dreams. They postulate qualities of intelligence and of virtue so unlike those which men possess that it would be just as intelligible to make plans for a society in which human beings were born equipped to fly like the angels, to feed on the fragrance of the summer breezes, and endowed with all possible knowledge.

Thus while the liberal philosophy is concerned with the reform of the laws in order to adapt them to the changing needs and standards of the dynamic economy, while the agenda of reform are long and varied, no one must look to liberalism for a harmonious scheme of social reconstruction. The Good Society has no architectural design. There are no blueprints. There is no mold in which human life is to be shaped. Indeed, to expect the blueprint of such a mold is a mode of thinking against which the liberal temper is a constant protest.

To design a personal plan for a new society is a pleasant form of madness; it is in imagination to play at being God and Caesar to the human race. Any such plan must implicitly assume that the visionary or someone else might find the power, or might persuade the masses to give him the power, to shape society to the plan; all such general plans of social reconstruction are merely the rationalization of the will to power. For that reason they are the subjective beginnings of fanaticism and tyranny. In these utopias the best is the enemy of the good, the heart's desire betrays the interests of man. To think in terms of a new scheme for a whole society is to use the idiom of authority, to approach affairs from the underlying premise that they can be shaped and directed by an overhead control, that social relations can be fabricated according to a master plan drawn up by a supreme architect.

The supreme architect, who begins as a visionary, becomes a fanatic, and ends as a despot. For no one can be the supreme architect of society without employing a supreme despot to execute the design. So if men are to seek freedom from the arbitrary dominion of men over men, they must not entertain fantasies of the future in which they play at being the dictators of civilization. It is the bad habit of an undisciplined imagination. The descent from fantasy to fanaticism is easy. Real dictators raised to power by the fanatics who adore them are only too likely to adopt the fantasy to justify their lust for power.

On the other hand, reasonable and civilized people who would like to make the best of the situation before them, but have no ambition for, or expectation of, the power to reshape a whole society, get no help from these architectural designs. The blueprint, be it as grandiose a work of genius as Plato's *Republic*, cannot hope to fit the specific situation. No a priori reasoning can anticipate the precise formulae which will reconcile the infinitely varied interests of men. The reconciliation has to be achieved by the treatment of specific issues and the solution will appear only after the claims and the evidence have been examined and fairly judged. Thus in Plato's great scheme each man was assigned his station and his duties; any architectural plan is necessarily based on the same presumption. But Plato's scheme worked only in Plato's imagination, never in the real world. No such scheme can ever work in the real world. For the scheme implies that men will remain content in the station which the visionary has assigned to them. To formulate such plans is not to design a society for real men. It is to re-create men to fit the design. For in real life men rest content in their station only if their interests have been successfully reconciled: failing that, they do not fit the design until they have been dosed with castor oil, put in concentration camps, or exiled to Siberia.

That is why the testament of liberty does not contain the project of a new social order. It adumbrates a way of life in which men seek to reconcile their interests by perfecting the rules of justice. No scheme which promises to obliterate the differences of interest can be deduced from it, no architectural design of society in which all human problems have been resolved. There is no plan of the future: there is, on the contrary, the conviction that the future must have the shape that human energies, purged in so far as possible of arbitrariness, will give it. Compared with the elegant and harmonious schemes which are propounded by the theoretical advocates of capitalism, communism, fascism, it must seem intellectually unsatisfying, and I can well imagine that many will feel about the liberal society as Emma Darwin felt when she wrote about the *Descent of Man*, "I think it will be very interesting, but that I shall dislike it very much as again putting God further off."

But though it must seem an insufficient ideal both to those who wish to exercise authority and to those who feel the need of leaning upon authority, it is the only practicable ideal of government in the Great Society. When huge masses of men have become dependent upon one another through the division of labor in countless, infinitely complex transactions, their activities cannot be planned and directed by public officials.

Thus it is true that the liberal state is not to be conceived as an earthly providence administering civilization. That is the essence of the matter. To the liberal mind the notion that men can authoritatively plan and impose a good life upon a great society is ignorant, impertinent, and pretentious. It can be entertained only by men who do not realize the infinite variety of human purposes, who do not appreciate the potentialities of human effort, or by men who do not choose to respect them.

The liberal state is to be conceived as the protector of equal rights by dispensing justice among individuals. It seeks to protect men against arbitrariness, not arbitrarily to direct them. Its idea is a fraternal association among free and equal men. To the initiative of individuals, secure in their rights and accountable to others who have equal rights, liberalism entrusts the shaping of the human destiny. It offers no encouragement to those who dream of what they could make of the world if they possessed supreme power. In the testament of liberty these ambitions have been assessed: the record of all the Caesars from Alexander to Adolf is visible. The world has known many societies in which each man has his station, his duties, and his ordained destiny, and the record shows that it is beyond the understanding of men to know all human needs, to appreciate all human possibilities, to imagine all human ends, to shape all human relations.

Yet if the ambitions of liberalism are more modest than those of authority, its promise is greater. It relies upon the development of the latent faculties of all men, shaped by their free transactions with one another. Liberalism commits the destiny of civilization, not to a few finite politicians here and there, but to the whole genius of mankind. This is a grander vision than that of those who would be Caesar and would set themselves up as little tin gods over men. It is a hope engendered in the human heart during the long ages in which the slowly emerging impulses of civilization, beset by barbarism, have struggled to be free.

. . . .

The recognition that all men are persons, and are not to be treated as things, has arisen slowly in the consciousness of mankind. It has made its way with difficulty against the recurrent testimony of immediate experience, against sophisticated argument, against the predatory and acquisitive instincts which men bring with them out of the animal struggle for existence. The passage from barbarism into civilization is long, halting, and unsure. It is a hard climb from the practice of devouring one's enemies to the injunction to love them. But in that long ascent there is a great divide which is reached when men discover, declare, and acknowledge, however much they may deny it in practice, that there is a Golden Rule which is the ultimate and universal criterion of human conduct. For then, and then only, is there a standard to which all can repair who seek to transform the incessant and indecisive struggle for domination and survival into the security of the Good Society.

The Golden Rule, sometimes in its positive form but more often in the negative form, has been enunciated among many peoples widely separated in time and space. In the Upanishads of Indian Brahmanism it is said: "Let no man do to another that which would be repugnant to himself. . . . In refusing, in bestowing, in regard to pleasure and to pain, to what is agreeable and disagreeable, a man obtains the proper rule by regarding the case as like his own." "My doctrine," says Gautama Buddha, "makes no distinction between high and low, rich and poor. It is like the sky. It has room for all, and like waves it washes all alike. . . . To him in whom love dwells, the whole world is but one family." The rule appears again and again in Confucius: "When one cultivates to the utmost the capabilities of his nature and exercises them on the principle of reciprocity, he is not far from the path. What you do not want done to yourself, do not do unto others."

If we ask ourselves why we should not do unto others what we do not want done to ourselves, the only possible reason must be that we have recognized them as inviolable persons, finally and essentially distinguished from things. Thus the Golden Rule is the moral maxim which establishes itself when men recognize others as autonomous persons, when they acknowledge the inalienable manhood of other men. The rule is meaningless where that recognition is absent. It can be preached from all the pulpits of the world and it will be without effect unless men acknowledge that there is an inalienable essence in all other men. But for this acknowledgment of the ultimate distinction between a person and a thing we should think no more of stepping on a man than of stepping on the carpet. Without it there is nothing in the human organism to which human rights can be ascribed or attached.

But wherever the sentiment of the indefeasible qualities of persons appears, there begins to spread through all institutions that exploit and oppress "the infection of an uneasy spirit." For six hundred years, says Whitehead, the ideal of the intellectual and moral grandeur of the human soul had haunted the ancient Mediterranean world. It troubled the conscience of Aristotle, and in order to vindicate human slavery he had to argue that slaves are by nature servile. The Stoic philosophers and lawyers, who initiated the abolition of slavery, taught that all men are "equal persons in the great court of nature," not in the sense that their faculties were identical or equivalent, but that in each man there was finally an inviolable and inalienable essence. The Stoics spoke quietly and in terms intelligible only to an elite. To the masses of the western world the news that all men are more than things was proclaimed by the Christian gospel and was celebrated in its central mysteries. It proclaimed the news to all men that they were not brute things, to all men without exception, the weak, the outcast, the down-trodden, the enslaved, and the utterly dejected. The influence of that gospel has been inexhaustible. It anchored the rights of men in the structure of the universe. It set these rights apart where they were beyond human interference. Thus the pretensions of despots became heretical. And since that revelation, though many despots have had the blessings of the clergy, no tyranny has posssessed a clear title before the tribunal of the human conscience, no slave has had to feel that the hope of freedom was forever foreclosed. For in the recognition that there is in each man a final essence—that is to say, an immortal soul—which only God can judge, a limit was set upon the dominion of men over men. The prerogatives of supremacy were radically undermined. The inviolability of the human person was declared.

Towards this conviction men have fought their way in the long ascent out of the morass of barbarism. Upon this rock they have built the rude foundations of the Good Society.

VII. Religion & Immortality

THE SUBJECT of religion and its connections to conservatism presents a knotty problem. For some conservative thinkers, religion has been the core of both their lives and their conservatism in a way uncommon in liberals and radicals. Their political, literary, and educational values have all been derived from religious faith. Indeed, whole volumes of scholarship have been written that stress the necessary connections between conservatism and religion.

For cultural conservatives in the first half of the twentieth century in America, however, this connection is not always present. For writers like Paul Elmer More or John Crowe Ransom, religion was central to their system of values. But for Irving Babbitt or H. L. Mencken religion not only was not central, it was an enemy, one subject to frequent and deserved attack. In the context of this book, religion is thus not necessarily central. It is, instead, only one of those concerns of life which make living worthwhile. Religion as a subject was always worthy of study, and it raised central issues of concern to all conservatives, but genuine faith had no necessary connection to an individual's essential conservatism. Babbitt and Mencken studied religion in great detail and responded to these issues with alternative, nonreligious assertions of value. Nock at one time was an ordained clergyman, but his beliefs changed slowly; he left the church and refused to discuss the subject directly for the last thirty-five years of his life. Santayana loved the tradition and ritual of Roman Catholicism yet refused to accept the theology as having any more validity than an epic poem.

In the first document in this section, More makes one of the most moving assertions of religious faith available in the literature of cultural conservatism. He too had been skeptical and heretical, but he ultimately made his peace with orthodoxy, and thus his words help express the way religious conservatives came to terms with the disorganization and chaos of modern life.

25. Rationalism and Faith

By Paul Elmer More

It should be made perfectly clear at the outset that, in dealing with religion from the sceptical point of view, I am not assuming the impossibility or invalidity of other methods of approach. I am deliberately taking the attitude of those who, as a result either of their own thinking or of unreflective submission to the thought of the age, find intellectual difficulties in the way of accepting the traditional dogmas of faith. Such men ordinarily are regarded, and indeed regard themselves, as sceptics. The question I would raise is whether their doubts do not in most cases spring rather from unexamined assumptions than from a true spirit of inquiry, and whether a thoroughgoing use of reason would not lead to a position more hospitable to the dogmas of religion than to the equally dogmatic tenets of rationalism so-called.

By the sceptical point of view, then, I mean something quite definite. Very briefly, scepticism comes down to this, that it draws a sharp distinction, and persistently maintains a sharp distinction, between knowledge and theory. Knowledge is limited to what we have, not by inference from something else, but directly and without the intervention of inferential reason; in the ancient terminology of the sect, knowledge is what we possess in the form of immediate affections. To take a familiar illustration: I have certain sensations, when looking at or feeling an object, which I express by calling the object red and hard and round. And these sensations I know that I have, whatever you or another may have. Again I have certain feelings of pleasure and pain, hope and fear, elation and depression, self-approval and disapproval, and all the rest. And these, too, no matter how we try to explain them, are simply there, immediate affections of the mind, indisputable facts. Thus much I know, and I know further that these sensations and feelings come to me in certain patterns and sequences, so that I can classify them and order my doings accordingly. The complete sceptic is perfectly justified in addicting himself to scientific pursuits, if by science we mean no more than experimentation among, and classification of, phenomena; and he is equally justified in adapting his life to a chosen scheme of ethics. But the sceptic stops there, and stops sharply. Any attempt to go behind the immediate data of

Note: Selections from Paul Elmer More, *The Skeptical Approach to Religion* (copyright © 1934, 1952, by Princeton University Press), pp. 2–26. Reprinted by permission of Princeton University Press.

experience, any theory which reason may fabricate of the nature of
the objects causing those sensations in his mind, or of himself as the
recipient feeling subject; still more, any inference as to the ultimate
nature of the world of which all phenomena and he himself are con-
stituent parts, may be true or may be false, but whether true or false
he, as sceptic, will not presume to say. Such is the sceptical position
which I accept, the self-denying ordinance at which, as it seems to
me, the rigorous use of reason must arrive; and I am seeking for an
approach to religion from this point of view.

.   .   .   .

First of all we must keep clearly before us the fact that the faith of
religion, as we are considering it, is not knowledge but inference, and
we should make no attempt to escape the implication of such an admission. But if faith stands thus on the same basis with rationalism,
as one alternative of two possible attitudes towards the paradox of experience, yet its procedure is not quite the same as that of the other
alternative. In a sense the religious man's inference from intuition rejects the result of observation as an illusion, just as the rationalist's
inference from observation rejects the result of intuition as an illusion. But the parallel is not exact. The inference of rationalism is by
its nature all-embracing and fanatically dogmatic; it simply sweeps
away the possibility of freedom and responsibility anywhere and
everywhere; it tells me categorically that my intuition is a pure illusion having no correspondence with the facts of existence, and that if
I think of myself as free and responsible I am merely a victim of self-
deception. Theoretically, if I accept the contention of rationalism, I
may seem to have reached a logical solution of the dilemma of experience, and I may thus bring a certain ease to my mind; but the simple truth must not be shuffled out of sight that I have accomplished
this by means of pure inference, and that the consciousness of myself as a responsible being capable of purpose remains uneliminated
and unaltered. I may by inference remove the immediate affection of
freedom from my theory of life; I shall continue to live nevertheless
precisely as if I had no such theory.

In contrast with this procedure the inference of faith is more modest and consistent; it is thus, in the proper use of the word, more reasonable than rationalism, as it is far less subject to the corrosive acid
of scepticism. It does not, at least it need not, so much reject as tran-
scend the immediate data of observation. It may, without betraying
its own demands, admit that the acorn, so far as we can see, develops
into an oak by a law which leaves to the acorn itself no freedom of
action and no responsibility for its growth; it may with perfect consistency admit, indeed in loyalty to itself is rather bound to believe,
that the cosmic evolution has left no visible material records of a conscious purposive mind at work in the cosmos itself. In other words,
faith normally does not transfer our consciousness of freedom and

responsibility and purpose to, or into, the observed phenomena of the objective universe, but rather infers the existence of a free and responsible agent, whose purpose is operative in the world while He Himself is transcendent to the world. The content of faith is thus theistic rather than pantheistic or deistic. To sum up the argument in more technical language; the inference from observation is in the direction of a materialistic or pseudo-spiritual monism, whereas the proper inference from intuition leads to a dualism of spirit and matter. This is the true meaning of cosmic teleology as different from immanent law, and it was against precisely this dualistic conception of teleology that the rationalizing philosophers of the seventeenth century thundered in the index.[1]

To the proposition that faith is intrinsically theistic every student of religion will assent, and he will admit with equal readiness certain corollaries, as they may be called, of theism.[2] The belief in such a God as we conceive by faith must react upon the immediate intuition of ourselves from which faith draws its content. Our sense of freedom is not quite the same when we think of ourselves as in a world under the governance of a divine Agent, but is directed into an effort to conform our will to the will of God. Our sense of responsibility takes on a more definite aspect of obligation to a supreme Ruler and Judge. The morality of self-satisfaction is thus transformed into the morality of duty. And with the recognition of duty there enters a new hope. The sense of purpose is caught up into, and justified by, a vaster teleology. The God of purpose, we trust, will not leave our deepest desires frustrate. In particular the instinctive belief in immortality, whether it comes to the primitive man by inference from the immediate consciousness of life or as a defensive reaction against the fear of death, acquires a new assurance from faith in an eternal and benevolent Lord of life.

To these corollaries of belief, which affect the human side, so to speak, of religion, the theist adheres spontaneously. But there are other implications of theism, affecting rather the supernatural factor of religion, to which theologians have not always been favourably inclined. Faith according to our definition starts from, and receives at least its initial content from, man's immediate intuition of freedom

1. In drawing this contrast between the uses of observation and of intuition I have omitted the emotional reaction of the poet, or of the poetic faculty within all of us, which brings a sense of something human and divine interfused through nature. This, I take it, is not the result of pure observation but is definable as the pathetic fallacy (though the word fallacy rather begs the question). It is a kind of halfway house between the scientific outlook and the fully teleological inference of faith. I have in mind to deal with this subject in an essay on Wordsworth.

2. I say nothing here of Buddhism which, in its early form, was neither theistic nor, in the full sense of the word, teleological. This subject I have dealt with elsewhere, in *The Catholic Faith*.

and responsibility and purpose. Now the consciousness of purpose can mean only this, that I have in my mind an ideal of righteousness, a conception of something better than my present state, a pattern of life more or less clearly outlined, which, in my moods of exaltation, perhaps oftener in my moments of repentance, I propose to attain by voluntary effort. Such a purpose may exhaust itself in transient regret or futile dreaming, but in one degree or another it comes to all men, even the most abandoned. Further the accompanying sense of responsibility, which is an inherent factor of self-applause or self-condemnation, implies that this ideal is not the arbitrary creation of my own fancy, but in some way possesses authority which I neglect at peril of my happiness. And still further, the accompanying sense of freedom has a double significance. It implies on the one hand that I am conscious of a power within myself to move on towards the fulfilment of my purpose. And it implies on the other hand, and simultaneously, the presence of obstacles on my path, of difficulties to be overcome; otherwise purpose would not be what it is, the proposal to achieve an end, but would be a self-accomplished desire; there would be no time-process, but an immediate fact.

Now if cosmic teleology is an inference from the teleological knowledge of myself, if faith is a transference of this triple form of consciousness to a Being who transcends the world, then we are bound by our faith to a corresponding conception of the nature and operation of such a Being. As a matter of fact, if we deal with the subject honestly, we shall see that the whole history of religion from the superstition of the most ignorant savage to the creed of the most enlightened man of today does actually follow this law of correspondence. We shall discover the same inference of purpose and freedom and responsibility in the mysterious object of primitive worship as in the God of the most advanced theism. For what is the daemonic presence, too vague perhaps even to possess a name, which excites at once the awe and the devotion of the earliest known man, and which he thinks he can in some degree control by means of magical formulae and rites? It is a something instinctively rather than consciously conjectured behind the world of his observation which is purposing to bring good or evil to the individual man or his people; something free and transcendent in so far as it is separated in his thought from the little mechanical world of his restricted observation; yet at the same time hampered somehow by that which it transcends and through which it works; something responsive in the sense that it may respond to the worshipper's prayers and threats, but responsible also to the worshipper's moral code in a manner which justifies him in showing on occasion indignation against the invisible power for what he regards as wrong-doing as well as gratitude for right-doing. The object of primitive faith is thus utterly anthropomorphic; but it scarcely can be called personal, just as primitive man has the vaguest notion of his own personality. And this is the point where progress enters. One may say that the change from superstition to religion and the gradual development of religion to the most refined theism can be measured by an ever clearer understanding of personality as involved in the intuition of purpose and freedom and responsibility, by an ever clearer conception of faith as a conscious inference of such a personality behind the mechanism of observed phenomena.

Growth in religion is thus in the direction of a deeper and broader anthropomorphism; *but not away from anthropomorphism.* And this is a corollary of faith that must not be forgotten. So long as God remains a purposeful Being—and to faith He can be only that—He must be imagined as working out a design, just as man is conscious of doing, through some sort of obstacle or hindrance and by the lingering processes of time. There can in fact be no conception of purpose without such limitation, though with deepening self-consciousness the inference of limitation may change in character. Similarly He must be held, like man, responsible to the moral law, though again the nature of the moral law will purify itself and deepen as human experience grows larger. And so God's freedom will correspond to man's liberty of choice, developed to that self-determination to choose only good which man sees as the far-off goal of his own endeavour. If ever theologians, whether Christian or non-Christian, growing restive under the restraints of anthropomorphism, have framed what seemed to them a higher definition of the Supreme Being, if ever they have declared His freedom to be absolute power to do as He would, if they have altered responsibility into absolute authority over good and evil as though moral distinctions were no more than the decrees of His unconditioned will, if they have transmuted purpose into absolute creativeness,—then they have done so, not by pursuing the humble inferences of faith from intuition, but by transferring to God the monistic inferences of absolute causality drawn from observation of the mechanical sequences of nature. That was the way of Calvin, for instance, in reaching his rationalized theology of determinism. Yet it is a notable fact that, whenever religion has not been utterly stifled by misapplied metaphysics, the true inferences of faith will, in the theologian's unguarded moments, break through the whole panoply of absolutism.

.   .   .   .

Such, I hold, are the inevitable corollaries of faith. The Christian may object that the whole content of his religion does not come to him by a spontaneous inference of faith alone but in part has been directly revealed by an act of divine grace. That may well be true; but the question thus raised of grace and revelation has been deliberately eschewed in this essay for treatment elsewhere, and at any rate is secondary to that of faith. Here I am only contending that the theism which, without being at all peculiar to Christianity, yet constitutes its necessary basis, comes by an inference of faith, and cannot demand the allegiance of faith unless it remains true to its origin.

Why, then, if faith is what I have described it to be, do we make such an inference, what warrant have we for its validity, and what compulsion lies upon us for taking religion seriously as a matter of any consequence to our intellectual and practical life?

Now the reply to these queries given by a large number of thinking men, of whom Professor John Dewey may be named as an eminent example, is at once simple and specious. The inference of faith they declare, is merely a "wishful belief," a "defence attitude." We are here in a world which affords no knowledge of any life beyond the span of our mortal years, and no knowledge of a supernatural Being who is governing it in accordance with our individual sense of freedom and responsibility to an end corresponding to our sense of purpose. We crave the existence of such a Being, and so we infer that He does exist. We are dismayed by the thought of our life as confined to the limits of birth and death, terrified by the great gulf of nothingness which yawns before us at the end of our course, tormented by our loneliness in a world where there is no personality responding to our human need of companionship. And so, losing heart, unwilling to face the hard facts, we create for ourselves a religion as a pure attitude of defence against the truth. We believe simply because we wish to believe, because we are afraid not to believe.

The issue is clear cut. The infidel has thrown down the gauntlet; for myself I am ready to accept the *défi* and to meet the challenger on his own ground. Whatever others may have said of mystical visions, whatever tales there may be of violent irruptions from the supernatural world, I can only report that for myself I can see no sure warrant for the beginning of religion except in faith, and no warrant for rejecting the infidel's identification of faith with desire. I say for myself; yet I think that the writer of the Epistle to the Hebrews was with me when he defined faith as "the substance of things hoped for." What is the meaning of these words except that faith is a deliberate act of confidence in our hopes, and what is the meaning of this but an acceptance of the challenge that we believe because we wish to believe? And I submit that the Church today holds the same position. At least I can put no other interpretation upon the words of a learned Jesuit which, though they were intentionally directed against myself, sound to me like a confirmation of what I would maintain. "You may," he says, "tell yourself, *intelligo ut credam*: but . . . the intimate understanding of Catholicity, which is the real understanding of it, comes only after your act of Catholic faith, after your adherence, after your *credo ut intelligam*." For what is this *credo ut intelligam* but an admission that the initial act of faith is, again, to believe because we wish to believe, hoping that possibly confirmation in experience may come later?

All this, you will observe, is no more than a corollary of the sceptic's statement that knowledge, demonstrable knowledge at least, is limited to our immediate affections, and that faith is therefore not knowledge but undemonstrable inference. Nor has reason any power to demonstrate that the inferred existence of a God is necessarily true. At least I can say that of all the rational attempts to demonstrate the existence of God—and I have read many from Plato's time to those of the present day—not one is logically coercive, not one of them bridges the gap between a demonstration of what would be in the world if anything there corresponded to what we know of ourselves by intuition, and demonstration of the fact that something does actually there exist corresponding to our intuition. Against that final doubt reason is perfectly powerless. It is, to illustrate my point, because of the inadequacy of A. E. Taylor's attempt to solve this problem rationally in his initial chapter on Actuality and Value, while he seems to imply that the validity of religion depends upon such a solution, that we go through the rest of this really noble work on *The Faith of a Moralist* with the unquieted sense of having been trapped by some concealed fallacy.

Again, admit the challenger's assertion that we believe because we wish to believe, because we are afraid not to believe. What then?

Well, first of all I would ask the challenger to play fair. I would say to him: You tell me that my faith is a mere refuge from the known facts. Very good. But you cannot make such an accusation and at the same time cloak yourself about in the pretended indifference of the self-styled "agnostic"; having taken this positive attitude, you cannot avoid the issue you have raised by asserting that we know nothing of the truth or falsehood of any proposition whatsoever and must therefore hold our judgement in absolute equilibrium. This is not a matter of idle curiosity, as if one were debating whether he should open his egg at the sharp or the flat end. Faith means belief in God and in the responsibility of my human soul to God, and religion, if it is anything more than a *flatus vocis*, means a life fashioned in accordance with that belief. Indifference to faith, equally with dogmatic denial of faith, is pragmatically a rejection of the demands of religion. You, the challenger, cannot hold me to the consequences of my position, while you slip easily from the infidel's stand of open contradiction to the self-styled agnostic's indifference of suspended judgement. There are not three parties to our dispute, but only two: to the honourable mind it must be either acceptance or non-acceptance of the inference of faith, with loyalty to the consequences of one or the other choice.

And in another matter I would ask the challenger to play fair. Again I would say to him: You cannot belittle my faith as a product of fear and as a defence-attitude, and then laugh at me for fleeing from a bogey of my own fancy. It is you who are fond of asserting that faith springs from a refusal to face facts. Or, if you would creep out of the implication of such an assertion by adding that it is not really facts from which I am fleeing but my own falsely pessimistic colouring of the facts; if, that is, you present the truth of life as simply this: that my conscious existence is measured by the quick transit from birth to

death, that I am only a sudden and momentary emergence into a
world which pursues its ruthless course with grand indifference to
what my desires may be, and with nothing at its heart which corresponds to my sense of personal freedom and responsibility, that my
life is like a bubble tossed up from a sea of waves clashing endlessly
and purposelessly beneath an empty sky, and of tides sweeping rest-
lessly hither and thither in obedience to no directing hand—if this is
the fact you would beg me to face, yet would insist that there is nothing to disquiet or discomfort me, nothing to fear, nothing to justify
me in running off to some imaginary refuge, then I would retort with
the charge that your optimism is less logical than my faith; I would
say that this optimism of yours, granting it to be genuine, either is
dependent on the dullness of an atrophied imagination or is itself a
kind of stubborn and joyless and very vulnerable defence-attitude.
And in this the judgement of mankind is with me, and it is you that
stand in arbitrary isolation. Not here and now only, but always and
everywhere, when men begin to reflect, their reaction towards a world
seen without God and without purpose is dark with despair and bitter
with resentment.

.   .   .   .

And so I take up the challenge. I must either believe or disbelieve
that there is within the world, or, rather, beyond the world, that which
corresponds to my intuition of freedom and responsibility; I must
either regard the universe as teleological, with all which this implies,
or I must regard it as without purpose. There is for the honest and
serious mind, for the practical rule of life, no middle ground. And
faced with the compulsion of choosing between such alternatives I
say to you, the champion of what you call facts, that your view is simply incredible. You ask me to believe that nature has planted in me,
and not in me alone but in all men, desires which I must eradicate as
pure deceptions, that I am the victim of a cosmic jest, only the more
cruel if unintended, that the ultimate fact of existence is a malignant
mockery. The genial Autocrat of the Breakfast Table once said that no
decent man could logically hold the doctrines of Calvin without going
mad. His gibe upon that parody of faith was not without point, but it
might be applied with even greater aptitude to the challenger of the
very principle of faith. Again I say: *de te fabula.*

I am not retracting the admission that faith, initially at least, is inference and not knowledge, or that a man believes because he wishes
to believe; I am only saying that, all things considered, the so-called
disbelief of the infidel is an inference which, if honestly examined,
demands an act of almost impossible credulity.

But the issue does not end here. Faith, to become religion, must be
something more than lip-assent to a greater probability. Religion requires a decision of the will to live in accordance with faith, an unre-
mitting determination to transmute a probability of belief into a truth

of experience. It is thus, as Pascal declared, a *pari*, a wager, a great
venture, in which a man stakes his all upon the realization of a hope.
And here it must be admitted that infidelity is much easier, less ex-
acting, than faith. The life of infidelity demands no such effort of the
will and no such renunciations as does the life of religion; it is rather
by comparison a letting of oneself go, a facile surrender to the stream-
ing impressions that crowd upon us from the outer world and to the
tides of sensation that ebb and flow within us. So it is that in moments
of depression and apparent failure, we hear the voice of doubt, like a
whisper in the ear, saying: After all faith at best is only a matter of
probability which we are under no obligation to accept; why then
take the harder course? Against such doubts the best remedy would
seem to be Plato's prescription of a handy sentence in the form of an
epôdê, or charm, to be repeated over and over again:

Χαλεπὸν τὸ πιστεύειν ἀμήχανον τὸ ἀπιστεῖν.
Difficilius discredere quam credere.
It is hard to believe, harder not to believe.
The alternative to faith, if honestly faced, is an act of impossible
   credulity.

You may remember the close of Socrates' argument in gaol with
the challenger of his faith:

> "These, my dear friend Crito, are the words that I seem to
> hear, as the mystic worshippers seem to hear the piping of
> flutes; and the sound of this voice so murmurs in my ears that
> I can hear no other. I know that anything more which you
> may say will be vain. Yet speak, if you have anything to say."
> "I have nothing to say, Socrates."
> "Leave me then, Crito, to fulfil the will of God, and to fol-
> low whither he leads."

WIDESPREAD SKEPTICISM *had been a common fear for the orthodox,* *at least since Darwinism arrived in America in the 1860s. In a sense,* *skepticism had always been a threat and always would be, but what* *was new by the 1920s was a growing apathy. More and more people* *no longer seemed to feel that religion was even worth refuting or ar-* *guing about at all. New doctrines of science, new ideas of pschology,* *"modernism" in general, had made religion unnecessary and incred-* *ible. The organized churches had responded frequently enough with* *secularized versions of the faith, where social service and good fel-* *lowship replaced orthodoxy and prayer as central concerns. Books like* *Lippmann's* A Preface to Morals *and Joseph Wood Krutch's* The Mod-ern Temper *summed up the new disillusionment; clergy like Harry* *Emerson Fosdick and John Haynes Holmes espoused the new, undoc-* *trinal liberalism in the churches.*

To many conservatives, but especially to the agrarians, these people *were the Enemy. They were city-dwelling Northerners and Easterners,* *often of Jewish or foreign background, and to the agrarians they did* *not speak with voices acceptable to hinterland Christianity. Ransom* *soon became the recognized leader on this issue, a Tennessee Jona-* *than Edwards defending orthodoxy and an inscrutable God against* *the Arminians of the urban East. The excerpt that follows distills his* *demand for a return to orthodoxy and a religion with Old Testament* *spirit and expresses his scorn for all kinds of religious liberalism.*

26. God without Thunder

By John Crowe Ransom

Is religion a cause or an effect, when we look at its relation to the whole conduct of life?

It is usual to take it as a cause, and a powerful cause too. For consider the usual meaning of religion. We mean by religion, usually, a body of doctrine concerning God and man. But the doctrine which defines God, and man's relation to God, is really a doctrine which tries to define the intention of the universe, and man's proper portion within this universe. It is therefore his fundamental philosophy, it expresses the conviction he holds about his essential destiny, and it is bound to be of determining influence upon his conduct.

In nearly every external respect, the conduct of life in the Western world has changed during modern times, for better or for worse, to a degree which is revolutionary. But while that change has been going on, it is interesting to inquire what religion has been doing.

Religion seemed during this time to change very slowly, and very little. The scientific successes of Western man were rapidly altering his attitude toward the world, and altering the program which he elected to carry out for himself in the world. But these alterations evidently were taking place in spite of his religion—his doctrines continued to make about the same demands as ever upon his attitude and upon his program. Westerners therefore seemed to be submitting themselves to a curious dichotomy: half of their minds was making a profession which was one thing and half was indulging in a practice which was another. The inevitable result was that religion fell into disrepute, for on these terms it clearly did not have the force which had been claimed for it in determining conduct. But probably the simple matter of fact was that an original body of religious convictions was being progressively disbelieved, while other religious convictions were forming unconsciously which would eventually rise to consciousness and call for expression. Inevitably the time would come when men would have to profess the principles which really governed them, and leave off the painful effort of adaptation which was required when they said one thing and tried to make it mean another.

Note: Originally published in *God without Thunder* (New York: Harcourt, Brace, 1930). Copyright © 1930, 1958, by John Crowe Ransom. Reprinted by permission of Harcourt Brace Jovanovich, Inc., from pp. 3–6, 28–29, 94–95, 124–125, 324–328.

That time has about come. The old doctrines are being more or less quietly dropped, the new doctrines are being more or less openly published. The war is nearly over, and the new doctrines have all but won. We are being invited now to abandon frankly a faith in which we really hadn't for a long time believed—and to subscribe to one in which we must have been believing very powerfully in secret, if our conduct means anything at all.

I will have to be much more specific.

The religion that is about to be superseded is orthodox Christianity. But since nearly every variety of Christianity is capable of claiming that title, let us apply the term severely: orthodox means the religion of the historically elder varieties that antedated modernism. Orthodoxy—the religion which now is losing in the Western world—is therefore such a religion as that of the Eastern or Orthodox Church. Perhaps a little less, it is that of the Roman and Anglican Churches, and perhaps still less that of several major nonconformist communions. From there orthodoxy tapers off towards the vanishing point, by varying degrees which I could not define, into Unitarianism; into many local Congregational units; into Christian Science; and into philanthropic societies with a minimum of doctrine about God, like the Young Men's Christian Association, welfare establishments, fraternal organizations, and Rotary.

And what is the characteristic doctrine of orthodoxy which is losing its ground? We may as well put this quite concretely: The doctrine which is now becoming so antiquated with us is that of the stern and inscrutable God of Israel, the God of the Old Testament.

The new doctrine which is replacing it is the doctrine of an amiable and understanding God. We wanted a God who wouldn't hurt us; who would let us understand him; who would agree to scrap all the wicked thunderbolts in his armament. And this is just the God that has developed popularly out of the Christ of the New Testament: the embodiment mostly of the principle of social benevolence and of physical welfare. The new religion makes this God the ruler of the world, reduces the God of the Old Testament to a minor figure in the Godhead, or even now and then expels him altogether.

Such a religion as this is clearly the one which adapts itself to the requirements of our aggressive modern science. It is the religion proposed by the scientific party. It is characteristically Occidental and modern. But as far as a religion can be, it is fundamentally irreligious, or secular, both in its doctrine and in its works.

The scientists, so much admired for the marvels they have worked, so very imposing in their unusual singleness of mind, have been steadily acquiring an ascendancy over public opinion. Their progress has been so regular that they have not generally found it necessary to resort to open battle with those who still defended the old doctrines, and the way of life which the old doctrines would have required of them. A change in religions is of course a revolution of the first importance in society, and might well be attended with violence. And in fact we have had a little of that. There was Dayton, Tennessee, which scared us with its revelation of the deep passions that might be involved. There is now the public religious conflict in Communist Russia. But on the whole, the new religion is on the point of having established itself in America, and in most Western societies perhaps, with unusual tact and with the minimum of outrage. The war has been fought now nearly to its finish, and yet it has been a war that grew more and more polite in its latter stages, with the purpose that at its conclusion nobody need openly admit defeat.

.   .   .   .

Our historical orthodoxy was an aggregate of supernatural stories, or myths. As soon as I make this statement, I remember painfully that there is a certain state of mind which will reply: "Myths are for children, and I am adult, and I do not care to hear about your historical orthodoxy." Probably this state of mind is not of the advanced mental age it supposes. But here it is enough to say: Myth is the mark of every religion that has functioned after the usual historic types. Our myths were taken partly from the Old Testament and partly from the New. We will examine in rather short order the part which was taken from the Old Testament, and which has to do with the question, Who was the God of Israel? I would fix attention upon only a few leading features, the ones which seem most peculiarly Hebraic, and the most foreign to the temper of our Occidental modernism.

I should add that our glance will have to be, so far as I am concerned, that of a layman, and not of an expert theologian.

The old God distinguished himself from the new God in at least three important particulars. First, he was mysterious, and not fully understood; there was no great familiarity with him which might breed contempt. Second, he was worshiped with burnt offering and sacrifice. And third, he was the author of evil as well as of good.

Perhaps all these are correlative features which imply each other.

.   .   .   .

There are probably sorcerers, magicians, and fakirs in the pay of every institutionalized religion, as its priests, and people who are taken in by them, as its defrauded believers. I should certainly not undertake to find an exceptional religion where this fact would not obtain. Nevertheless, I do not think it a fair conclusion that the classes together "constitute the Church."

And now it is time to discuss Fundamentalism. My own view is that all first-class religionists are Fundamentalists, and that it is the Fundamentalists, properly speaking, who constitute the Church. These Fundamentalists, as I see it, do not believe in magic. And yet I would feel obliged to define them in the usual terms. The Fundamentalists are those who regard their God as an actuality, and treat their super-natural fictions as natural objects. How then is it possible to clear them of the usual reproaches heaped upon them by anthropologists?

I will try to imagine the religious history of a good Fundamentalist as a perfectly intelligent course of action. There seems to be nothing preposterous in that combination.

The Fundamentalist is a man who, in the first place, had the meta-physical acuteness to rise from the scientific laws to the Principles. To get that far he employed philosophy, in its most ordinary kind of service.

But he was not only a philosopher, for he had religious desires; and so he allowed his Principles to take their spontaneous mythical forms. There was some courage and decision involved in this step too. He had to release his imagination, and honor the forms under which it represented the Principles.

And still he had not done all. The enjoyment of myths in general does not quite make a Fundamentalist. The act that yet remained for him was *to pick out of all the myths a particular one to profess and to keep*. This act he performed; and at that stage he became our full-fledged Fundamentalist.

. . . .

Much more might be written about the doctrine conveyed in the Garden myth, as one which is embodied again and again in a whole tissue of Old Testament myths—while it remains itself the grandest of all the embodiments. But I must make a more general point which does not have to do directly with myths.

The Scriptures do not consist only in "histories" or myths or doc-trine. They are the work of a race of writers who loved nature, and a very large fraction of them consists in pastoral poetry, or a litera-ture about nature. Religionists are almost inevitably agrarians rather than industrialists—they find a God readily when they make contact with the elemental soil, and with more difficulty as their habitations and occupations increase in artificiality and in distance from the soil.

There is nothing mysterious in the curse which attaches to the arti-ficial habitation, and to the occupation with business rather than with agriculture. There is just one thing wrong with an artificial en-vironment: it is much simpler than any natural one, and it produces in the man whom it environs a false illusion respecting the simplicity of nature. I will modernize a little. In the office room in which I write, the six inclosing surfaces, the doors, the lamps, the furniture, the shelves, and the books are for the most part of a severe rectilinear pattern, or at least of such geometrical and regular patterns as lend themselves to the easiest production by man's tools and processes. And they have textures which are smooth and homogeneous—another mark of the mechanical product. If I leave this room, I must walk through a building whose appointments are of the same simplicity. If I leave the building, I am in a city where I am almost as little in contact with nature: the streets are paved, the buildings are rectilinear, and the flora arrange themselves dutifully according to the prescriptions of the Street Commissioner and the Park Commissioner.

The modern American city or industrial district is certainly the most impressive transformation of natural environment that has yet appeared on this planet. It is no wonder if it tickles its inhabitants so pleasantly with the sense of their ruthless domination of nature, and the ease with which they can manage its God.

But any city, even a small city of the old Jewish world, approaches this degree of transformation. Its effect is to insulate its inhabitants against observation of a fact which it is well for the realist to take always into account: the infinite variety of nature. The agricultural population is constantly aware of this fact, and accordingly its temper differs from the temper of industrialists and city-folk: it is humble, religious, and conservative. Its God is inscrutable. The nature it knows is not the nature that the city-folk think they have mastered. Neither in the manner of their habitations nor in the forms of their occupation do the city-folk make contact with elemental nature. And if even the city-folk are visited sometimes by an unaccountable nostalgia for the soil, and would like to return at week-ends to visit the old nature from which they have emancipated themselves, they do it far too patronizingly, they do not really recover the old attitude towards nature: they only take what may be called a picnic view of nature.

.   .   .   .

We have moved far from the habits of those days and those climates to which the Scriptures were congenial. Culturally their language and their images seem strange to us now. And we have heard so much fun made of them! There is a real effort required now to enter into them sympathetically even when we consider that metaphysically they are sound. Perhaps we would greatly relish, and indeed it is probable that we are continually on the lookout to see if we will not discover somewhere, a brand-new myth, not shop-worn, not yet ridiculed, and not unrepresentative of what little taste we may have yet for the enjoyment of myths. But that is an event upon which it is impossible to make any calculations.

A new religion being totally impracticable as a thing to propose, the only recommendation that it is in my power to make is this one: We had better work within the religious institutions that we have, and do what we can to recover the excellences of the ancient faith. The churches must be turned from their false Gods towards their old true Gods—whenever, and however, and so far as this proves to be practicable.

Is it possible then for all the religious institutions yet to be saved? There is undoubtedly a good deal of difference in their respective chances of obtaining this happiness. The further they have come from orthodoxy, the smaller their chances.

But why should one not dispose of this vexing problem by saying, ever so simply: Let the West go into the Greek communion, where orthodoxy still largely prevails.

Like other dispositions that are excessively simple, that solution is not in the least practicable. The West will scarcely do what I might ask in this matter. At best only a few Westerners might do it. Where is this Greek communion? It is too far away from my part of the world, and I would have to expatriate myself to join it, or lead an emigration of a few like-minded fellow-citizens to go and become Greeks. The only local example of a church of this faith with which I have any actual acquaintance is situated in a Wyoming mining town: I cannot pronounce the names of its members, I can scarcely exchange with some of them any conversation in the same tongue, and I find very little in common with them except that, so far as I understand, I admire their Gods. The thought of joining them is, in brief, abhorrent.

Or why not advise the Western world to enter the Synagogue, if the Synagogue might be so kind as to receive it, and find the God of Israel in his greatest purity? Once more, and with all respect, the word suggests itself: abhorrent. For better for worse, a man is a member of his own race, or his own tribe. He will have to prosper or suffer as it prospers or suffers. The religion that he requires must have the character of being his own social institution. If there is not a religious institution that suits him quite near at home, he will have to go without one.

Besides, there might be some disagreeable questions to raise and answer. Would Judaism admit Christ the Logos into its Godhead, even in his subordinate capacity? And does Judaism still cherish the ancient God of Israel in his stern and inscrutable majesty? Or has Judaism softened him down, and degraded him, and identified him with its rather secular and commercialized existence?

I will mention another possibility. Why should not the Western world go Roman? But again that is too simple. My Western world does not want to do anything of the kind. The history of the Western world is a history of political separation from the Roman church, which is now definitely a rejected polity (as well as a faith), and against which we have for a good many generations cultivated a powerful antagonism. We have prejudices; and if I for my part might overcome these prejudices, would my community as a whole do this also? I have friends, and I hear of men whose sound judgment I esteem highly, who are going back to Rome. Sometimes I may feel envious of their spiritual advantages. But the most of my friends and kind are not doing this and will not. Therefore I am not willing to do it, and neither will I advocate it.

And next: Why not bid the West go Anglican, or Episcopal? I am now getting much nearer home—much nearer to the actual milieu in which I live. I am an Anglophile, and I wish my country might be more so. But I am not so Anglophile as I am American. And I find myself sometimes, as I find my neighbor more frequently, abhorring Anglicanism and Episcopacy. For reasons perhaps that are social and political, and inarticulate but deep—for inherited reasons. Therefore I propose no such thing. I still seek the religion that will be the expression of the social solidarity of my own community.

There is Presbyterianism; and Methodism; and Baptistry; there are plenty of other sectarian possibilities. These bodies are evidently close to the genius of my kind of community. But they have declined rather far from orthodoxy, as I see it—and as what Western religious body has not? They secularize themselves more and more every day. It is hard to give them an endorsement.

There are two objectives at which the religious purpose of an intelligent private citizen has to drive. One is scarcely more important and indispensable than the other. But while it might well be possible to realize one of them, it is, according to our present prospects, almost impossible to realize both of them at once. One is a religion to which the private citizen might by personal conviction be intensely loyal, with Gods whom he may fear and love, and whose commandments represent for him the deepest wisdom. The other is simply a religion with the sanction of his own natural society behind it.

Under these circumstances it will be a bolder man than I who has an extremely specific or concrete proposal to offer to the Western cis-Atlantic world seeking its religious expression.

I have already made the best suggestion I can; it is a comparatively tame one, it does not look in the least heroic, and it does not promise any quick and spectacular consequences. But I will repeat it, a little more fully, and it will have to be the only contribution that I know how to offer.

With whatever religious institution a modern man may be connected, let him try to turn it back towards orthodoxy.

Let him insist on a virile and concrete God, and accept no Principle as a substitute.

Let him restore to God the thunder.

Let him resist the usurpation of the Godhead by the soft modern version of the Christ, and try to keep the Christ for what he professed to be: the Demigod who came to do honor to the God.

IF SANTAYANA *ever encountered Ransom's book, he left no record of it. He would doubtless have put it aside with a kind of amazement that so intelligent a man could seem to endorse religious ideas and institutions that led to narrow-mindedness and even to bigotry in so many of their followers. Yet Santayana too could defend orthodoxy, if of a startlingly different kind. In any strict theological sense, Santayana had no religion or faith at all. He was a pagan and a naturalist and was frank about saying so. But he also adored myth and beauty and regarded the best aspects of Christianity as among the most profound and worthy achievements of the human spirit. He was a Spanish Roman Catholic by birth and allegiance, yet a heretic to his bones. Such a stance helped him survive life in Protestant America and gave his remarks on both religion and culture a genuine bite often absent from the comments of others.*

I have chosen excerpts from six private letters to give some indication of Santayana's complex views on religion and immortality. They have been strung together from letters to, in order, Henry Ward Abbott, August 6, 1889; William James, December 6, 1905; Susana Sturgis De Sastre, December 7, 1911; J. Middleton Murry, November 1, 1927, and December 11, 1929; and the Marchesa Iris Origo, May 1933.

27. Excerpts from Six Letters

By George Santayana

. . . . . I must quarrel with your criticism of neo-paganism. In my
case it may be true that it is forced (although I do not feel it so myself), I may not be able to free myself entirely from the oppression of
a false idealism. But the question is a broad one: my lingering superstitions or yours are personal accidents. I protest against the notion
that what is really joyous and lovely in life is for ever vitiated to all
men because a fictitious and fanatical system has had great influence
in the world. Your position is hardly tenable. You admit, do you not,
that paganism is rational and satisfactory for men who have not been
Christians? So that for our children, if we brought them up without
Christianity, paganism would be natural and rational. That is, paganism is the human and spontaneous attitude of an intelligent and cultivated man in the presence of the universe. So that your consistent
pessimism is but the unnatural reaction after an unnatural excitement and strain. The Hebrew religion and its twin offspring, and
more than all, the Hebraising sects of Christianity, represent a false
moral interpretation of life, a weight of responsibility and a consciousness of importance, which human nature repudiates. The Jews had
the incredible conceit of believing they had made a covenant with
nature, by which the mastery of the earth and all the good things
thereof were secured to them in return for fidelity to a certain social
and religious organization. Freed from its religious and irrational nature this covenant might stand for something real. Nature does award
her prizes in return for fidelity to certain ethical laws: only these
laws are natural: they are variable according to circumstances, and
discoverable only by experience and study of history. But a religion,
as it develops, loses hold of the natural significance and justification
of its first principles. The fiction grows, the truth dwindles. So with
the Hebrew idea. From recognition of the conditions of worldly success it waxed into the assertion of an inscrutable inward law with
transcendent and imaginary sanctions. The crushing weight of delir-
ious exaltation is still felt, especially in Protestant communities.
Catholicism is rational in its morals: its superstitions are in the field
of fancy and emotional speculation: in conduct it has remained rational, granting the reality of the conditions of life believed in. In fact

Note: Originally published in *The Letters of George Santayana*, edited
by Daniel Cory (New York: Scribner's, 1955), pp. 33–35, 81–82, 110–111,
226, 246–248, 281. Reprinted by permission of Mrs. Margot Cory.

I have never been well able to understand the moral superstition of conscience and duty. Only when reading of or seeing cases of insanity has it become clear to me. X, for instance, has moral delirium, a fearful belief in right and wrong, without external sanctions, and of pathological origin. A touch of this insanity is what pervades society. And will you pretend to assert that life is not worth living if we are not mad? That only superstitious terrors give it value? that actual goods are worthless and fictitious and imaginary goods—in which is no enjoyment, no peace, and no loveliness,—are alone valuable? I confess, that seems to me pure madness. The world may have little in it that is good: granted. But that little is really and inalienably good. Its value cannot be destroyed because of the surrounding evil. But the greatest of all evils is surely that lunacy that convinces us that this little good is not good, and subverts natural standards in favor of unnatural and irrational standards. It is a form of insanity. And you know how the insane tinge sometimes all their experiences with a pathological horror or emptiness. That is just what you would have us do in the name of consistency. It seems to me that even supposing that our illusions are pleasant and consoling (which is not the case with moral illusions, although it may be with purely imaginative and speculative fictions) the lesson of life is to give them up quietly and settle down, a sadder but a wiser man, on the new basis. And believe me, in respect to paganism, the new basis is the best basis. It admits more noble emotion, more justifiable ambition, more universal charity, than the old system. I cannot go on forever: but I should like to show you how we deceive ourselves in thinking that immortality, for instance, really added to our lives any value. An old man's enthusiasms, if he has any, are *naturally* for the world he leaves behind him, not for himself. Cf. Gladstone. F. Harrison may be a fool, but positivism, if truly pagan, seems to me good. But Goethe is the real spokesman of neo-paganism. I follow him.

.   .   .   .

I forgot yesterday to answer one of your questions, which I remember may be of importance to you. The lectures are at five o'clock in the afternoon on Tuesdays and Saturdays. I have no doubt they would change the hour for you if you wished. To everything they say "comme vous voudrez," and things here, as in England, seem to go by prerogative. You could also give as many or as few lectures as you chose—the great Hyde consenting.

Another omission. Blood's poem,[1] after about six readings, has become intelligible to me, and I like the thought very much, also the diction, but the *composition* is deplorable. Why can't people begin and end, and give one some indication of what they are talking about? As to the Tychism of it, it seems to me a good surface philosophy, a

1. *Reveries of One*, by B. P. Blood.

good expression of consciousness and the look of the flux. Of course what must be, if it must be, would never be known beforehand; and the machinery that may actually support our feelings doesn't deprive them of their dramatic novelty and interest, any more than the print-ed *dénouement* of a novel, extant in the last chapter, takes away from the dreamful excitement of perusing it and of wondering what will come next.

Now that I am launched I will say a word about some of the criti-cisms in your letter. You are very generous; I feel that you want to give me credit for every thing good than can possibly be found in my book.[2] But you don't yet see my philosophy, nor my temper from the inside; your praise, like your blame, touches only the periphery, accidental as-pects presented to this or that preconceived and disparate interest. The style is good, the tone is supercilious, here is a shrewd passage, etc., etc. And you say I am less hospitable than Emerson. Of course. Emerson might pipe his wood-notes and chirp at the universe most blandly; his genius might be tender and profound and Hamlet-like, and that is all beyond my range and contrary to my purpose. I am a Latin, and nothing seems serious to me except politics, except the sort of men that your ideas will involve and the sort of happiness they will be capable of. The rest is exquisite moonshine. Religion in par-ticular was *found out* more than 100 years ago, and it seems to me intolerable that we should still be condemned to ignore the fact and to give the parsons and the "idealists" a monopoly of indignation and of contemptuous dogmatism. It is they, not we, that are the pest; and while I wish to be just and to understand people's feelings, wherever they are at all significant, I am deliberately minded to be contemptu-ous toward what seems to me contemptible, and not to have any share in the conspiracy of mock respect by which our intellectual ig-nominy and moral stagnation are kept up in our society. What did Emerson know or care about the passionate insanities and political disasters which religion, for instance, has so often been another name for? He could give that name to his last personal intuition, and ig-nore what it stands for and what it expresses in the world. It is the latter that absorbs me; and I care too much about mortal happiness to be interested in the charming vegetation of cancer-microbes in the system—except with the idea of suppressing it.

A more technical point. You say "activity" can be spiritual only. Is your activity, or sense of activity, not rather an ἐνέργεια [actuality] than a δύναμις [potentiality]? Of course I should be the first to agree that activity, in the sense of actuality and conscious stress, belongs only to consciousness or even to the rational and reflective energy of thought. But *efficiency*, in the sense of regular predictable contiguity with other specific events, belongs only to δύναμις, to the potential

2. *The Life of Reason.*

(= the potent.) In a dream there is the sense of activity, there is commotion and actualization, ἐνέργεια; but there is no δύναμις, no material efficacy, save through the underlying metabolism in the brain; the story in the dream stops short; its purposes evaporate. This may be contrary to common sense, meaning ordinary ways of expressing oneself; but it seems to me quite of a piece with common sense of a progressive sort, with science. It might be contrary to common sense to say that the sun is larger than the earth, but not to the common sense applied to the full situation. So this doctrine seems to me reasonable in its method and result, though as yet paradoxical in its language.

.   .   .   .

As to your supposition that I am removing myself "farther from God," apparently in some deliberate manner, I certainly have no consciousness of such a plan. My opinions in philosophy have not changed essentially for twenty years, although they may have settled and grown less plastic with time. In respect to the Church, I think I am in greater sympathy with it politically than I was previously, because the radical people I know are proving to be such Hottentots and so wholly ignorant of the art of living and of the art of thinking. The Church is an integral part of European civilisation, as it has been for the last thousand years and more. The "satanic" onslaught on it which you lament is a symptom of a general transformation, which will take hundreds of years to become definable in its results or ideals, and which is tending to destroy not the Church only but all institutions, including private property and national governments. The French Revolution was a first and violent shock of this earthquake; others will follow from time to time, I suppose, until, long after we are dead, everything we know and care about has disappeared. Now, I sympathise with the self-preserving instinct of formed things more than with the destructive forces of nature, such as democratic envy, fury, and ignorance are. Therefore I sympathise with the Church more than with its enemies: but I think the latter must prevail more and more in the world in our time. I also think that after the deluge, life and order are bound to reassert themselves in some form—doubtless a wholly new one. I should not be hostile to that new order for not being Christian, as I am not hostile to ancient Greece. But we don't know what that new order may some day be, and meantime the revolution is destroying everything noble and beautiful which actually exists, or which can exist in our day. It is producing nothing but vulgarity, shallowness, and a suicidal waywardness in the "emancipated souls"—like those of the Infanta Eulalia. These people are positively *loathsome*. They do not understand the creative and moral principle of anything, least of all of what they are themselves.—They are *silly traitors*. Yet, without in the least knowing what they are about, they are ploughing up the ground in which the seeds of new things are to take root. For, as Hamlet says, "so runs the world away."

.   .   .   .

. . . A heretic, I should say, had to be a believer: he had to maintain a principle while denying some of its consequences. I am a free-thinker or sceptic: and my sympathies in religion are with the ortho-doxies—not with one, but with each in contrast to its heresies. I am therefore not a heretic: but you are right that my share in the spiritual life is more vicarious than personal, if a complete ascetic renunciation is understood to be involved in it. Such insight as I may have comes from poetic indolence, or speculative ecstasy. I *can* feel the sweetness of saying no, and the greater joy of leaving the daisies growing in the field rather than plucking them to wilt in my button-hole.—I thought my little book[3] made my position quite clear: but I have a more formal treatise, about to appear, called *The Realm of Essence*, in which I speak more than once of my personal attitude towards the ambition of those who aspire to be pure spirits. I do *not* share it.

.   .   .   .

I have read "God"[4] with much interest, and am happy to think that perhaps my books have been of use to you in your heroic struggles with so many misfortunes and perplexities. My own course has been relatively smooth: I have had no "mystical experience" and have not been obliged to extricate myself from the tangle of Protestantism and Moralism. For that reason, probably, I am not able to share your enthusiasm for D. H. Lawrence, Dostojewski, Nietzsche, or even Goethe. They may be invaluable in bringing one to the conclusion that things moral are natural, and simply the fruition of things physical—in which latter the psyche, or principle of life, must be included. But I gathered all that in my youth from Aristotle and from my own reflection (as I have described at length in "Dialogues in Limbo") and those romantic solvents were unnecessary to my own liberty. I see their strength, but I don't need their influence. Goethe of course is full of wise reflexions, like Bacon: but when his romanticism droops, he becomes, like Bacon, a ponderous worldling: not a ray of spirituality in either of them. I am puzzled about what you find in Keats: is it there? As to your reconstruction of Christ, you know that I have no faith in such things. Like everybody else, I like to assimilate the sense of the Gospel to my own insights: and I have no objection to *poetic* interpretations of Jesus, if they continue his legend and are faithful to his sacred character as tradition preserves it—according

3. *Platonism and the Spiritual Life.*
4. *God: being an introduction to the science of Metabiology.* J. Middleton Murry (1929).

to the maxim of Horace about fidelity to characters once established
by the poets. But these reconstructions have no historical truth: documents are lacking, and the imagination of the modern poet is hopelessly transformed. On single abstracted points we may, of course,
have reasons for forming particular judgements: and there are *ideas*
which we may study and understand in themselves, apart from the
biography of their author, who probably did nothing but adopt them.
What you call Christ's "amazing" idea of God seems to me to be one
of these. In substance it is the commonplace of all Eastern religion:
you say yourself that it is found also in India and China; yes, and in
the Stoics and the Mohammedans: in fact in everybody except the
unmitigated Jews. It is the universal *"sursum corda"—"habemus ad
Dominum."* If we ventured on hypotheses about the personal context
in which this idea existed in Christ, we might say that it was merged
with that of Jehovah and (as you explain) with that of a Messiah:
and there was also a good deal of assimilation of the divine Being to
the governing principles of this world. For instance, besides your
favourite text about the sun and rain, there are texts about the wheat
and tares, the harvest, and the burning. Elevation above human interests did not exclude perception of what those interests required:
they required conventional morality, and even an established church.
I was glad to see you so bravely identifying genuine Christianity with
Rome; but there is one point which, if I had the pleasure of talking
with you, I would try to convince you of: and that is that the "supernatural" is the most harmless thing in the world, and not arbitrary.
It is merely the ultra-mundane: it is governed by its own principles,
of which there is a definite science, and it is the truly and fundamentally natural, of which our conventional or scientific nature is
only a local, temporary, and superficial mode. Of course, the *revelation* of what this ultra-mundane sphere contains is "fishy" and itself
inspired from below: it is like our modern Spiritualism; but that
doesn't prevent the general notion of an existing sphere beyond our
sphere, but touching it and sometimes penetrating into it, from being
legitimate, if only the evidence for it were not drawn from the wrong
quarter.

You are a modern, an "intellectual," and I am an old fogey: that is
probably the reason why I balk at your emphasis on "newness." Aren't
you confusing newness with freshness or spontaneity? True religion,
true philosophy, like true love, must be spontaneous, it must be fresh:
but why should it be new? There is no harm in a new species of rose,
if nature drops into it, or horticulture succeeds in bringing it forth
under electric reflectors, and by judicious grafting: but surely the
beauty even of the new roses, if genuine, and not simply a vile worldly fashion, is independent of the accident that such a form was previously unknown. Evolution is a fact, and we must be grateful to it
for the good things it brings forth: but the good in each of these
things lies in their own perfection and harmony with themselves; and

the date of them makes no difference in their happiness. Am I wrong?

I have just received Whitehead's new book on "Process & Reality", in which I expect to find much instruction. His point of view is in some respects like yours, and you must value so expert an ally. But why such "newness" in vocabulary? Both you and he bewilder us with your pseudo-technical terms, most of which, I am sure, could be avoided by a little precision in the use of old words.

.   .   .   .

. . . . . We have no claim to any of our possessions. We have no claim to exist; and as we have to die in the end, so we must resign ourselves to die piecemeal, which really happens when we lose somebody or something that was closely intertwined with our existence. It is like a physical wound; we may survive, but maimed and broken in that direction; dead there.

Not that we ever can, or ever do at heart, renounce our affections. Never that. We cannot exercise our full nature all at once in every direction; but the parts that are relatively in abeyance, their centre lying perhaps in the past or in the future, belong to us inalienably. We should not be ourselves if we cancelled them. I don't know how literally you may believe in another world, or whether the idea means very much to you. As you know, I am not myself a believer in the ordinary sense, yet my *feeling* on this subject is like that of believers, and not at all like that of my fellow-materialists. The reason is that I disagree utterly with that modern philosophy which regards *experience* as fundamental. Experience is a mere whiff or rumble, produced by enormously complex and ill-deciphered causes of experience; and in the other direction, experience is a mere peephole through which glimpses come down to us of eternal things. These are the only things that, in so far as we are spiritual beings, we can find or can love at all. All our affections, when clear and pure, and not claims to possession, transport us to another world; and the loss of contact, here or there, with those eternal beings is merely like closing a book which we keep at hand for another occasion. We know that book by heart. Its verses give life to life.

I don't mean that these abstract considerations ought to console us. Why wish to be consoled? On the contrary, I wish to mourn perpetually the absence of what I love or might love. Isn't that what religious people call the love of God?

MANY CONSERVATIVES *were thoroughly irritated by the forces of modernism. Santayana proved as able to poetize their insights as he was those of the Catholic church. In an essay which, as far as I know, has never appeared in any Santayana collections, he made a conservative case for Freud and some of the usable myths of psychoanalysis. As with all of Santayana's writings, this piece has a graceful effortlessness which makes even death seem but a pleasant ending to the party of life. "The point is to have expressed and discharged all that was latent in us," whether "calling it having one's day, or doing one's duty, or realizing one's ideal, or saving one's soul. . . . Wisdom and genius lie in discerning the prescribed task and in doing it readily, cleanly, and without distraction."*

28. A Long Way Round to Nirvana

By George Santayana

That the end of life is death may be called a truism, since the various kinds of immortality that might perhaps supervene would none of them abolish death, but at best would weave life and death together into the texture of a more comprehensive destiny. The end of one life might be the beginning of another, if the Creator had composed his great work like a dramatic poet, assigning some lines to one character and some to another. Death would then be merely the cue at the end of each speech, summoning the next personage to break in and keep the ball rolling. Or perhaps, as some suppose, all the characters are assumed in turn by a single supernatural Spirit, who amid his endless improvisations is imagining himself living for the moment in this particular solar and social system. Death in such a universal monologue would be but a change of scene or of metre, while in the scramble of a real comedy it would be a change of actors. In either case every voice would be silenced sooner or later, and death would end each particular life, in spite of all possible sequels.

The relapse of created things into nothing is no violent fatality, but something naturally quite smooth and proper. This has been set forth recently, in a novel way, by a philosopher from whom we hardly expected such a lesson, namely Professor Sigmund Freud. He has now broadened his conception of sexual craving or *libido* into a general principle of attraction or concretion in matter, like the Eros of the ancient poets Hesiod and Empedocles. The windows of that stuffy clinic have been thrown open; that swell of acrid disinfectants, those hysterical shrieks, have escaped into the cold night. The troubles of the sick soul, we are given to understand, as well as their cure, after all flow from the stars.

I am glad that Freud has resisted the tendency to represent this principle of Love as the only principle in nature. Unity somehow exercises an evil spell over metaphysicians. It is admitted that in real life it is not well for One to be alone, and I think pure unity is no less barren and graceless in metaphysics. You must have plurality to start with, or trinity, or at least duality, if you wish to get anywhere, even if you wish to get effectively into the bosom of the One, abandoning your separate existence. Freud, like Empedocles, has prudently intro-

Note: Originally published as "A Long Way Round to Nirvana or, Much Ado about Dying," in the *Dial* 75 (November 1923): 435–442.

duced a prior principle for Love to play with; not Strife, however (which is only an incident in Love), but Inertia, or the tendency towards peace and death. Let us suppose that matter was originally dead, and perfectly content to be so, and that it still relapses, when it can, into its old equilibrium. But the homogeneous (as Spencer would say) when it is finite is unstable: and matter, presumably not being coextensive with space, necessarily forms aggregates which have an inside and an outside. The parts of such bodies are accordingly differently exposed to external influences and differently related to one another. This inequality, even in what seems most quiescent, is big with changes, destined to produce in time a wonderful complexity. It is the source of all uneasiness, of life, and of love.

"Let us imagine [writes Freud[1]] an undifferentiated vesicle of sensitive substance: then its surface, exposed as it is to the outer world, is by its very position differentiated, and serves as an organ for receiving stimuli. Embryology, repeating as it does the history of evolution, does in fact show that the central nervous system arises from the ectoderm; the grey cortex of the brain remains a derivative of the primitive superficial layer. . . . This morsel of living substance floats about in an outer world which is charged with the most potent energies, and it would be destroyed . . . if it were not furnished with protection against stimulation. It acquires this through . . . a special integument or membrane . . . The outer layer, by its own death, has secured all the deeper layers from a like fate. . . . It must suffice to take little samples of the outer world, to taste it, so to speak, in small quantities. In highly developed organisms the receptive external layer of what was once a vesicle has long been withdrawn into the depths of the body, but portions of it have been left on the surface immediately beneath the common protective barrier. These portions form the sense-organs. [On the other hand] the sensitive cortical layer has no protective barrier against excitations emanating from within. . . . The most prolific sources of such excitations are the so-called instincts of the organism. . . . The child never gets tired of demanding the repetition of a game. . . . he wants always to hear the same story instead of a new one, insists inexorably on exact repetition, and corrects each deviation which the narrator lets slip by mistake. . . . According to this, *an instinct would be a tendency in living organic matter impelling it towards reinstatement of an earlier condition*, one which it had abandoned under the influence of external disturbing forces—a kind of organic elasticity or, to put it another way, the manifestation of inertia in organic life.

1. The following quotations are drawn from *Beyond the Pleasure Principle*, by Sigmund Freud; authorized translation by C. J. M. Hubback. The International Psycho-Analytic Press, 1922, pp. 29–48. The italics are in the original.

"If, then, all organic instincts are conservative, historically acquired, and directed towards regression, towards reinstatement of something earlier, we are obliged to place all the results of organic development to the credit of external, disturbing, and distracting influences. The rudimentary creature would from its very beginning not have wanted to change, would, if circumstances had remained the same, have always merely repeated the same course of existence. But in the last resort it must have been the evolution of our earth, and its relation to the sun, that has left its imprint on the development of organisms. The conservative organic instincts have absorbed every one of these enforced alterations in the course of life, and have stored them for repetition; they thus present the delusive appearance of forces striving after change and progress, while they are merely endeavouring to reach an old goal by ways both old and new. This final goal of all organic striving can be stated too. It would be counter to the conservative nature of instinct if the goal of life were a state never hitherto reached. It must be rather an ancient starting point, which the living being left long ago, and to which it harks back again by all the circuitous paths of development . . . *The goal of all life is death.* . . .

"Through a long period of time the living substance may have . . . had death within easy reach . . . until decisive external influences altered in such a way as to compel [it] to ever greater deviations from the original path of life, and to ever more complicated and circuitous routes to the attainment of the goal of death. These circuitous ways to death, faithfully retained by the conservative instincts, would be neither more nor less than the phenomena of life as we know it."

Freud puts forth these interesting suggestions with much modesty, admitting that they are vague and uncertain and (what it is even more important to notice) mythical in their terms; but it seems to me that, for all that, they are an admirable counterblast to prevalent follies. When we hear that there is, animating the whole universe, an *élan vital*, or general impulse toward some unknown but single ideal, the terms used are no less uncertain, mythical, and vague, but the suggestion conveyed is false, whereas that conveyed by Freud's speculations is true. In what sense can myths and metaphors be true or false? In the sense that, in terms drawn from moral predicaments or from literary psychology, they may report the general movement and the pertinent issue of material facts, and may inspire us with a wise sentiment in their presence. In this sense I should say that Greek mythology was true and Calvinist theology was false. The chief terms employed in psychoanalysis have always been metaphorical: "unconscious wishes," "the pleasure-principle," "the Oedipus complex," "Narcissism," "the censor"; nevertheless, interesting and profound vistas may be opened up, in such terms, into the tangle of events in a man's life, and a fresh start may be made with fewer encumbrances and less morbid inhibition. "The shortcomings of our description,"

Freud says, "would probably disappear if for psychological terms we could substitute physiological or chemical ones. These too only constitute a metaphorical language, but one familiar to us for a much longer time, and perhaps also simpler." All human discourse is metaphorical, in that our perceptions and thoughts are adventitious signs for their objects, as names are, and by no means copies of what is going on materially in the depths of nature; but just as the sportsman's eye, which yields but a summary graphic image, can trace the flight of a bird through the air quite well enough to shoot it and bring it down, so the myths of a wise philosopher about the origin of life or of dreams, though expressed symbolically, may reveal the pertinent movement of nature to us, and may kindle in us just sentiments and true expectations in respect to our fate—for his own soul is the bird this sportsman is shooting.

Now I think these new myths of Freud's about life, like his old ones about dreams, are calculated to enlighten and to chasten us enormously about ourselves. The human spirit, when it awakes, finds itself in trouble; it is burdened, for no reason it can assign, with all sorts of anxieties about food, pressures, pricks, noises, and pains. It is born, as another wise myth has it, in original sin. And the passions and ambitions of life, as they come on, only complicate this burden and make it heavier, without rendering it less incessant or gratuitous. Whence this fatality, and whither does it lead? It comes from heredity, and it leads to propagation. When we ask how heredity could be started or transmitted, our ignorance of nature and of past time reduces us to silence or to wild conjectures. Something—let us call it matter—must always have existed, and some of its parts, under pressure of the others, must have got tied up into knots, like the mainspring of a watch, in such a violent and unhappy manner that when the pressure is relaxed they fly open as fast as they can, and unravel themselves with a vast sense of relief. Hence the longing to satisfy latent passions, with the fugitive pleasure in doing so. But the external agencies that originally wound up that mainspring never cease to operate; every fresh stimulus gives it another turn, until it snaps, or grows flaccid, or is unhinged. Moreover, from time to time, when circumstances change, these external agencies may encrust that primary organ with minor organs attached to it. Every impression, every adventure, leaves a trace or rather a seed behind it. It produces a further complication in the structure of the body, a fresh charge, which tends to repeat the impressed motion in season and out of season. Hence that perpetual docility or ductibility in living substance which enables it to learn tricks, to remember facts, and (when the seeds of past experiences marry and cross in the brain) to imagine new experiences, pleasing or horrible. Every act initiates a new habit and may implant a new instinct. We see people even late in life carried away by political or religious contagions or developing strange vices; there would be no peace in old age, but rather a greater and

greater obsession by all sorts of cares, were it not that time, in ex-
posing us to many adventitious influences, weakens or discharges our
primitive passions; we are less greedy, less lusty, less hopeful, less
generous. But these weakened primitive impulses are naturally by far
the strongest and most deeply rooted in the organism: so that although an old man may be converted or may take up some hobby,
there is usually something thin in his elderly zeal, compared with the
heartiness of youth; nor is it edifying to see a soul in which the
plainer human passions are extinct becoming a hot-bed of chance
delusions.

In any case each fresh habit taking root in the organism forms a
little mainspring or instinct of its own, like a parasite; so that an
elaborate mechanism is gradually developed, where each lever and
spring holds the other down, and all hold the mainspring down together, allowing it to unwind itself only very gradually, and meantime keeping the whole clock ticking and revolving, and causing the
smooth outer face which it turns to the world, so clean and innocent,
to mark the time of day amiably for the passer-by. But there is a
terribly complicated labour going on beneath, propelled with difficulty,
and balanced precariously, with much secret friction and failure. No
wonder that the engine often gets visibly out of order, or stops short:
the marvel is that it ever manages to go at all. Nor is it satisfied with
simply revolving and, when at last dismounted, starting afresh in the
person of some seed it has dropped, a portion of its substance with
all its concentrated instincts wound up tightly within it, and eager to
repeat the ancestral experiment; all this growth is not merely material
and vain. Each clock in revolving strikes the hour, even the quarters,
and often with lovely chimes. These chimes we call perceptions, feelings, purposes, and dreams; and it is because we are taken up entirely
with this pretty music, and perhaps think that it sounds of itself and
needs no music-box to make it, that we find such difficulty in con-
ceiving the nature of our own clocks and are compelled to describe
them only musically, that is, in myths. But the ineptitude of our
aesthetic minds to unravel the nature of mechanism does not deprive
these minds of their own clearness and euphony. Besides sounding
their various musical notes, they have the cognitive function of indicating the hour and catching the echoes of distant events or of matur-
ing inward dispositions. This information and emotion, added to the
incidental pleasures in satisfying our various passions, make up the
life of an incarnate spirit. They reconcile it to the external fatality
that has wound up the organism, and is breaking it down; and they
rescue this organism and all its works from the indignity of being a
vain complication and a waste of motion.

That the end of life should be death may sound sad: but what
other end can anything have? The end of an evening party is to go to
bed; but its use is to gather congenial people together, that they may
pass the time pleasantly. An invitation to the dance is not rendered

ironical because the dance cannot last for ever; the youngest of us and the most vigorously wound up, after a few hours, has had enough of sinuous stepping and prancing. The transitoriness of things is essential to their physical being, and not at all sad in itself; it becomes sad by virtue of a sentimental illusion, which makes us imagine that they wish to endure, and that their end is always untimely; but in a healthy nature it is not so. What is truly sad is to have some impulse frustrated in the midst of its career, and robbed of its chosen object; and what is painful is to have an organ lacerated or destroyed when it is still vigorous, and not ready for its natural sleep and dissolution. We must not confuse the itch which our unsatisfied instincts continue to cause with the pleasure of satisfying and dismissing each of them in turn. Could they all be satisfied harmoniously we should be satisfied once for all and completely. Then doing and dying would coincide throughout and be a perfect pleasure.

This same insight is contained in another wise myth which has inspired morality and religion in India from time immemorial: I mean the doctrine of Karma. We are born, it says, with a heritage, a character imposed, and a long task assigned, all due to the ignorance which in our past lives has led us into all sorts of commitments. These obligations we must pay off, relieving the pure spirit within us from its accumulated burdens, from debts and assets both equally oppressive. We cannot disentangle ourselves by mere frivolity, nor by suicide: frivolity would only involve us more deeply in the toils of fate, and suicide would but truncate our misery and leave us for ever a confessed failure. When life is understood to be a process of redemption, its various phases are taken up in turn without haste and without undue attachment; their coming and going have all the keenness of pleasure, the holiness of sacrifice, and the beauty of art. The point is to have expressed and discharged all that was latent in us; and to this perfect relief various temperaments and various traditions assign different names, calling it having one's day, or doing one's duty, or realizing one's ideal, or saving one's soul. The task in any case is definite and imposed on us by nature, whether we recognize it or not; therefore we can make true moral progress or fall into real errors. Wisdom and genius lie in discerning the prescribed task and in doing it readily, cleanly, and without distraction. Folly on the contrary imagines that any scent is worth following, that we have an infinite nature, or no nature in particular, that life begins without obligations and can do business without capital, and that the will is free, instead of being a specific burden and a tight hereditary knot to be unravelled. This romantic folly is defended by some philosophers without self-knowledge, who think that the variations and further entanglements which the future may bring are the manifestation of spirit; but they are, as Freud has indicated, imposed on living beings by external pressure, and take shape in the realm of matter. It is only after the organs of spirit are formed mechanically that spirit can exist, and can distinguish the better from the worse in the fate of those organs, and therefore in its own fate. Spirit has nothing to do with infinity. Infinity is something physical and ambiguous; there is no scale in it and no centre. The depths of the human heart are finite, and they are dark only to ignorance. Deep and dark as a soul may be when you look down into it from outside, it is something perfectly natural; and the same understanding that can unearth our suppressed young passions, and dispel our stubborn bad habits, can show us where our true good lies. Nature has marked out the path for us beforehand; there are snares in it, but also primroses, and it leads to peace.

Bibliographical Essay

The books and articles recommended below hardly exhaust the subject of cultural conservatism between 1900 and 1945. I have merely attempted to make suggestions for further reading that best relate the given individuals to larger cultural issues. I have intentionally omitted a large number of relatively technical studies and many books that do not seem to add much to the general data available in standard intellectual histories. I have also included a few articles that might easily have been included in the text of this book, had there been room.

For a chapter-length study of many of the figures in this book, interpreted along the general lines of the Introduction, see Robert M. Crunden, *From Self to Society, 1919–1941* (Englewood Cliffs: Prentice-Hall, 1972). For a book-length study of cultural conservatism throughout all of American history, see Ronald Lora, *Conservative Minds in America* (Chicago: Rand-McNally, 1971). Lora's book unfortunately was released in a paperback text series and has not been widely reviewed or distributed. It is in many ways a solid, thoroughly researched volume, and its bibliography goes far beyond anything I have attempted here.

Three other books since World War II have attempted to cover much of the subject, although less directly. Clinton Rossiter, *Conservatism in America* (New York: Knopf, 1962), is the best of these in many ways, but it dwells chiefly on the spirit of conservatism prevalent in the revolutionary era, and in pursuing this spirit into the twentieth century it inevitably distorts recent cultural conservatism, at times out of all recognition. Russell Kirk, *The Conservative Mind* (Chicago: Regnery, 1968), is religious in emphasis rather than political, and thus not only overemphasizes the importance of Christianity for conservatism but entirely omits essential figures and tends to ignore irreligious strains in the figures it does treat; it also overemphasizes the importance of Edmund Burke. Allen Guttmann, *The Conservative Tradition in America* (New York: Oxford University Press, 1967), is much less comprehensive than its title indicates, is methodologically inconsistent, and simply leaves too much out to be very useful.

In many ways, conservatism should be studied as part of the whole culture of its time, not isolated as in most of these books. Two excellent treatments of conservatism in this context are classics: Frederick

J. Hoffman, *The Twenties* (New York: Free Press, 1962), and Alfred
Kazin, *On Native Grounds* (New York: Reynal & Hitchcock, 1942).
A more recent and somewhat more restricted example is Richard
Ruland, *The Rediscovery of American Literature* (Cambridge: Harvard University Press, 1967). All these books are essentially literary
in emphasis and thus tend to neglect subjects like architecture and
philosophy.

A number of recent anthologies have brought together documents
labeled "conservative," with often very great differences among themselves and when compared to this book. Most of them are present-
minded, polemical, and keyed to political more than cultural considerations. See, for example, Frank S. Meyer, ed., *What Is Conservatism?* (New York: Holt, Rinehart & Winston, 1964); William F.
Buckley, Jr., ed., *American Conservative Thought in the Twentieth
Century* (Indianapolis: Bobbs-Merrill, 1970); David Brudnoy, ed.,
Viewpoints: The Conservative Alternative (New York: Holt, Rinehart
& Winston, 1973); Jay Sigler, ed., *The Conservative Tradition in
American Thought* (New York: Putnam, 1970); and A. G. Heinsohn,
ed., *Anthology of Conservative Writing in the United States, 1932–
1960* (Chicago: Regnery, 1962).

For overviews of the New Humanism, see Hoffman and Kazin; the
best longer study is the unpublished Ph.D. dissertation, John David
Hoeveler, Jr., "The New Humanism: An Aspect of Twentieth Century
American Thought," University of Illinois, 1971 (Ann Arbor #72-
6954). For Irving Babbitt, begin with Frederick Manchester and
Odell Shepard, eds., *Irving Babbitt, Man and Teacher* (New York:
G. P. Putnam's Sons, 1941), and the two key articles by T. S. Eliot,
"The Humanism of Irving Babbitt" and "Second Thoughts about
Humanism," in Eliot's *Selected Essays* (New York: Harcourt, Brace,
1950). Other relevant articles, occasionally quite critical, are Henry
S. Kariel, "Democracy Limited: Irving Babbitt's Classicism," *Review
of Politics* 13 (October 1951): 430–440; Wylie Sypher, "Irving Bab-
bitt: A Reappraisal," *New England Quarterly* 14 (March 1941): 64–
76; and Walter Lippmann, "Humanism and Dogma," *Saturday Review
of Literature* 6 (March 15, 1930): 817–819. Babbitt's view of H. L.
Mencken appears in "The Critic and American Life," *Forum* 79
(February 1928): 161–176.

Byron C. Lambert has edited a useful recent anthology of Paul
Elmer More's work, *The Essential Paul Elmer More* (New Rochelle:
Arlington House, 1972). Of the several books on More, the best is
Arthur Hazard Dakin, *Paul Elmer More* (Princeton: Princeton Univer-
sity Press, 1960). Briefer discussions appear in Whitney J. Oakes,
"Paul Elmer More," in *The Lives of Eighteen from Princeton* (Prince-
ton: Princeton University Press, 1946), pp. 302–317; Folke Leander,
"More—'Puritan à Rebours,'" *American Scholar* 7 (Autumn 1938):
438–453; and M. D. C. Tait, "The Humanism of Paul Elmer More,"
University of Toronto Quarterly 16 (January 1947): 109–122. More's

own comment on humanism can be found in "A Revival of Humanism," *On Being Human* (Princeton: Princeton University Press, 1936).

The best starting place for George Santayana is his charming series of memoirs, collectively entitled *Persons and Places*, published in three volumes (New York: Scribner's, 1944, 1945, 1953) and then reissued in one volume. It should be supplemented for biographical detail by Daniel Cory, ed., *The Letters of George Santayana* (New York: Scribner's, 1955) and *Santayana: The Later Years* (New York: Braziller, 1963). A good selection of his writings is Richard C. Lyon, ed., *Santayana on America* (New York: Harcourt, Brace, 1968). There are a number of scholarly books on various aspects of his philosophy, especially his aesthetics, but the best general discussion remains George W. Howgate, *George Santayana* (Philadelphia: University of Pennsylvania Press, 1938), a volume written prior to Santayana's own memoirs, but one of which the subject generally approved.

Ralph Adams Cram has been unjustly neglected by scholars of both conservatism and architecture. His autobiography, *My Life in Architecture* (Boston: Little, Brown, 1936), gives most of the important facts and will always be useful, but it is hardly adequate for the whole subject. There is some biographical material scattered in several of his essays, chiefly those collected in *Convictions and Controversies* (Boston: Marshall Jones, 1936). The best secondary treatment is the essay by Walter Muir Whitehill in Edward T. James, ed., *Dictionary of American Biography*, supplement 3 (New York: Scribner's, 1973), pp. 194–197. Harold F. Sheets is currently completing a Ph.D. dissertation on Cram at the University of Texas at Austin.

H. L. Mencken edited his own selected version of his writings in *A Mencken Chrestomathy* (New York: Knopf, 1956), and it remains the best. There are several others, all useful, some overlapping. *The Days of H. L. Mencken* (New York: Knopf, 1947) brings together three volumes of autobiographical writing which are mellow and undogmatic in tone. Guy J. Forgue has edited *Letters of H. L. Mencken* (New York: Knopf, 1961), with emphasis on material of literary importance. The most enjoyable study of Mencken's career is William Manchester, *Disturber of the Peace* (New York: Collier, 1950); the most recent scholarly volume is Carl Bode, *Mencken* (Carbondale: Southern Illinois University Press, 1969), a book that manages the incredible feat of making the man seem dull; the best memoir is Sara Mayfield, *The Constant Circle* (New York: Delacorte, 1968), a volume of charm and perception although limited in scope. Two recent specialized studies are Fred C. Hobson, *Serpent in Eden: H. L. Mencken and the South* (Chapel Hill: University of North Carolina Press, 1974), and Douglas C. Stenerson, *H. L. Mencken: Iconoclast from Baltimore* (Chicago: University of Chicago Press, 1971).

Albert Jay Nock has contributed a superb autobiography in *The Memoirs of a Superfluous Man* (New York: Harper & Bros., 1943). Van Wyck Brooks, *Days of the Phoenix* (New York: Dutton, 1957), has a chapter on Nock and the journal he edited, the *Freeman*; for more extended treatment, see Susan J. Turner, *A History of the Freeman* (New York: Columbia University Press, 1963). I have analyzed Nock at length in *The Mind and Art of Albert Jay Nock* (Chicago: Regnery, 1964), as has Michael Wreszin in his rather more critical *The Superfluous Anarchist* (Providence: Brown University Press, 1972). Wreszin has condensed his position in a useful article, "Albert Jay Nock and the Anarchist-Elitist Tradition in America," *American Quarterly* 21 (Summer 1969): 165–189.

The individuals involved in the fugitive/agrarian/distributist movements in America have received extended treatment from several viewpoints. On the agrarians, the best source in many ways is Virginia Jean Rock, "The Making and Meaning of *I'll Take My Stand*: A Study in Utopian-Conservatism, 1925–1929," unpublished Ph.D. dissertation, University of Minnesota, 1961 (Ann Arbor #64-3833). This dissertation contains a substantial amount of biographical data on each figure, uses many unpublished sources, and is absolutely essential for any serious advanced student in the field; unfortunately much of the material remains undigested, and the valuable material is sometimes swamped by the redundant quotations. Some of this primary material was subsequently published in John T. Fain and Thomas D. Young, eds., *The Literary Correspondence of Donald Davidson and Allen Tate* (Athens: University of Georgia Press, 1974). Four key published books cover various aspects of these movements: Louise Cowan, *The Fugitive Group* (Baton Rouge: Louisiana State University Press, 1959), was a volume well received by surviving members of the group; John M. Bradbury, *The Fugitives* (Chapel Hill: University of North Carolina Press, 1958), and John L. Stewart, *The Burden of Time* (Princeton: Princeton University Press, 1965), the most exhaustive treatment, struck the survivors as overly critical and insensitive, although there is no reason other readers need adopt this attitude; Alexander Karanikas, *Tillers of a Myth* (Madison: University of Wisconsin Press, 1966), provides the most comprehensive brief overview.

The *American Review* was for several years in the thirties a key journal of agrarian opinion both within and without the South; Albert E. Stone traces its history briefly in "Seward Collins and the *American Review*: Experiment in Pro-Fascism, 1933–1937," *American Quarterly* 12 (Spring 1960): 3–19. Radcliffe Squires, ed., *Allen Tate and His Work* (Minneapolis: University of Minnesota Press, 1972), is one of the few volumes devoted to a single author that has enduring value. For two significant opinions by nonsouthern conservatives, see T. S. Eliot, "Tradition and Orthodoxy," *American Review* 2 (March 1934): 513–528, and H. L. Mencken, "Uprising in the Confederacy," *American Mercury* 22 (March 1931): 279–281.

Most of the writing about T. S. Eliot tends to be narrow explication for students of his poetry. John Crowe Ransom has a section on Eliot in *The New Criticism* (Norfolk: New Directions, 1941), illuminating what one conservative can find in another. Louis A. M. Simpson also treats Eliot extensively within a biographical framework in *Three on the Tower* (New York: William Morrow, 1975). Of book-length treatments, Russell Kirk provides a New Conservative's look at Eliot in *Eliot and His Age* (New York: Random House, 1971). John Margolis concentrates on the *Criterion* period in *T. S. Eliot's Intellectual Development, 1922–1939* (Chicago: University of Chicago Press, 1972). A useful anthology is Allen Tate, ed., *T. S. Eliot: The Man and His Work* (New York: Dell, 1966). William M. Chace has gone into useful interdisciplinary detail in his well-received volume, *The Political Identities of Ezra Pound and T. S. Eliot* (Stanford: Stanford University Press, 1973).

Walter Lippmann has been the subject of many studies, but few have much to do with his conservatism; indeed, a number of commentators seem embarrassed by it. Marquis Childs and James Reston edited *Walter Lippmann and His Times* (New York: Harcourt, Brace, 1959), which contains several illuminating articles. Of the book-length studies, the best are Charles Wellborn, *Twentieth Century Pilgrimage: Walter Lippmann and His Public Philosophy* (Baton Rouge: Louisiana State University Press, 1969), and Benjamin F. Wright, *Five Public Philosophies of Walter Lippmann* (Austin: University of Texas Press, 1973).